ETHICAL INVESTIGATIONS

NOEL ROWE

Ethical Investigations

ESSAYS ON AUSTRALIAN LITERATURE AND POETICS

Edited by Bernadette Brennan

VAGABOND PRESS

THE PUBLISHER would like to thank the executors
of Noel Rowe's estate, Kevin Rowe and Stephen Fahey, as well as
Bernadette Brennan and Justin Gleeson, for making possible
the posthumous publication of Noel Rowe's
A Cool and Shaded Heart: Collected Poems and
*Ethical Investigations: Essays on Australian
Literature and Poetics.*

ISBN 978-0-9805113-1-4

Vagabond Press, Sydney

Contents

Preface

NOEL ROWE WAS A poet, critic, editor and Senior Lecturer in Australian Literature at the University of Sydney. He graduated from the University of Sydney with a B.A. First Class Honours and University Medal in 1984 and went on to complete a PhD at that institution in 1989. In his doctorate, supervised by Leonie Kramer, Rowe examined the religious character of the poetry of James McAuley, Francis Webb and Vincent Buckley. Rowe was appointed as an Associate Lecturer in the Department of English at the University of Sydney on February 26, 1990. He gained promotion to Lecturer in 1993 and Senior Lecturer in 1997. He continued to teach in the Department until a few weeks before his death in July 2007.

During the 1970s Rowe trained for seven years to become a Marist priest. He was ordained in 1977 and left the priesthood in 1992. Those years of theological study informed in a unique and powerful way Rowe's approach to literature and to life. His understanding of the relationship between literature and theology, most clearly outlined in the essay 'Are There Really Angels in Carlton? Australian Literature and Theology', is evident throughout this collection. As early as 1993 Rowe was arguing that theology needed to be 'sensitive to the ways in which literature can create its meanings, be aware of the demonic possibilities in writing, and come to terms with texts which deconstruct the words and worlds of traditional theology.' This collection demonstrates how he developed that argument and explored its implications across a diverse range of Australian texts. These essays chart Rowe's appreciation of the development of an Australian theology in literature spanning a fifty year period—a development that establishes imaginative connections between writers as different as Vincent Buckley and Christos Tsiolkas.

In these essays Rowe seeks to enliven the appreciation of the profound analogies he recognised in religious and poetic processes. He offers alternative readings of the poetry of McAuley, Webb and Buckley from those that originate when the poetry, and the poet, is labelled 'Catholic' and made to try and fit established systems of belief. He encourages readers to appreciate the way in which belief is an act of imagination and imagination an act of belief. In 'Believing More and Less: The Later Poetry of Vincent Buckley' Rowe argues that 'Catholicism stays in Buckley's imagination as one of the idioms of sensation' and shows how Buckley's poetry challenges the separation of the 'sacred' and the 'secular' which 'so deeply characterises and confounds Western religious imagination'. 'James McAuley: The Possibility of Despair' uncovers the negativity that informs McAuley's writing. This essay recognises a strand of despair present in McAuley's writing from the outset and argues that when McAuely's poetry is writing belief it is negotiating a space between 'hope and despair, doctrinal and mystical, theological and atheological'.

As a reader, poet and teacher Rowe was deeply attracted to the poetry of Francis Webb. Here we have two previously unpublished essays on Webb. The first, 'Francis Webb's "Harry": Can Imbecility Be Made Innocent?', offers a reading of 'Harry' and affirms that Webb's poetry is never transcendent but remains always with 'the suffering of language'. The second, '"Are you from the Void?" A reading of "Sturt and the Vultures"' has been published only as a tape recording. In this essay Rowe states that after fifteen years of reading Webb's poetry he remains dissatisfied with his analysis and, therefore, turns to negative theology as a form of criticism that might do justice to 'the tattered eloquence of the poetry'. Between these two essays is 'Francis Webb and the Will of the Poem' where Rowe elucidates the degree to which the 'Suffering Servant' model informs Webb's vision.

Vivian Smith was Rowe's teacher, then colleague and, for many years, beloved friend. Rowe's respect and admiration for both Smith and his poetry is palpable in 'Patience and Surprise: The Poetry of Vivian Smith', an essay in which he recognises how the formal aspects of Smith's verse operate to open the poetry up to possibilities of imaginative release. In 'Justice, Sacrifice and the Mother's Poem' we are offered a perceptive and poignant reading of Murray's 'The Steel' within the broader context of Murray's writing. Rowe identifies Murray's preoccupation with blood sacrifice before concluding that, contrary to accepted critical opinion, the speaker of Murray's poem is not interested in scapegoating the doctor. This essay, like all of Rowe's later criticism, is an example of what he terms 'ethico-literary interpretation' or 'ethographic' reading.

Rowe was particularly interested in the relationship between literature and ethics; a relationship, like that between literature and theology, based on an equal and reciprocal dialogue. In '"No one but I will know": Hal Porter's Honesty' he articulates how 'narrative-as-ethics' operates, drawing attention to how imagery, structure and perspective incorporate acts of power that have ethical as well as textual value. 'Just Poetry', written for a book on the relationship between writing and justice, demonstrates through its discussion of the poetry of Eva Johnson, Rosemary Dobson, Judith Wright and Francis Webb, how poetry works through images, metaphor, tone and speaking positions to create a relational ethic. In '"Will this be your poem, or mine?" The give and take of story' Rowe tackles persuasively and piercingly the fraught question of who has the right to speak for whom.

In 2005 I read Christos Tsiolkas' *Dead Europe* and knew immediately that this powerfully disturbing, thrilling narrative would excite Rowe's intellectual interest and called for a reader with Rowe's literary and theological knowledge. Rowe read the novel and was energised by it. He reveled in the challenge of writing about it, a challenge that resulted in the extended essay 'Sacrificing Grace: Christos Tsiolkas' *Dead Europe*', in which Rowe identifies the multilayered and ethically-complex issues the novel grapples with, particularly its engagement with anti-Semitism.

Noel Rowe died on July 11, 2007. He was 56 years old. As evidenced by both the criticism and the poetry he was writing in his last years he was approaching the peak of his creative powers. As a concluding aside in his essay on Seamus Heaney's poetry he wrote: 'The dead are always with us. We often feel that we would like to talk with them again. Perhaps poetry allows us to feel that we almost have.' In both his poetry and his critical work Noel Rowe continues to keep the lines of communication open to us.

Bernadette Brennan
March 2008

Acknowledgments

'"Will this be your poem, or mine?" The give and take of story' was first published in 'New Reckonings: Australian Literature Past, Present, Future'. *Australian Literary Studies* 23:2, 2007. 1–14.

'Are There Really Angels in Carlton? Australian Literature and Theology' was first published in *Pacifica* 6, 1993. 141–164.

'Believing More and Less: The Later Poetry of Vincent Buckley' was first published in *Meridian* 10:1, May 1991. 4–18.

'James McAuley: The Possibility of Despair' was first published in *Southerly* 60:2, 2000. 26–38.

'Francis Webb and the Will of the Poem' was first published in *Southerly* 47:2, 1987. 180–196.

'"Are you from the Void?" A reading of "Sturt and the Vultures"' was delivered as a conference paper at the Francis Webb Conference, Australian Catholic University, Strathfield, 14 November, 1997.

'Patience and Surprise: The Poetry of Vivian Smith' was first published in *Southerly* 47:2, 1986. 178–194.

'Justice, Sacrifice and the Mother's Poem' was first published in *The Poetry of Les Murray: Critical Essays*. L. Hergenhan and B.Clunies Ross (eds.). A Special Issue of *Australian Literary Studies* 20:2. St Lucia: University of Queensland Press, 2001. 142–165.

'Just Poetry' was first published in *Just Words?: Australian Authors Writing for Justice*. Bernadette Brennan (ed.). St Lucia: University of Queensland Press, 2008. 46–61.

'"No-one but I will know": Hal Porter's Honesty' was first published in *Australian Humanities Review* 41, February 2007. http://www.lib.latrobe.edu.au/AHR/archive/Issue-February-2007/Rowe.html

'Will this be your poem, or mine?'

THE GIVE AND TAKE OF STORY

THE QUESTION OF WHO owns story is perhaps best answered by telling story. In 'Poems of the River Wang', Rosemary Dobson tells this story of Wang Wei and P'ei Ti:

Two poets walking together
May pause suddenly and say,
Will this be your poem, or mine?

May offer courteously,
Please take it. No, you first. (186)

It is a story in which the two poets figure the dialogic inclinations of analogical activity. 'Poems of the River Wang' is one of twelve poems making up 'The Continuance of Poetry' (1981), the sequence Dobson wrote to commemorate David Campbell and their joint project translating Russian poetry.[1] As a way of honouring her dead colleague, Dobson borrows freely from his writing, incorporating, for example, his image of the daylight moon. She takes as a way of giving back.

---

1. David Campbell and Rosemary Dobson, *Moscow Trefoil: Poems from the Russian of Anna Akhmatova and Osip Mandelstam*, Natalie Staples (trans.). (Canberra: ANU Press, 1975). David Campbell and Rosemary Dobson, *Seven Russian Poets* (St Lucia: UQP, 1979).

'The Continuance of Poetry' shows how poems in a sense dispossess themselves in order to make their way across borders. Translation, conversation, and continuance become its metaphors. So too does cross-pollination:

Poems blow away like pollen,
Find distant destinations,
Can seed new songs
In another language. (186)

Dobson's title is somewhat self-reflexive: 'continuance' is a word she elsewhere uses to indicate the cross-cultural and cross-temporal exchange that happens in minds in museums. In 'On Museums: 3. Their Purpose' museums offer 'resonant conversation / From the articulate past' and their purpose is to be 'the lightning- / Conductors of continuance' (192). The sequence, then, takes its place within these metaphors, suggesting that culture might best be imagined as something that involves the give and take of a good conversation. A few years after finishing 'The Continuance of Poetry', Dobson published an essay, 'Imitations and Versions of Russian Poetry,' in which she confesses:

For my part, I had, and have, a very strong belief in translation as a means of cross-pollinating literature, and furthering the exchange of cultures … It may be remarked that in my own poetry I have 'taken' from European literature and art. All poets, however, 'take' to some degree from other cultures, other languages. The importance of poetry shared and, as with all the other arts, as a means of communication between peoples—these are convictions I hold to very firmly (97).

This is consistent with other of Dobson's poems. For example, 'Folding the Sheets' draws a picture of women matching corners of sheets washed in Burma, Lapland, India and China. In China women who wash 'on either side of the river' are united through a poem: whatever side of the river they are on, they 'Have washed their pale cloth in the White Stone Shallows / 'Under the shining moon'.' (176) 'White Stone Shallows' is the title of the poem by Wang Wei:

> In the clear White Stone Shallows
> Green reeds almost near enough to touch
> The people on both sides of the river
> Wash their silk here under the shining moon. (Robinson 30)

Dobson's act of translating Wang Wei is itself translated into a moment when the women, in a collective voice, speak of the cooperation required to fold the world's sheets: 'We stretch and pull from one side and then the other— / Your turn. Now mine.' (176) 'Your turn. Now mine.' 'Will this be your poem, or mine?' If this is a dialogic world, it is a world realised in the give and take of imaginative exchange, in that communion of self and other we call analogy.

To open her sequence, Dobson borrows another image from Campbell. Returning from his burial, the speaker of 'A Good-bye' remarks:

> There will be time enough and time enough later
> For crossing the threshold to lamplight and conversation. (183)

For some reason, this makes me think of Gwen Harwood—possibly because of the 'lamplit presences' that emerge in her poem, 'The Violets' (247–48) and make their way into the title of her autobiographical essay. I have, however, no grounds for thinking Harwood borrowed from Campbell: lamplight was a not an uncommon experience and no one owns the image. I do, however, think she borrowed the ending of 'Impromptu for Ann Jennings' (231–32)—'our children walk the earth'—from Campbell's 'We Took the Storms to Bed' (Campbell 67–8). And she herself confessed that this striking image, from 'I am the Captain of My Soul' (CP 40–41), was not hers:

> 'We have seen,' say Eyes, 'how in Venice

the steps of churches open and close
like marble fans under water.' (40–41)

Vivian Smith used the image of marble fans when he wrote to Harwood
from Venice in the late 1950s (Kratzmann 89). Harwood took it; she did
not ask his permission. If the aesthetic good were simply determined by
the ethical good, this might be described as a minor instance of stealing.
It would certainly seem to be different from borrowing 'our children walk
the earth', since Smith's image was not in the public domain. Of course,
stealing is hard to establish in a climate of intertextuality and Harwood's
poetry does take into itself a vast range of references, from fellow poets
as well as from biblical, philosophical and musical sources, some of them
identified and some not. Her poetry also takes unto itself different voices,
as in 'Variations on a Theme' (190–93), which does mischievous variations
on a 'pop goes the weasel' theme using the styles and voices of Vincent
Buckley, Rosemary Dobson, Vivian Smith, James McAuley, A.D. Hope,
Francis Geyer, and Gwen Harwood. Harwood wrote men (Eisenbart and
Kröte) and she wrote as men (Francis Geyer and Walter Lehmann), and
was, as everyone now knows, adept at othering herself.

Gwen Harwood was in Philip Martin's mind when he gave a 1985
ASAL conference paper called 'Speaking as a Woman', which began:
'Obviously, women writers can speak as women … and as men.' Here
he has written '[Gwen Harwood]' in the margin. In choosing his topic,
Martin made a strategic error. As far as I know, no one questioned
Gwen Harwood's rights to imaginative freedom, but Martin himself was
attacked for presuming to speak on behalf of women. This was, after all,
when women writers such as Jennifer Strauss, Fay Zwicky, Kate Llewellyn
and Sylvia Kantaris were taking back the stories of Guenevere, Mrs Noah,
Eve and Mary, as *The Penguin Book of Australian Women Poets* was about to
demonstrate. Martin's main point, however, was to affirm a writer's rights
and responsibilities in regard to imaginative freedom. In speaking as a
woman, he was trying 'to see others as they see themselves' (1), a need
he related to 'the fact that we live with others, in community' (11). He
nevertheless acknowledged the limitations of the endeavour, admitting

that 'there are some areas of women's experience that a man is very unlikely to write about convincingly' (1). When he discussed his own poem, 'Going to Meet Her Lover', he claimed only that he had felt 'something like [...] but not exactly like' (emphasis his) what his protagonist feels. He is arguing for analogy, not identity. At this point his paper contains another marginal annotation:

> I explained that the poem was based closely on what a woman I know well had told me, and that I often write poems on behalf of others, since it's an ancient and honourable practice for poets to do so. (8; emphasis in original)

I want to pick up that annotation. Is it still considered honourable to write on behalf of others? Or have we reached the stage where such an act is more likely to be interpreted as appropriation than as empathy?

Katharine Susannah Prichard may have thought she was writing on behalf of oppressed Aborigines, grounding *Coonardoo* in a realist's observation, trying to incorporate Language, doing her best to make Coonardoo a sympathetic character. Yet most contemporary criticism would accept that this characterisation, now seen as the construction of a subjectivity (I am not sure they are the same), represents a failure to create a genuine Indigenous female subjectivity and is little more than a vehicle for a compensatory white female sexual fantasy. Now we examine Prichard's story for its legitimacy anxieties (Hodge and Mishra 55–6), its racialised compassion (Brewster 153), its sexual exoticism (Sheridan 331), and its failure to be popular, evidently an indicator of its failure to have any significant political and cultural impact (Shoemaker 40). I have no real dispute with these readings, though I think we also need to remember what Nettie Palmer wrote at the time. Believing the book represented a movement away from portraits of the pitiable or comical black, Palmer remarked: 'The blacks in *Coonardoo* are seen as individual characters, not as diagrammatic forms' (Smith 375). This could, of course, be dismissed as patronising, but I think Nettie Palmer is right and *Coonardoo* deserves some credit for helping shift white imagining of black from type to individual. That credit ought not depend on how many copies were sold and read—it is a qualitative, not a quantitative achievement. Moreover, to dismiss Palmer's judgment as patronising is to dismiss it on ethico-political grounds, ignoring the fact that it is a statement about quality of writing. While Palmer's discussion contains assumptions that might now be labelled racist, her focus is on what she calls 'the aesthetic quality of the work'. Among the qualities she admires are that the book is 'shaped and firm', has lyrical form, 'stays as a whole in the mind', and weaves 'a tapestry of language'. As a writer, Prichard is attempting to liberate her character through particularity, physicality, language and even interiority. She is attempting an imaginative engagement with an individual other. In doing so, she unwittingly commits an ideological offence (but it might also be the case that it is easier to write a pure idea than to write a credible individual). This may affect the value of her writing, but it does not affect its quality. As Etienne Gilson remarks:

> The only good that art as such has to pursue is the perfection of the work. Its responsibility is no more to promote moral perfection, which is the good of the will, than to say the truth, which is the good of knowledge. Its own good is that of an object to be constructed in such a way that its sense apprehension will be pleasing to an intelligent being. Nothing prevents the artist from putting his art at the service of a moral or religious cause, far from it, but good causes may be promoted by poor art, and the artistic quality of the works which serve such causes owes nothing to their dignity. Inversely, and still more so, works of a kind which corrupt morality do not rise in artistic value for doing so, but the disapproval they deserve should be taken from the point of view of ethics, not of art. (43–44)[2]

If the critical reception of *Coonardoo* shows one thing, it is that stories do not always subscribe to the best intentions of authors—or, indeed,

---

2. While I do not think the distinction between art and ethics is quite as clear-cut as Gilson would have it, I think we need such a distinction as part of the discussion.

critics. This is true even of our allegedly more enlightened era. When Carmel Bird edited *The Stolen Children: Their Stories* (1998) she would have had more information than Prichard had in regard to issues of permission and voice that attend the use of Indigenous story. Yet her book releases ambiguities comparable to those that attach to Prichard's novel. Bird's edition bears an uncanny resemblance to Prichard's novel in the deference it pays white authorities. In her 'Foreword to the First Edition', Prichard defers to Ernest Mitchell, then Chief Inspector for Aborigines for Western Australia, affirming that 'no one in this country has wider knowledge and more sympathetic understanding of the Western and Nor'-West tribes'. Bird does something similar in her use of Ronald Wilson and such commentators as Veronica Brady and Frank Brennan. Cath Ellis has argued this turns the book into a struggle between Indigenous and non-Indigenous voices. If so, it is a struggle that ends in ambiguity. At one level, the book is a work of mediation, which is to say power flows through the stories. At another level, the editor's power is exercised over the stories and appropriation becomes an issue. While Bird makes her editorial position clear, recording that she received appropriate permissions and declaring the moral and ameliorative purpose of story, what she does not declare, and what seems to have gone unnoticed, is that the stories are arranged so that as the volume progresses the voices become more and more reconciled. In other words, individual Indigenous stories are told into and within an underlying narrative of hope. Whose story is this? If it is Bird's, is it another white fantasy designed to evade the hard realities of reconciliation or/and is it part of that give and take necessary for the longer work of cross-cultural conversation? And can we ever really escape this kind of situation where in order to receive other stories we have in some way to tell our own?

Since Prichard's day, Indigenous writers have done much to secure protocols that articulate and protect the conditions under which Indigenous cultural material might become available to non-Indigenous writers. Such protocols are clearly justified, but they could introduce another problem: they could encourage an assumption that the possibilities of writing are dependent on and determined by the racial identity of writers, so that discussion of who owns story could become a displaced exercise in identity politics, an exercise that privileges ethico-political over aesthetic values. Ethico-political and aesthetic concerns are clearly related, but they are also distinct, and it does not help discussion if the concerns of the one are resolved in terms proper to the other. Inasmuch as story participates in self-determination, issues of history, truth, authority, voice and subjectivity are central. And to some extent such issues become aesthetic concerns because a white writer who ignores them is unlikely to imagine well. But they are not the primary concern of writing as such. The primary concern of writing is to make from words something so possible and so beautiful that it convinces a reader to accept it as if it were true in itself and good of its own accord.

This is not an argument in favour of artistic irresponsibility. There is, after all, a sense in which writing acquires analogical depth and complexity to the degree that it is responsive, to the degree that it does justice to its subject. So I acknowledge claims that Indigenous sacred and secret material should not be available to white writers and I agree that white writers ought not use Indigenous spiritual characters and ought obtain appropriate community approval and permission for material they do use. In such instances, ethico-political concerns take precedence. There are, however, two instances where, in my view, ethico-political concerns have begun exercising an improper authority over aesthetic concerns. While it is undeniable that Australian literature has a history of negative representation of Aboriginal people, I cannot see how this justifies an argument against non-Aboriginal writers using Indigenous material (Heiss 198). It seems to me the history of negative representation is reason for more good writing by whites—and 'good' in this context cannot mean other than writing based on the best efforts of mutual appreciation. Inasmuch as these negative representations are writing faults, they can only be remedied by writing, in this case white writing that engages in a more equitable conversation with Indigenous story. A 'this is mine, not yours' approach is not a solution, or at least not an imaginative solution. Moreover, complaints about negative representation often get very close to assuming character is allegory, type rather than individual, which may be why critics now say 'representation' more often than they say 'characterisation'. In their attempts at characterisation, writers have to allow (do they not?) that some individuals are imperfect, even evil, but that the individual does not represent the race, gender, sexual orientation or religion?

I am also uneasy with the argument that non-Indigenous writers should not use Indigenous characters. Sandra Phillips maintains:

> For a non-Indigenous author to achieve a true feel to their representation on Indigenous subject matter and ... character... they would need to be very enculturated with Indigenous culture. And if they are not, they are writing as outsiders to that culture and their representation would be vastly different to the representation defined, developed and refined by an Indigenous writer. (qtd. in Heiss 197)

Certainly writers have a duty of learning which is partly how they do justice to their subject. It is, however, unrealistic to imply that this duty can only be acquitted when an outsider becomes an insider. Imagination, as Philip Martin noted, engages with the 'something like'; it is not an exercise in complete identification. Analogy includes difference. Moreover, this argument makes a claim that may need more careful consideration: it makes a claim to truth in representation, opposing the true to the different and concluding that because non-Indigenous representation will be different it should be disallowed. This leaves me wondering whether all forms of representation depend equally on empirical truth and whether truth itself is only ever one and the same. Are there not, for instance, different truths within Indigenous writing, and is Indigenous self-representation always and necessarily accurate and adequate? It seems to me terms such as truth and representation will need more discussion if they are to encourage imaginative collaborations between Indigenous and non-Indigenous writers. Otherwise they are more likely to extend the problem, taking us to a place where truth and story are 'mine, not yours'.

It is difficult to explore this question in a country which has done so much to bury Indigenous history. Thea Astley, in *A Kindness Cup*, reminds us that Australian history is grounded in a contest for story. Judith Wright, in 'Two Dreamtimes' (315–18), acknowledges the inequity of this: even as she honours the stories Oodgeroo has shared with her, she cannot extricate herself from a story of conquest. In a sense the poem dramatises two different kinds of power, that which is released in the sharing of stories and that which is executed by the knife which, at the end, Wright offers to her Indigenous interlocutor. One of the difficulties with an inequity of this kind, which is like an original inequity, is that it will continually unsettle the similitudes analogy might want to build between Indigenous and non-Indigenous experience. Perhaps the work of writers is to make analogies that will be at once equitable and effective.

Taking a cue from Gillian Whitlock's remark that public intellectuals known for Holocaust study published some of the first and best responses to The Stolen Generations discussion, I want now to consider earlier attempts to compare the experience of Aborigines to that of the Jews. Judah Waten, in 'Black Girl', sketches a situation where the innocence of childplay is contrasted with and then contaminated by the adult suspicions of Mr Johnson, who has a padlocked gate and a distaste for difference that encompasses 'abo kids' (135) and Jewish women. At first it seems as if innocence will prevail. Ignoring Johnson's prejudice, the 'Australian' and Jewish migrant children head off to play with the Aboriginal girl, Lily Samuels, and her siblings, but Harry, Johnson's son, is soon engaged in what is effectively a property conflict with Charlie, Lily's brother. This conflict prompts Harry's father to declare:

> 'I told them to keep away from those stinking, thieving abos. But they didn't do what I told them. Abos shouldn't be allowed to live among white people.' (138)

Waten is doing something more than representing a character's racist outlook. The figure of Ishmael, Abraham's exiled son, is like a metaphor moving through *Alien Son*, linking characters, positioning the narrative, and bringing the oppressed together. The narrator is keenly aware that his place in Johnson's padlocked community is almost as uncertain as Lily's. At this point, however, the story becomes more complex: the narrator loses innocence as he watches older boys trying to rape Lily and gains instead a 'heart heavy with guilty secrets' (143). Suffering does not necessarily make for companionship. In this way, 'Black Girl' might be said to demonstrate at once the importance and the problem of exploring analogies between Aboriginal and Jewish stories. At much the same time as Waten was developing *Alien Son*, Yosl Bergner was painting works such as 'Aborigines in Fitzroy' and 'Group of Aborigines', which, according to Frank Klepner, neither patronise nor romanticise their subject because Bergner's Polish-Jewish background 'allowed him to cross this gap from his own circumstance to that of the Aborigines' (97). Noel Counihan, writing to Bernard Smith, commented:

> For the first time these abused people are being painted by a painter with an understanding of their suffering and exploitation. It has taken a Polish Jew to interpret the Aboriginal realistically, sympathetically, as a struggling people, without patronage or sentimentality. (qtd. in Klepner 97)

Are these examples of cross-cultural imagining or merely exercises in appropriation? (And is it really so easy to make such clear separations when we are trying to describe and evaluate imaginative activity?) Each instance requires its own answer, but it seems to me a key criteria is whether there is enough give and take to make the analogy ethically proportionate, and more importantly for the writer, imaginatively captivating, credible and satisfying? Waten and Bergner have exercised the right of analogy, and, for what it's worth, it seems to me in this case the grounds for comparison do sufficient justice to both parties: displacement, racism, scapegoating, and extermination. The two stories, Aboriginal and Jewish, are not the same but they can live together.

In some stories the Holocaust has an understandably theological status, as Helen Demidenko/Darville discovered when she published and promoted *The Hand That Signed the Paper*. Too much has already been written about her book, but I will add one brief comment about the way in which it becomes a work of theft. As everyone knows, the author stole a Ukrainian identity and through public appearances and interviews inserted a fictional autobiography into what appeared as autobiographical fiction. The novel itself, however, performs a more serious theft. Whatever else it is, the Holocaust is a narrative of evil, and Demidenko's novel works against this, opposing her family story against the stories of Jewish survivors, until evil becomes not only ordinary but excusable. The novel ends with a disturbing evasion as the narrator's uncle is decriminalised by death:

> At Treblinka itself, as Vitaly told me, nothing remains. Even the memorial is poorly kept, now no communist regime needs it for moral capital. … While I am walking towards the memorial, a Trabant with unified Germany numberplates clatters past. It sports a new bumper sticker—My other car is also a piece of shit. The car shudders to a stop. The driver, a young man with black curly hair, leans across and opens the door. We drive to the site, to the pines and broken rocks. He says, 'My aunt died here.' I say, 'My uncle was a guard here.'
>
> I ask, 'Why?'
>
> He says, 'She was a Quaker. A pacifist. She couldn't fight so she hid Jews from the authorities. Eventually they caught her. They said if you want to be friendly with Jews, we'll make you into a Jew. And?'
>
> 'My uncle? He volunteered. He was a poor peasant.'
>
> He looks at me sharply, but not angrily. 'Are you sorry?'
>
> 'Yes,' I said. 'I am.'
>
> 'Is he?'
>
> 'He's dead.'
>
> 'Too late to ask him now.' (156–57)

True to Vitaly's word, nothing does remain. Vitaly's death means that he and his narrative cannot be interrogated further. Fiona's expression of sorrow is an attempt to provide a substitute resolution for the story's central moral problem. That problem, to do with individual choice and culpability, remains disguised while ever Vitaly can continue to be represented, as he is here, as 'a poor peasant'. Such a representation is really a final reiteration of the novel's thesis that oppressive circumstances can make ordinary people capable of extraordinary evil, a thesis attached to the fallacy that explaining evil is as good as justifying it. Moreover, immediately prior to this ending, Fiona has been writing against war crimes trials and constructing her uncle's death in such a way as to take him out of history and offer him to the Church, whose sacrament of 'divine mercy' will allow him to escape justice. Before that Fiona and Vitaly have been discussing the trial and he has declared that 'if you leave people alone they don't do bad things'(154), admitted that he cannot explain why he did what he did and confessed that he is 'trying' to be sorry. In this context, '[t]oo late to ask him now' removes the reader's right to persist with the ethical questions the novel evokes and evades, offering instead a twist on the image of Vitaly's face as a 'peaceful death mask' (156). Obviously I am not convinced by postmodern readings: it seems to me the novel has a central viewpoint on evil and that it pursues that viewpoint; what others see as polyvalence I am more inclined to suspect as evasion. In my view, *The Hand That Signed the Paper* steals and then devalues the Holocaust. It takes away its moral core.

Another victim of *The Hand That Signed the Paper* may well have been Christos Tsiolkas's *Dead Europe*, which should have won more prizes than it did. Some have again complained of anti-Semitism, but I cannot see how such a reading can be maintained without conflating character and narrator. Tsiolkas's treatment of the Holocaust seems to me profound because of the way he opens up analogies between that story and so many others in his book. Tsiolkas himself raises the question of who owns story in an interview with Richard Watts:

Anti-Semitism was the first racism that I ever learned but because I'm Gentile, I'm not Jewish, I asked myself, do I have the right to deal with this subject? That led me back to an engagement with a monotheistic god, which is the god of the Jews, and Muslims and the Christians. I realised that I have every right, especially as a gay person, to talk about some of the brutality occurring because of religious belief and, because I grew up in a religious family, I feel a sense of legitimacy in being able to write about God.

This is yet another appeal to the rights of analogy. Tsiolkas deploys a comparison between racism and homophobia which he extends by claiming that persecution is caused by religion, thus relating the story of the Holocaust to the three grand narratives of Judaism, Islam and Christianity. This answer mimics the analogical activity that characterises his novel and makes his use of Holocaust material work (which, in aesthetic terms, justifies his writing). *Dead Europe* employs narrative parallels, such as those that link the story of Abraham to ancient and modern accounts of sacrifice, interreaching images, such as those interweaving stories of blood, until Eucharistic and vampiric discourses are con/fused, and wide-ranging allusions, such as those to Odysseus, Dante, Faustus, Cavafy and the cinema of Roman Polanski. The result is a remarkable example of how stories exist in an economy of exchange, belonging to everybody and nobody. Tsiolkas's novel understands that you cannot lock a story down as if it were an isolable cultural product, something like an individual identity. Writing and reading take place not so much within one story as between many. This is simply because the ambitions of story are more convivial than imperial: story, as a work of analogy, likes company.

One of the major difficulties I have had in formulating this argument is that the word 'writing' will not submit to my will. Whereas I have tried to use it to indicate an act of making with words, most critics are likely to think the word refers to a thing made with words. Certainly critics focused on ethico-political textual effects and contexts are inclined to think of writing as the finished product. Valid as it is, such a focus can diminish appreciation of how writing, and story, work. Gilson distinguishes between 'the art that makes things (*ars artefaciens*) rather than the things which art makes (*ars artefacta*)' (13). In Gilson's terms, writing is a making before it is a knowing or willing, so its primary concern is not a truth to be known or a good to be willed. Its primary concern is beauty. Once upon a time there was a language to describe what made writing beautiful. Jacques Maritain, for example, records how Aquinas identified three conditions for beauty: integrity, proportion, and clarity. This clarity, or claritas, he explains as the splendour of intelligibility recognised by the Platonists (*splendor veri*), by Augustine (*splendor ordinis*) and Aquinas (*splendor formae*) (Maritain 20).

Gilson speaks of integrity, inasmuch as the beautiful lacks nothing essential to its nature, harmony, inasmuch as the form of the whole brings unity to the parts, and claritas or radiance, which is like the 'affective tonality' of a beautiful work (28–34). Both acknowledge that claritas is a metaphor and that it has to do with the way beauty compels our attention. Neither suggests that beauty's appeal is easily explicable. I doubt this approach will convince many contemporary critics since it involves or is easily associated with too many suspect notions, such as truth, coherence, and order. I doubt it convinces me, but I do think we need to rediscover a way of talking about beauty. Allowing that it can come in all shapes and sizes, from the classical to the postmodern, there is still something to be said for beauty as the impossible desire of writing (as *ars artefaciens*), since it acknowledges the fact that as writers are making their works, they are weighing individual words, fashioning structures that provide an appropriate proportion, establishing and varying rhythm, connecting images, particularising characters, controlling perspectives, and matching style to subject. Which is to say that beauty, even if it resists understanding, is what brings most writers into and through their dark nights of creativity.

I realise that in introducing the idea of beautiful or good writing I am resuscitating a corpse and that as soon as that corpse starts to walk it is likely to be run over by careering anxieties about elitism, traditionalism and canonicity. But I need to think in aesthetic terms because I spend so much of my time caring about whether this word or that works best in terms of rhythm, resonance, and feeling. I also suspect that the resistance to the notion of good writing is based on a suspicion of political effects mediated through and around the thing written, rather than on an appreciation of how much the act of making with words is driven by the need and desire to get it right. Finally, I want to end my days in the company of good writing. I cannot share current utilitarian assumptions that writing is only good if it is good for someone or something. I believe writing is, primarily, not what used to be called a *bonum utile* or useful good, but a *bonum honestum*, a good unto itself.

As I was trying to finish this essay, I overheard a conversation in a doctor's waiting room. A father was reading a story in the hope of helping his small daughter cope with a stomach pain. It was a story about Mister Dizzy, which he suddenly interrupted in order to ask his daughter, 'What colour is the opposite of black?' She hardly had to think before she answered, with huge confidence, 'Pink.' 'No,' he said, 'The opposite of black is white, because they are so different.' For all the difficulties surrounding the question of story, I hope I have succeeded in offering a small word in favour of pink.

Works Cited

Astley, T. *A Kindness Cup*. Melbourne: Thomas Nelson, 1974.

Bird, C. (ed.) *The Stolen Children: Their Stories*. Sydney: Random House, 1998.

Brewster, A. 'Aboriginal Life-Writing and Globalisation: Doris Pilkington's *Follow the Rabbit-Proof Fence*'. *Southerly*, 62:2, 2002.153–161.

Campbell, D. *Collected Poems*. North Ryde, NSW: Angus & Robertson, 1989.

Demidenko, H. *The Hand That Signed the Paper*. St Leonards, NSW: Allen & Unwin, 1994.

Dobson, R. *Collected Poems*. North Ryde, NSW: Angus and Robertson, 1991.

——. 'Imitations and Versions of Russian Poetry: The Record of an Experiment'. *Australian Literary Studies* 11.1,1983. 94–99.

Ellis, C. 'A Strange Case of Double Vision'. *Overland* 158, 2000. 75–79.

Gilson, E. *The Arts of the Beautiful*. Champaign, Illinois: Dalkey Archive Press, 2000.

Harwood, G. *Collected Poems 1943–1995*. A.Hoddinott and G.Kratzmann (eds.). St Lucia: University of Queensland Press, 2003.

——.'Lamplit Presences', *Southerly* 40:3, 1980. 247–54.

Heiss, A. 'Writing About Indigenous Australia—Some Issues to Consider and Protocols to Follow: A Discussion Paper'. *Southerly* 62:2, 2002. 197–205.

Hodge, B and Vijay Mishra. *Dark Side of the Dream*. Sydney: Allen & Unwin, 1991.

Klepner, F. *Yosl Bergner: Art as a Meeting of Cultures*. Sydney: Macmillan, 2004.

Kratzmann, G. (ed.) *A Steady Storm of Correspondence: Selected Letters of Gwen Harwood 1943–1995*. St Lucia: University of Queensland Press, 2001.

Maritain, J. *Art and Scholasticism with Other Essays (1924)*. J.F. Scanlon (trans.). 1960. Montana: Kessinger Publishing, 2006.

Martin, P. 'Speaking as a Woman'. ASAL conference paper, 1985. Manuscript in possession of the author.

Prichard, K.S. *Coonardoo*. (1928). Sydney: Angus and Robertson, 1985.

Robinson, G.W.(ed. and trans.). *Poems of Wang Wei*. London: Penguin, 1973.

Sheridan, S. 'Women Writers'. *The Penguin New Literary History of Australia*. L.Hergenhan (ed.). Ringwood, Vic.: Penguin, 1988. 319–326.

Shoemaker, A. *Black Words, White Page*. St Lucia: University of Queensland Press, 1989.

Smith, V. (ed.) *Nettie Palmer*. St Lucia: University of Queensland Press, 1988.

Tsiolkas, C. *Dead Europe*. Sydney: Random House, 2005.

Waten, J. 'Black Girl'. *Alien Son*. 1952. North Ryde, NSW: Collins/Angus & Robertson, 1990. 133–43.

Watts, Richard. 'A Fortunate Son'. *Age* 3 July 2005. http://www.theage.com.au/news/books/a-fortunate-son/2005/07/03. Accessed 25 May 2006.

Whitlock, G. 'In the Second Person: Narrative Transactions in Stolen Generations Testimony'. *Biography* 24.1, 2001. 197–214.

Wright, J. 'Two Dreamtimes'. *Collected Poems 1942–1985*. North Ryde, NSW: Angus & Robertson, 1994. 315–18.

Are There Really Angels in Carlton?

AUSTRALIAN LITERATURE AND THEOLOGY

THERE HAS, IN RECENT years, been an increasing interest in what is sometimes called 'Australian theology', an enterprise which is particularly attracted to connections between religion and culture and to theological readings of Australian literature. I have mixed feelings about this development. While it has been a long time coming, it now seems, in its individual manifestations, to have been shaped too swiftly, almost as if it has made up its mind before exploring its heart. While it investigates important links between theology and culture, it often uses 'Australian' as if it signified a uniform, shared meaning (just as it often refers to 'our' history and experience in a way which conceals important exclusions). While it introduces theology to new subjects, even new language, it seems to have little effect on theological method itself. I may be wrong, but I do not get the impression that the conversation between theology and culture is one between equal partners. Theology does not seem to take its own metaphorical status seriously: it does not appreciate the degree to which metaphor is constituted negatively, nor does it know how to break its images before they turn into idols. Rather, theology seems to maintain its privileged speech-position, presuming it can sacralise culture, or inculturate itself, without having to question, perhaps abandon, its own preference for systematic, universal and transcendent meanings.

In particular, I am concerned about the manner in which Australian theology is using Australian literature. The hidden agenda in much theological selection of Australian writing is a preference for texts to

sustain the realist epistemology and metaphysical symbolism which
still underwrite most of our theologies. If this issue is not brought more
effectively and openly into play, the conversation between theology and
literature will simply continue along what are already becoming familiar
lines: a hopeful reading of the taciturn stoicism (or is it survivalism?) in
Lawson's writing, a careful mention of Baynton's work to show we are
not entirely bushed, nor mated, a longer pause on Hope's 'Australia' as if
to prove the prophets have come at last from the desert, a meditation on
White (the semi-Christian mystic, not the drag queen), then a Wright
turn, through the land we love, to the Centre and 'Aboriginal Spirituality'.
All is then secured, with great equanimity, by generous references to
Murray and Wholespeak. Wholespeak, however, does more than provide
theology with a new transcendent subject: it exposes theology's desire for
a mythopoeic mode, some way of writing which helps it free itself from its
own ratiocinated, sanctified mode. If one can ask, and I think one can, why
certain spiritual apologists should expect traditional Aboriginal culture
to turn gospel and save Christianity from its self-administered doctrinal
overdose, one can also ask why poets should be expected to save those
theologians who are not prepared to mend/rend their ways and want to
appropriate only that Australian writing which comes obediently into the
light and the Word. Would it not be worthwhile for theology a little to
reconsider its alliance with the angels?

I accept that theology might be more comfortable with the angels: with
those texts which foreground clarity, coherence, and formal beauty. But such
texts will provide too limited and too easy an access to Australian writings.
They will not challenge theology to a radical reconsideration of its own
methodologies. The fundamental challenge is to develop methodologies
which are genuinely interdisciplinary, methodologies which distribute
authority more evenly and properly between theology and literature. This
will take time. In the meantime, literature can offer Australian theology
three more immediate challenges: a dialogue with postmodern texts which,
in various ways, enact the 'death of God'; a realisation that the religious
imagination (as distinct from the theological imagination) can need its
demons as well as its angels (even when it seems to be very much on the

side of the angels); an awareness that literature is not simply a storehouse of themes (theological or otherwise).

All readings of literary texts are partial, but some are more partial than others, particularly those which hurry towards a systematic reading of themes and forget that literature can make and unmake its meanings through such features as structure, image, intonation, and narrative perspective. There are theologians who have set out to explore Australian literature in the hope of arriving at those true symbols of our culture which might best be sacralised, and they have not always avoided the temptation to treat literature as a storehouse of themes, they have not always remembered that liminality informs how meaning is made, not simply what meaning is made. It is, then, ironic to see Peter Kirkwood translating the poetry of Les Murray and Bruce Dawe into a list of limit-situations which are taken to reveal the theological seeds of Australian culture. After reading what Murray and Dawe have to say about Isolation, Black Australians, Affluence, Migrants, Leisure, Sexuality, Land, War and Unemployment, I was left distracted by the fact that neither seems to say much about unemployment, and that Murray does not seem to say as much as Dawe about sexuality. And I was wondering what had happened to the more particular, more profound religious sense, the unsystematised but real liminality, playing in Dawe's and Murray's works.

Kirkwood's rather too clear and certain framework strangles discussion of Dawe's comedy of death, his prophetic imagination, his way of evoking and evading belief through a vernacular inflection, and his use of life-cycles as a way of ritualising suburban life. Consequently, the theology attributed to the poetry is not a thinking which rises from the primary energies and images of the poems themselves, but a thinking which is using the poems to illustrate its own general frame of argument. It is not a theology which helps us evaluate Dawe's attempt to mythologise Australian life. It is significant that Dawe's 'Life-cycle' consistently attracts readings which disagree as to whether its use of myth is serious or parodic, just as 'And a Good Friday Was Had By All' has its admirers, who think its merger of irreverence and awe effective, and its critics, who think its comic form inappropriate to and subversive of its subject, the crucifixion of Christ.

Quite often a reading of Dawe's work has to account for the play between a public, performing voice and a private, silent awareness which is rarely congruent with the public voice. Dawe's work, in short, shifts along a margin between social surfaces and reticent desire which may suggest a lot about Anglo-Australian sensibilities, as also about the real position of religious language in Australia, its need to unearth myth, respect the ordinary, and use irreverence to crack open the sacred once again.

Since 1985, when Kirkwood first published his essay, Les Murray has established his position as one of this country's leading poeticotheologians and has himself explained many of the theological implications of his poetry: its commitment to the common dish, its meditative dreaming of place, its embodiment of Wholespeak, and a belief in equanimity which encloses an affirmation of transcendence. Even so, a more careful consideration of why land and silence were so often partnered, why poems were so often structured to focus on an horizon, why vernacular phrases were arrested and changed into something approaching prayer, something 'absolutely ordinary', might have produced a theology which retained some of the poetry's own 'quality of sprawl'.

Another article which addressed a literary figure was Brian Thompson's 'Patrick White' which began by reminding itself: 'Only after a critical appreciation of White's novels as literature are we justified in drawing specifically theological conclusions.' However, critical appreciation is achieved within the space of two pages and this conclusion drawn:

> What can we conclude from this analysis of some of the works of Patrick White? Perhaps White is saying that Australians, like other people, have the potential for spiritual greatness. But the achievement of this involves the learning of a basic lesson, taught by Jesus, that has to do with a wheat grain falling to the ground and dying. As White puts it: 'When man is truly humbled, when he has learnt that he is not God, then he is nearest to becoming so.' (32)

White's novels do, indeed, have a lot to say about 'the potential for spiritual greatness', but they do not say it in a manner which leaves conventional

Christian theology comfortable, so that Thompson's theological interpretation becomes a falsification of White's spiritual insight. White himself persisted in linking his spirituality to his homosexuality, not because of any serious commitment to gay politics, but because of his belief in the androgynous capacities of his own imagination and, more privately, because of his recognition that 'My inklings of God's presence are interwoven with my love of the one human being who never fails me.' (*Flaws* 145) White also situated his belief within the deconstructive movements proper to symbolic perception:

> What do I believe? I am accused of not making it explicit. How to be explicit about a grandeur too overwhelming to express, a daily wrestling match with an opponent whose limbs never become material, a struggle from which the sweat and blood are scattered on the pages of anything the serious writer writes? A belief contained less in what is said than in the silences. In patterns on water. A gust of wind. A flower opening. I hesitate to add a child, because a child can grow into a monster, a destroyer. Am I a destroyer? This face in the glass which has spent a lifetime searching for what it believes, but can never prove to be, the truth. A face consumed by wondering whether truth can be the worst destroyer of all (*Flaws* 70).

This implies a radically negative and pluralist theology, consistent with White's novels in the way they so often enact fragmentation as the way to punitive awareness, so often combine serious and parodic versions of the same 'truth', and so often ground religious vision in an inexpressible personal experience which leaves itself open to all religious systems, but contained by none. *Voss*, for example, is concerned not so much with the matter of belief as with the mode. Certainly, there is a great deal of Christian symbolism deployed throughout the novel, but its meaning is placed and displaced within the fragmentary mode which White favours. There is, indeed, a clear warning against the dogmatic instinct to turn truth into a monument:

What kind of man is he? wondered the public, who would never know. If he was already more of a statue than a man, they really did not care, for he would satisfy their longing to perch something on a column, in a square or gardens, as a memorial to their own achievement. They did, moreover, prefer to cast him in bronze than to investigate his soul, because all dark things made them uneasy, and even on a morning of historic adventure, in bright, primary colours, the shadow was sewn to the ends of his trousers, where the heels of his boots had frayed them (117).

While at one level this supports the sanctity-through-suffering readings which theology often finds in *Voss*, it also signals that shadowing and fraying will be constitutive factors within any real meaning discovered in 'the country of the mind'. It seems to me that such a 'literary' reading of the text should inform any 'theological' reading, but recent works of Australian theology tend to neutralise this iconoclastic element of *Voss*. John Thornhill explores the novel's 'Christ motif', suggesting that the established churches may have diluted the narrative power of the gospel and implying that White's work can revive this story which remains for Thornhill 'the ultimate measure' of Australian experience. Tony Kelly approves Voss's declaration that 'in this disturbing country … it is possible more easily to discard the inessential and attempt the infinite', but seems unaware of the inflated character of this belief and does not set it against what soon follows: 'The German began to think of the material world which his egoism had made him reject. In that world men and women sat at a round table and broke bread together.' Denis Edwards uses White to locate God in the spiritual desert, then, bravely, quotes that most mischievous of texts, *Memoirs of Many in One*, to support a belief that 'we are all born in search of a vocation'. As theological readings, these pieces represent new material done in the old way (Thornhill, Kelly, Edwards). As readings of White's fiction, they present a problem. While they may seem to sit easily with metaphysical readings of the 'quest' theme in Australian writing, these readings are, nevertheless, too redemptive: they want to appropriate White's images of fracturing, but they do not want to follow White as far as the fracturing of images. So they do not really confront the complexity of White's own theological manoeuvres. Let me illustrate this with David Marr's account of the theological implications of *The Vivisector*:

> Duffield's belief follows the pattern of White's loss and rediscovery of faith. 'As an old man he realises that his belief in God has been there all the time 'like a secret relationship'.' This God is fallible— 'everyone can make mistakes, including God'—and man is one of God's blunders, a kind of Frankenstein monster. This God is also cruel: 'Otherwise, how would men come by their cruelty—and their brilliance?' Where White believed the churches went wrong was in rejecting so much that is sordid and shocking, 'which can still be related to religious experience'. An artist who celebrates the world by depicting it in all its squalor and beauty, draws close to God. The pursuit of truth is an act of worship (472–73).

I presume that mainstream theology would not accept this identification of cruelty and fallibility with the divinity. Yet it is fundamental to White's religious imagination. Marr's White involves 'God' in the structures of ambivalence which mark White's images of experience, sexuality and creativity. It is this ambivalence which protects the images from becoming idols and forms an alliance between pietas and parody, just as the Frankenstein reference combines a volatile mixture of Romantic ambition and Modernist travesty to produce White's version of the Monster/Creator. In other words, White's richly-textured fictions (which are also his theologies) are generated from a coincidence of iconographic and iconoclastic impulses.

Les Murray's work needs to be scrutinised along similar lines. Before going too much further with Murray's theology of place and equanimity, theologians need to consider whether the poetry's calm, rural communal vision is not protected by Murray's own version of the scapegoat ritual, whether there is not an exclusivist edge to 'the common dish', sharpened by an antipathy towards the city and the academy, and whether there is not a violent and demonic sub-current working within Murray's theologies of sacrifice and grace (theologies which may be partly motivated by a desire to redeem the absence of the mother). There are many other examples of Australian texts, and subtexts, which have incorporated what might be called 'demonic' energies. This does not mean they are 'works of the devil', but that they include, need, perhaps recognise and respect the ugly and untidy, the irrational and repressed, the unspoken and unspeakable, in their writing. For example, the Joe Wilson stories of Henry Lawson may appear to be about endurance before an unrelenting landscape, but a more suspicious reader (one who weighs well the fact that, in the narrator's time, Mary is dead) may discover that Joe is making the landscape a fate-symbol in order to displace his guilt. Martin Boyd's *A Difficult Young Man* (1984) celebrates, in part, a spiritual vision of culture, but it also betrays its own fascination with violence, working this into its discussion of sacrifice in a manner which implicates the cultivated desire for beauty in a primitive instinct for appeasement. There is a sense in which the novel demonstrates René Girard's thesis that 'Human culture is predisposed to the permanent concealment of its origins in collective violence'(29). Thea Astley's *The Acolyte* (1980) is also fascinated with violence and its relation to sacrifice, though it stresses the destructive character of sacrifice. Astley rarely restrains her instinct to view the eucharist through parodic distortions, so that one often encounters passages like this in which the acolyte finds little to redeem his victimisation:

> I want to break into obscene cries about his half-baked genius, his gluttony for worship, my pity for him, my latest understanding, my own dismemberment, but I look at him struggling to rise, groping about for his stick, his face redrawn with the shock of truth, and I sense him to be right and me to be wrong, but it is too late for anything like that now. We both munch the eucharist and no grace enters our souls (154).

Can theology help articulate the complex relationship between aversion and attachment which seems to operate in such parodic uses of theological discourse?

Approach from the Other Side

It may help to approach from the other side, to take writing which seems quite sure of its belief in God and remember how Blake, reading *Paradise Lost*, observed that Milton was of the Devil's party though he did not know it. James McAuley's reputation as a conservative has obscured the way in which his writing uses despair to help sculpture belief. It might be helpful to read his work as a search for a negative theology, following the 'lean plough' of 'Envoi', the 'bare attentiveness' of 'Nativity', the surrendered lyricism which qualifies the polemical Thomism of 'A Letter to John Dryden', the 'despair / Older than any hope I ever knew' of 'Because' and the negatively affirmative, 'At least there's nothing that I would unsay' which becomes something of a summation in one of his last poems, 'Parish Church'. Such a reading might do more justice to a poetry which requires the mind to submit to 'the grammar of existence' even though it never displaces its early awareness that the world is 'eaten hollow with despair'. Such a reading might also allow theology to make more respectful use of doubt and despair as creative elements, instead of repressing them to such an extent that their subversive potential can only be realised destructively, in sentimental and pathological subtexts. Whereas in McAuley's poetry the play of negative and affirmative energies actually creates the work, in Christopher Koch's *The Doubleman* ((1985) it comes close to undoing it. The novel presents as a confrontation between occultism and Christianity, in which the preferred option is represented as a refusal of demonic rituals. What the novel shows is that a rejection of the demon does not necessarily mean an affirmation of the divinity, that it may, in fact, afford the demon a subtler fascination. When Richard Miller finally confronts the occultist, Darcy Burr, he is doing so, not as a convinced Christian, but as a disillusioned and very tired man, whose decisive denial of this incarnation of evil is described: 'he'd become merely tedious, and I turned my head away'(326). This is, to say the least, an unconvincing victory for belief. In fact, belief is represented through a mode that could hardly be called incarnational: it is a matter of theological mysteries, Latin liturgies, prayers for the defeat of Satan, and the emotional dissatisfactions and intellectual doubts of so many of its former devotees. Belief is, in short, confused with a nostalgia for transcendence. Occultism, on the other hand, is presented and well realised as a rather ordinary illusion, companion to the sense of strange presences, the lust for power and wealth, the enthralling force of jealousy, suspicion and memory. Occultism, therefore, operates in the text with a great deal of tension, immediacy, and psychological credibility. The result is that the novel's imaginative impulse pulls away from its theological design, and one more text can be added to the list of those possessed by Milton's Satan.

The Presence of Angels

On the other hand, there are still angels. Australian theology might profitably ask why writers as diverse as Vivian Smith, Michael Dransfield, Robert Adamson, John Tranter, Helen Garner, Gerard Windsor, Tim Winton, Patrick White and David Malouf have appealed to the image of the angel. In what sense is theology itself a subtext in their writing? For some, like Tranter and Adamson, it may be that angels are like ghosts from a theological script which has been rejected, just as Brennan's mythological enterprise and Prichard's visionary socialism might be said to conceal a theological subtext. (The other side of a de-constructive reading may be that, as our affirmations summon the shadow of their negations, our negations summon the shadow of their affirmations.) For others, like Smith and even Dransfield, the angels may indicate a persistent desire for a transcendent aesthetic, in much the same way as Shaw Neilson's poetry replaces its thunder-blue god with natural manifestations of heavenly beauty and calm or David Malouf's fiction celebrates the annunciating power of the imagination itself. So angels (and their cousins, the ordinary mysteries) may indicate a site of theological significance. They may indicate the place where literature wants to interrogate theology, asking whether, because of its somewhat defensive dependence on the analytic, it has lost its reverence for the aesthetic, whether it needs to reveal beauty as much as truth, and whether, to do this, its language needs to be epiphanic rather than (more than) correct.

When Helen Garner's angels appeared in *Cosmo Cosmolino* (1992), they considerably disturbed the atmosphere. One anonymous critic declared 'As soon as writers discover religion, their work goes downhill'(qtd. in Chenery 17). Such a comment is significant, not because it demonstrates an antagonistic ignorance towards religion, but because it exposes the degree to which such critics assume an alliance between realism and scepticism. This makes them first cousins to those theologians who assume an alliance between realism and belief. Garner's angels announce, to theologians and critics alike, the supreme hypotheses with which to disrupt the expectations of empirical and metaphysical realism. Don Anderson has observed that Garner's fiction has, within its realism, always been concerned with the possibilities of transformation and transcendence, and that 'The angels in this book are objects of "metaphysico-aesthetic" desire, rather than of epistemological certainty' (47).

Cosmo Cosmolino is more honest than realist, just as it is more honest than religious. Even as it converts biblical images and cadences into its own body, it refuses the traditional rhetoric of religion. This refusal is partly and partially conveyed through character viewpoint: when Janet attacks Ray's fundamentalist beliefs (because they silence his personal voice and sustain a separation of spirit and matter) and when she cannot find any meaning in phrases like 'Our Father', or at least any meaning which can correspond to her sense of the open darkness. But this character viewpoint receives, if not authorial endorsement, narrative reinforcement. The novel disrupts the frames which normally divide the real and unreal—Does Maxine really fly and are her visions just hallucinations? Is there really a dark column behind Janet's shoulder? Is the 'angel of mercy' which the first narrator meets real or imagined (and does the distinction hold)?—and thus commits itself to a perspective which breaks religion and realism back to a radical experience of liminality. In its style and vision, *Cosmo Cosmolino* is in search of transfigurations. Here is Ray seeing Kim's cremation:

> Something in there was wrinkling. The small end of the coffin, fragile as an eggshell, was crinkling into a network of tiny cracks. While Raymond stared, greedy in his swoon of shock, the panel

collapsed; it gave way to the swarming orange argument, and where it had been he saw a dark-cored nimbus of flame, seething, closer to him than an arm's reach. Its twin centres, their shod soles towards them, were her feet. In the passion of their transfiguration they loosened. They opened. They fell apart (44).

Ray's experience, which also contains a vision of two funeral workers in a 'corona of light', is related to his recognition of death, and his 'angels' are mediators of that recognition, unexpected invitations to stare into the burning furnace. *Cosmo Cosmolino* is also a novel which resists such epiphanies. When the novel first appeared many commentators were preoccupied with the dark column which appears periodically at Janet's shoulder. Whether or not this is a literal column, it may be Garner's true version of the Exodus symbol, true because Janet is undergoing a passover: she has had a tubal ligation which has left her with 'a terrible sense of having been rushed, rushed past herself into a future with no outcome' (54), she is grieving for and disillusioned about collective households and their seventies ideals, and she is more and more overcome with a sense of impermanence. Janet is the realist: 'All she believed in was the physical, the practical, the stoical' (52). But Janet is honest in a way which puts pressure on her realism: 'We had not learnt the words with which to speak of death' (56). And so the novel searches for words to speak of death and arrives instead at the dark column, appropriate because it resembles a fissure: 'Behind her left shoulder a fissure opened in the room's density. I will die. I will die and leave nothing behind: I will be forgotten.'(88). Having bought from Maxine a drawing which shows the dark column, Janet finds that the illumination is receding into reality:

This was Maxine's pastel drawing, her gift, and Janet had rushed out at once and paid an arm and a leg to have the thing decently mounted and framed; but the framing had not worked out satisfactorily at all, for the picture was so dark and so densely layered that once enclosed behind the sheet of glass, it vanished. It completely disappeared. No wonder Maxine had trouble making ends meet. The drawing had retreated into its own mystery, and all Janet saw, when she looked up at it from her chair, was herself: her thought-darkened face, her penitential haircut, and a deep and detailed reflection of the room behind her (176).

If it is possible to read this as a parable about the limited way in which realism frames the mysterious, it is important to realise that the parable could equally apply to the limits of dogmatism. In her introduction to the screenplay for *The Last Days of Chez Nous*, Garner records how she had imagined a row of pencil cypress trees to be visible from the main characters' bedroom windows, 'a reminder of darkness, of stillness, of death and thus of the question of God, and the soul.' When shooting began, there were no cypresses to be found and a church spire was substituted. Garner observes:

A spire, no matter how indistinct and beautiful, is literal. It represents a known religion, a particular theology, with all the sectarian and social meanings that this entails. The mystery of the image is lost (xii).

Tim Winton's *Cloudstreet* (1991) takes the well-worn image of the river, places it within a classical religious text—'Shall we gather at the river /Where bright angel-feet have trod...'—and then rewrites its mystery. Winton's rewriting is convincing partly because he conveys the river's presence through descriptions which are luminously physical:

With the cord of her dressing gown she ties you to the tree, Fish, even while you sleep because she knows what you'll do. You don't even see her, do you? But she sees you, boy, and she knows what you'll be dreaming of here by the river, the beautiful, the beautiful the river. There's always someone with their fingers in the belt loops of your pants. You're aching with it while those dark angels laugh on the water without you. The river. Remember, wherever the river goes every living creature which swarms will live, and there will be many fish, for this water goes there, that the waters of the sea will become fresh; so everything will live where the river goes (178).

Winton reinforces this sense of the river by having characters return again and again to its waters and by the novel's narrative sprawl which gathers into its spacious simplicity moments that are numinous, playful, fantastic, vernacular, and poignant. The river is the place of miraculous catches of fish, of the black angel walking on water, the place where the nets of deepest possibility are played out. The river (which is above as well as below) is also the place from which the story is told: the ultimate narrator is the holy fool, Fish, who is both drowned and saved (baptized?), so that he sees everything through the (eternal) river, the transcendent perspective of the dead, even though he is held back from his desired vision by the river of time. (It seems that Winton has learnt one of Les Murray's tricks and is making a holy pun on the vernacular phrase, 'a fish out of water'.) When Fish finally succeeds in returning to the river, the moment of death is shown to be the moment of narrative:

Fish goes out sighing, slow, slow to the water that smacks him kisses when he hits. Down he slopes into the long spiral, drinking, drinking his way into the tumble past the dim panic of muscle and nerve into a queer and bursting fullness. And a hesitation, a pause for a few moments. I'm a man for that long, I feel my manhood, I recognize myself whole and human, know my story for just that long, long enough to see how we've come, how we've all battled in the same corridor that time makes for us, and I'm Fish Lamb for those seconds it takes to die, as long as it takes to drink the river, as long as it took to tell you all this, and then my walls are tipping as I burst into the moon, sun and stars of who I really am. Being Fish Lamb. Perfectly. Always. Everyplace. Me (424).

The image of the river, while reclaiming its terrible as well as its quickening power, is allowed to write the novel. One result of this is that the novel's consideration of such theologico-Australian questions as luck and work is fully embodied and profoundly imagined. Another result is that because the story is so profoundly imagined (gathered, as it were, at the beautiful river), this tall yarn is told as if it really could happen, as if it is not actuality which is most real, but possibility.

This belief in possibility is confirmed, not only by the narrative's transcendent perspective (the eyes of death are liberating), but also by Winton's sense of play. The text is loaded with his witty, wonderful reinventions of biblical precedents (perhaps faith is itself a reinvention) such as the miraculous catch of fish, the walking on the water, the lamb of God, the angel, the Emmaus journey, the tent and the house, to say nothing of the pentecostal pig and the manner in which the drowned man is signed both Fish and Lamb. Whereas Garner's transformations of the column and the annunciation are fundamentally serious, because they occupy the space left by collective households, Winton's are fundamentally comic, because they belong to the river, which is always there. Winton's is finally a comedy of faith: while it engages with serious issues, such as the spirituality of place, work and luck, and shows a fine sense of evil and compassion, its resolution is comic: the Pickles and Lambs are at last reconciled through a wedding and a meal, Fish has returned to the river, and Oriel is undoing her backyard tent and re-entering the house, now redeemed by love.

Playful Imaginations

It would be a pity if Australian theologians used the biblical resonances in Winton and Garner to bolster a traditional religious rhetoric (as if these writers simply signalled a 1990s recovery of religion) or borrowed their luminous passages to reinstate a conventional sense of mystery (as if the novels do not rescue mystery from convention). It would be a pity if, reading Garner's work, theologians did not attend more carefully to the ambiguities and liminalities of imagined experience and develop a more honest imagination. It would be a pity if, reading Winton's work, theologians took its spirituality of place and did not incorporate something of its playful vision and strategy.

Winton's sense of play is not subversive in the postmodern manner of books which deliberately confuse the distinction between fiction and reality, write themselves as self-conscious texts, frustrate expectations of a single, coherent subject by infusing subjectivity and narration with fragmentation and multiplicity, and prefer to see themselves as versions within a quasi-transcendent act of writing. Such texts, deconstructing the objective world of the father's word, challenge theology to imagine the death of God. Janette Turner Hospital's *Borderline* (1987), for example, uses the borderline as a metaphor for meaning, particularly as it resists the framing intentions of the painter-father and the narrator-son. Father and son are competing to make the final meaning of an event (or person), assuming a god-like control and forgetting they are themselves creations in someone else's dream. At the very moment the son goes to finish and possess his story, he finds his father has already painted it. Even so the father's authority has already been dislodged by an earlier story within the story, a story of Perugino which in many ways writes the novel:

> She was searching the crowds for Perugino, who had smuggled an Umbrian girl into Florence. The girl had been murdered by the Medicis. She watched for a man obsessed with a woman in black, haunted by the memory of her eyes (149).

This tiny parable unsettles the father's creation in two ways: it proposes that fiction involves 'an infinite number of possible configurations' (269); and it allows Felicity, the very much created woman, to look back at her male creators and their desire. The narrator-son is Jean-Marc, and even though he compares himself to the evangelist, he is actually a piano-tuner. So his desire for an authorised, sacred text is inflated: he is someone who simply facilitates playing. Similarly, his determination to tell the real story of Felicity is shown to be his way of writing over her absence, of putting his mark on her 'otherness' or 'essence'.

Theologians might find this too metafictional to be of any metaphysical use, but I find it highly significant that one of Australia's most theological writers, Gerard Windsor, should write the death of the father and the struggle with the father's text. *Family Lore* (1991) shows how the death of the father exposes the absence behind language (one of its most compelling images is the father's shroud, never used and now possessed by the son). At one level, the text resists this absence and tries to reconnect with the father and, given developments in narrative theology, it is significant that Windsor uses a form which is somewhere between the essay and the story. At another level, the book proceeds as a competition, with the narrator debating with his characters and the son trying to secure his version of family lore against (but also within) the father's authority. This authority is ambiguous in its effects: it guarantees tradition and supports a surgical logic, but it is also patriarchal and self-centred. If it is also distant, this is itself ambiguous, allowing both father and son to diagnose each other with accuracy, but without contempt. In expressing these losses and recoveries, *Family Lore* grieves for a theological understanding of the father and may name the condition of much contemporary theology. It may be that God has died, but this may only be the God of fathered texts, who may have died from overuse, as well as from all the exercise needed to control the earth-mother whose story lies concealed beneath the authorised version of the heavenly father.

Feminist Mischief

While such a grand assertion may turn out to be only mischief, Australian theology will need a sense of mischief if it is to appreciate how some feminist writers are gleefully overturning the sanctified readings which have become attached to primary Christian myths. Kate Llewellyn's 'Eve' may appear to be just a bit of a joke, but it manages to reposition the preferred reading of the Fall: innocence becomes boring and brainless, original sin becomes an option for experience, an option made by an active and intelligent woman. The story of a satanic temptation is neatly sidelined, because it has been subsumed into Eve's decision on behalf of the necessary, and interesting, ambiguities of experience, the double-sidedness of knowledge:

no it had to end
Eve showed she was the bright one
bored witless by Adam
no work
and eternal bliss
she saw her chance
they say the snake tempted her to it
don't believe it
she bit because she hungered
to know
the clever thing
she wasn't kicked out
she walked out. (Hampton and Llewellyn 160)

Theology may find the right kind of mischief in Bruce Dawe's 'Mary
and the Angel' (244) which uses the Annunciation myth as a way of
satirising that belief in fertilisation technology which has allowed us to
write a very different version (some might say, inversion) of the virginal
conception. But theology might have more difficulty appropriating Sylvia
Kantaris's 'Annunciation', which makes from the same myth a refusal of
logocentric readings of mystery, preferring instead the 'body's arch and
flow', and ending with a mischievous poke at phallocentric dogmatism:

I must be simple to have told them anything.
Just because I stressed the miracle of it
they've rumoured it about the place that I'm
immaculate—but then they always were afraid
of female sexuality.
I've pondered these things lately in my mind.
If they should canonize me
(setting me up as chaste and meek and mild)
God only knows what nonsense
they'll visit on the child. (Hampton and Llewellyn 145)

One could discuss whether this implies denial of Christ's divinity, one could suggest that it demonstrates a contemporary preference for immanence over transcendence, but that would still be working within familiar language and neglecting the manner in which the poem, by breaking Christological dogmas back to their mythic substrata, is interrogating the whole venture of religious language, as well as arguing that much of women's profound experience cannot be sacralised through the predominantly male imaging of the divinity.

Judith Wright's work has become a valuable resource for Australian theologians wanting to consider questions of race and place, but very few seem to notice her powerful poem, 'Ishtar':

> When I first saw a woman after childbirth
> the room was full of your glance who had just gone away.
> And when the mare was bearing her foal
> you were with her but I did not see your face.
>
> When in fear I became a woman
> I first felt your hand.
> When the shadow of the future first fell across me
> it was your shadow, my grave and hooded attendant.
>
> It is all one whether I deny or affirm you;
> it is not my mind you are concerned with.
> It is no matter whether I submit or rebel;
> the event will still happen.
>
> You neither know nor care for the truth of my heart;
> but the truth of my body has all to do with you.
> You have no need of my thoughts or my hopes,
> living in the realm of the absolute event.
>
> Then why is it that when I at last see your face
> under that hood of slate-blue, so calm and dark,

so worn with the burden of an inexpressible knowledge —
why is it that I begin to worship you with tears? (103)

The goddess allows Wright to articulate the ambiguities of the sacred—
presence and absence, indifference and intimacy, life and death—and
the liminality which can attend bodily experiences such as childbirth
and menstruation, associating them with 'the realm of absolute event'.
Carol P. Christ has argued that the affirmation of the goddess means
'the acknowledgement of the legitimacy of female power as a beneficent
and independent power' (121), and thus a reclamation of women's bodies,
wisdom, and heritage. Christ is aware of the threat which theology poses
to theology, and remarks:

> To theologians, these differing views of the 'meaning' of the symbol
> of Goddess might seem to threaten a replay of the trinitarian
> controversies. Is there, perhaps, a way of doing theology that would
> not lead immediately into dogmatic controversy, would not require
> theologians to say definitively that one understanding is true and
> the others are false? Could people's relation to a common symbol
> be made primary and varying interpretations be acknowledged?
> The diversity of explications of the meaning of the Goddess
> symbol suggests that symbols have a richer significance than any
> explications of their meaning can express, a point literary critics
> have long insisted on. This phenomenological fact suggests that
> theologians may need to give more than lip service to a theory of
> symbol in which the symbol is viewed as the primary fact and the
> meanings are viewed as secondary (123).

This seems to me the crucial point: if theology is to dialogue profoundly
with poems like 'Ishtar' and 'Annunciation', it may need to admit that it is
itself a sacred fiction and to uncover, in its own metaphorical activities, that
radical pluralism which enables different tongues to speak the divine 'truth'.
    Of course, I cannot deny that theology is as free as Eve to put aside
the stories it finds 'witless' and to select those which most serve its own

independence of method and concern. (I am aware, that is, that I am indulging my own preference for literary method, just as I am also aware that I am, for the purposes of this argument, using 'theology' as if it were a uniform activity.) However, if the selection of stories becomes too predictable, theology diminishes its chances to dialogue with Australian culture because it diminishes its capacities to imagine difference. A theology involved in that diversity of diversity, 'migrant writing', for example, is a theology involved in translation. This is not simply because it has now to recognise writers such as Dimitris Tsaloumas and Rosa Cappiello who can use a language other than English. It is also because terms we would normally accept as part of the 'English language' are often more different than we realise: we may, for example, focus on familiar themes of 'homeland', 'exile' and 'displacement' and overlook the fact that these themes attract a cultural loading which distinguishes Judah Waten's use of them from Vincent Buckley's use from Ania Walwicz's. Hopefully, then, theology is being translated even as it translates, assessing its own power-centres and (Anglo-Celtic) privileges of naming even as it condemns racism, exposing within itself 'the politics of representing the other as always negative and subsidiary' (Gunew 169) even as it proclaims 'the capacity of the gospel to overcome all barriers of race and culture' (Thornhill 188).

Black Writing and Godtalk

A sensitivity to the power presumptions of Godtalk is particularly important when theology enters into conversation with Black writing. Whether it is advocating Aboriginal culture as instinctively 'gospel' (a current example of the 'Noble Savage' image) or crying for justice, Christian theology has still to take great care that it is not merely sustaining its own guilt and its own nostalgia for meditation, its own way of imagining justice, its own story. Theology can easily accommodate the pathos of Oodgeroo's 'We are Going', although it may find it more difficult to imitate the way the poem is positioned, formally as well as politically, on the margins of the speaking subject. (There is, surely, an irony in the way churchspeak so readily deploys its own powerful discourse on behalf of 'the poor and marginalised'.) Theology can easily accommodate Maureen Watson's 'Memo to J.C.' and Bobbi Sykes' 'Rachel' (Gilbert 49, 36) incorporating their protests about oppressive and hypocritical missionaries into its own social justice agenda, although it needs also to leave well alone, and hear such writers claiming to speak for themselves. Theology may find it difficult to redeem Robert Walker's 'Solitary Confinement' (Gilbert 128), which in many ways tells its readers to shove their sympathies and invests black prison experience with an irreconcilable alienation, unless theology can constitute itself from a sense of helplessness, and perhaps a sense of anger.

Theology's conversation with Black cultures is really a form of inter-religious dialogue, and there is a point at which it is not appropriate to frame such a dialogue in Christian terms, just as there is a point at which it is not appropriate to contain Buddhist writings within Christian boundaries. After all, there is another poem by Judith Wright, 'Eli, Eli', which imagines that Christ's suffering was to watch people drowning in the river of time and freedom and not save them:

He watched, and they were drowning in the river;
faces like sodden flowers in the river—
faces of children moving in the river;
and all the while, he knew there was no river (46).

This ending does more than construct a Christ who suffers the human misuse of freedom; it constructs a Christ who is imbued with a Buddhist awareness that the river of suffering is the river of illusion or unrecognised nothingness. The poem's title may well suggest that we are to conclude that Christ was abandoned by his God because that God was also part of the 'no river'. Certainly Robert Gray, who makes even greater use of Buddhist teaching in his poetry, would consider God an illusion. Gray's poetry might easily prove attractive to Australian theologians because of its precise, meditative awareness of Australian landscapes, especially if that awareness is written like this:

The paperbarks climb
slowly,
and are spreading out, like incense-smoke (77).

However, to be more than selective reading, theology would need also
to acknowledge these lines, which occur in the same poem, 'Dharma
Vehicle':

'No God, no soul'
It is all like a mountain river,
travelling very far, and very swiftly;
not for a moment does it cease to flow.
One thing disappears and determines what is arising,
and there is no unchanging substance
through all of this,
nothing to call permanent,
only Change.
That which is the substance of things
abides as nothing
and has nowhere
a nature of its own.
Its essential nature is Nothingness.

Whereas Gray uses Buddhism as if it is a philosophy of materialism,
Beverly Farmer, in *A Body of Water* (1990), uses Buddhism as if it is a
version of idealism and tries to combine a philosophy of no-self and a
text which is watching itself write itself. While one could read the book's
emphasis on process as an exemplification of the notion that 'The Path
is the Practice' (48), and its formlessness as another version of the river
of impermanence, once could also interpret its self-consciousness as a
covert egotism. Even so, one would need to grant that Farmer's text, in
its desire to be free of self-consciousness and egotism, may be naming
a more general spiritual dissatisfaction, a wider movement towards the
Way which is found 'by discarding concepts, thoughts, words, ideas' (251).

It is not enough to caricature this movement as 'sentimentalism' or 'anti-rationalism' (and forget that the Christian mystical tradition also speaks of this Way, though in language which is so close to contradiction that it has been marginalised by the dogmatic tradition). It is not enough to translate and reduce Buddhism to Western theological categories like 'atheism' and 'nihilism'. Nor is it enough to say with Panikkar that the Buddha did not so much deny God as refuse the question—mainly because Panikkar's argument is more complex, involving a recognition that the principles of identity and non-contradiction, so fundamental to the Western theological traditions, are themselves analogical manoeuvres which provide an unreliable basis for any affirmation or negation in regard to transcendent reality. It is, rather, necessary to consider Panikkar's principles of dialogue: that dialogue must be authentic—'without superiority, preconceptions, hidden motives or convictions on either side', that dialogue must happen at a level deeper than dogmas and at the risk of dogmas, and that it must involve genuine conversation in faith (as distinct from conversation about beliefs). Above all, dialogue involves a risk:

> religious dialogue must be genuinely religious, not merely an exchange of doctrine or intellectual opinions. And so it runs the risk of modifying my ideas, my most personal horizons, the very framework of my life... This amounts to saying that dialogue must proceed from the depths of my religious attitude to these same depths in my partner (50).

It is necessary to enter the desert of Eckhart's 'For the sake of God let go God', receive a different tongue, and so speak within and beyond the traditions.

Dialogue between Theology and Literature

In similar fashion, theology and literature, if they are to engage in genuine dialogue, will need to modify their horizons. I realise that there are theologies being written which incorporate literary material in sensitive ways and which highlight the imaginative character of their own endeavour. But I am not aware of Australian theology (I am not necessarily speaking of Australian theologians) investigating methodologies which are interdisciplinary in such a manner that authority is evenly distributed between literature and theology. Might it help, for example, to consider the work of Giles Gunn. Gunn claims that our appreciation of the relationship between religion and literature might be deepened if we saw the 'hypothetical' character of each. After proposing four main models of literary theory—mimetic, pragmatic, romantic, semantic—he examines how each emphasises a different aspect of religion. Because of its commitment to language as creative, the semantic model usually stresses our symbol-making capacity as analogous to a religious process. The romantic model highlights the visionary element of religious experience and expression, while the pragmatic model imagines religion as revealing supernatural truths since it sees literature as servant to the integral values of life. For the mimetic model, the religious character of a literary work is sought in the work's inner movement and dramatic structure, since it is here that the work imitates what is essential to reality. Gunn urges a principled eclecticism in all questions of theory and method, stressing that the real problem for methodology is not one of clarity, but one of catholicity.

Gunn then advances a fifth model, the 'hypothetical', which is designed to complement the other four. Literature entertains possibility. It creates a circuit of belief and desire between actual and possible worlds. Gunn gives three reasons for suggesting that the hypothetical can mediate between literary and religious modes. Literature is religious, first of all, because of its commitment to 'vital possibility', its half-conscious faith in all that lies beyond the range of immediate perception, 'that experiential component which constitutes at once the substance of our hope and the ground of the imagination itself' (85). Secondly, argues Gunn, we will only assent to the hypothetical, in literature as in religion, if it is commensurate with our deepest sense of self, a sense of self which is shaped by what we take to be ultimately real and meaningful. Finally, we experience in literature something analogous to the religious experience of reality as alternate.

That experience is had through the metaphysic of the text: 'this executive principle, which is responsible for the work's coherence both in formal and ideal terms, functions analogously to the notion of ultimacy in religious experience' (86).

Another possibility would be, with T. R. Wright, to explore literary forms as sites for the interaction of literature and theology. Affirming the degree to which form is meaning, Wright works with narrative, poetic and dramatic modes, not simply to demonstrate the religious dimension inherent in works like *The Prelude*, but also to suggest the manner in which formal changes register shifts in cultural and religious history. For example, he argues that formal changes which occur in the novel (from metaphysical to realist to metafictional modes) correspond to directions which have opened up within religious sensibilities since the nineteenth century. While it may be comforting to agree with Wright that modern novelists like Waugh, Greene and O'Connor defend the 'reality' of the supernatural and contest the dominance of a liberal humanism in which religious claims are the consequence of an ambitious and erroneous epistemology, it has become increasingly important to follow further, as Wright does (but all too briefly), and to initiate some dialogue between theology and metafictional writings, which absorb notions of 'reality' into their own self-conscious fictive procedures. Is theology a lie and might some such recognition liberate theology from its anxieties about absolute reality? Wright also engages with absurdist drama, suggesting that *Waiting for Godot* is, formally, 'a play about the desperate but unfulfilled desire to be saved' (193), a judgement which is saved from theological cliché by Wright's earlier remark:

> Absurd plays … do not argue about the death of God and the meaninglessness of life. They present traditional theological language as absurd and inappropriate, failing to address the reality of the human condition. They can be seen themselves, however, to be returning to 'the original, religious function of the theatre', to make people aware of their 'precarious and mysterious position in the universe' (188).

In this way, considering how literary form functions to create meaning, Wright attempts to uncover a language and a concern which theology and literature share, even if the more sceptical of contemporary theorists might think Wright still too attached to 'the referential dimension of language' (39) and prefer Roland Barthes:

> by refusing to assign a 'secret', an ultimate meaning, to the text (and to the world as text), (writing) liberates what may be called an antitheological activity, an activity that is truly revolutionary since to refuse to fix meaning is, in the end, to refuse God and his hypostases—reason, science; law (147).

Wright acknowledges the influence of Barthes, citing this very passage (4) with its death of God—death of author equation. It is this very equation which is used by Mark C. Taylor in his effort to develop his a/theology and disputed by Kevin Hart in his attempt to deconstruct deconstruction and recover negative theology as at once constitutive of and deconstructive of positive, metaphysical theology.

Taylor argues that notions of God, self, history, and book, are interdependent and grounded in a pattern whereby 'Christian theology is repeatedly inscribed in binary terms'—some of the opposites being God/World, Eternity/Time, Being/Becoming, Presence/Absence, Transcendent/Immanent, and Identity/Difference (8). Deconstruction does not so much prefer the neglected term in these relationships as occupy the margin between them, in such a way as to subvert 'the coherence, integrity, and intelligibility of this network of oppositions' (11). Taylor, then, sets out to deconstruct Western theology by playing out notions which are very much other than the four traditional concepts: the death of God, the disappearance of the self, the end of history, and the closure of the book. He then attempts an a/theology in which he reformulates 'God as writing, self as trace, history as erring, and book as text' (13). Hart thinks Taylor goes too far, allowing deconstruction to become a counter-construction and forgetting its intrinsic need to remain a strategy for reading. In this, Hart engages in a deconstruction of Derrida and contemporary readings of Derrida, to point out that deconstruction can be neither theistic nor atheistic without becoming again caught in the very 'totalisation of meanings' it wants to resist. When he further proposes that negative theology is deconstructive, he is not suggesting that theology appropriate deconstructive strategies simply to correct its own metaphysical excesses, nor that we argue for an anti-metaphysical theology—'an inversion of a metaphysical hierarchy remains immanently within metaphysics' (125)—but that, since 'it is the onto-theological constitution of metaphysics which determines the concept of God' (96), we re-evaluate the role of negative theology, which he sees as revealing a non-metaphysical theology at work within positive theology:

A non-metaphysical theology would accordingly be one which would show that metaphysics obliges us to take God as a ground; it would uncover a sense in which God could be apprehended as a non-ground; and it would show that the conceptions are systematically related (104).

It is the final movement, the demonstration that ground and non-ground, presence and absence, are irreducibly entwined, which incorporates the conversation between deconstructive readings of literature and theological interpretation. And theology, as interpretation, becomes involved in the breaking/making of meaning. Just as a sign does and does not repeat its originating presence without showing that the very possibility of such repetition is at once the possibility of some identifying and some differing, an interpretation does and does not repeat its originating text. The more it aspires to an original meaning, the more it releases those eccentric and heretical readings which will confuse and disperse its towered world.

Literature has not yet really had the chance to dialogue with theology at this level of methodology, to discuss how each embodies, not simply marginal concerns, but marginal meanings. I am not saying any one of these works, and they are simply examples, has the answers, only that they are raising the questions. Nor am I saying that Australian theology must dialogue with deconstruction, only that an Australian theology which wants to work with literature will need to acknowledge and appreciate the effects of postmodernism in more recent writing or it will find itself drawn to literature (especially of the forties and fifties) which can be used to reaffirm its own metaphysical fictions. If this happens, Australian theology will simply reauthorise theology's conventional methods and use literary material as a new way of sustaining, if not old conclusions, an established way of talking. It will not, in its own textual procedures, be sufficiently kenotic to become incarnate in culture(s). It will want the meaning of the crucifixion, but not the crucifixion of meaning.

Works Cited

Anderson, D. 'Strange Angels'. ABC Radio 24 Hours. July, 1992.

Astley, T. *The Acolyte*. St Lucia: University of Queensland Press, 1980.

Barthes, R. *Image-Music-Text*. New York: Hill and Wang, 1977.

Boyd, M. *A Difficult Young Man*. Ringwood: Penguin, 1984.

Chenery, S. 'The Cosmos of Helen Garner', *The Australian Magazine*. Feb 29–March 1, 1992. 17.

Christ, C.P. *Laughter of Aphrodite*. San Francisco: Harper and Row, 1987.

Dawe, B. *Sometimes Gladness*. Melbourne: Longman Cheshire, 1989.

Edwards, D. *Called to be Church in Australia*. Homebush: St Paul Publications, 1989.

Farmer, B. *A Body of Water*. St Lucia: University of Queensland Press,1990.

Garner, H. *Cosmo Cosmolino*. Ringwood: McPhee Gribble, 1992.

——. *The Last Days of Chez Nous*. Ringwood: McPhee Gribble, 1992.

Gilbert, K.(ed.) *Inside Black Australia*. Ringwood: Penguin,1988.

Girard, R. 'The Gospel Passion as Victim's Story.' *Cross Currents*. Spring, 1986.

Gray, R. *Selected Poems*. Sydney: Angus and Robertson, 1990.

Gunew, S. 'The Migrant Experience.' K. Goodwin and A. Lawson (eds.), *The MacMillan Anthology of Australian Literature*. Melbourne: Macmillan, 1990.

Gunn, G. *The Interpretation of Otherness*. New York: Oxford University Press, 1979.

Kelly, T. *A New Imagining*. Melbourne: Collins Dove, 1990.

Kirkwood, P. 'Two Australian Poets as Theologians: Bruce Dawe and Les Murray.' *Compass* 19, 1985. 31–44. Reprinted in *Discovering an Australian Theology*. Peter Malone (ed.). Homebush: St Paul Publications, 1988.

Hampton, S and K. Llewellyn. *The Penguin Book of Australian Women Poets*. Ringwood: Penguin, 1986.

Hart, K. *The Trespass of the Sign*. Cambridge: Cambridge University Press, 1989.

Koch, C. *The Doubleman*. London: Chatto and Windus, 1985.

Lawson, H. 'Water Them Geraniums.' J. Barnes (ed.), *The Penguin Henry Lawson Short Stories*. Ringwood: Penguin, 1986. 142–67.

Marr, D. *Patrick White: A Life*. Sydney: Random House, 1991.

McAuley, J. *Collected Poems*. Sydney: Angus and Robertson, 1973.

Murray, L. *Collected Poems*. Sydney: Angus and Robertson, 1991.

Oodgeroo Noonuccal (Kath Walker). *We Are Going*. Brisbane: Jacaranda Press, 1964.

Panikkar, R. *The Silence of God: The Answer of the Buddha*. New York: Orbis Books, 1989.

———. *The Intra-Religious Dialogue*. New York: Paulist Press, 1978.

Taylor, Mark C. *Erring: A Postmodern A/theology*. Chicago: University of Chicago Press, 1984.

Thompson, B. 'Patrick White.' *Compass* 14, 1980.

Thornhill, J. *Making Australia: Exploring our National Conversation*. Newtown: Millennium Books, 1992.

Turner Hospital, J. *Borderline*. St Lucia: University of Queensland Press, 1987.

White, P. *Flaws in the Glass*. Ringwood: Penguin, 1981.

———. *Voss*. London: Eyre and Spottiswoode, 1957.

Windsor, G. *Family Lore*. Melbourne: Minerva, 1991.

Winton, T. *Cloudstreet*. Ringwood: McPhee Gribble, 1991.

Wright, J. *Collected Poems 1942–1970*. Sydney: Angus and Robertson, 1971, 1979.

Wright, T. R. *Theology and Literature*. Oxford: Basil Blackwell, 1988.

Believing More and Less

THE LATER POETRY OF VINCENT BUCKLEY

The finest theologian Australia has produced is, arguably if ironically, a poet and layman, Vincent Buckley ... Buckley's overtly religious writings of the late fifties and sixties would be well worth collecting as a rare example of a highly original mind working in an Australian context on religious ideas. —GERARD WINDSOR

WHEN GERARD WINDSOR SUGGESTED this in 1981, Vincent Buckley was still widely recognised as a leading figure in Australian Catholicism, even though he had already declared that he felt no allegiance towards Catholicism as an organization (Booth; Davidson). During the fifties and early sixties, Buckley had worked on *The Catholic Worker* and *Prospect*. He had opposed hard-line Communism, but also the Movement and Santamaria's version of political activism. He had been deeply committed to 'The Apostolate' at Melbourne University, seeking to integrate Christian ideals and university life, giving critical respect to both, encouraging a realism at once spiritual and social. 'The Apostolate' was inspired by a theology of Incarnation, and Buckley's writings[3] provided further explorations and applications of this primary Christian metaphor.

---

3. Buckley's poetic writings include: *The World's Flesh* (Melbourne, Angus & Robertson, 1954), *Masters in Israel* (Sydney, Angus & Robertson, 1961), *Arcady and Other Places* (Melbourne, Melbourne University Press, 1966), *Golden Builders and*

In 'The World Awaiting Redemption' he argued that the Incarnation elevated the whole of creation and called for a Christian Humanism grounded in profound appreciation of 'the world'. In 'The Image of Man in Australian Poetry' he attempted an incarnational metaphysics, arguing that our metaphysical condition was 'localised in (our) actual physical surroundings, embodied in (our) sensuous and spiritual reactions to (our) world' (*Essays* 1). In *Poetry and Morality* he suggested that literature and Christianity had in common an incarnational mode. At the same time, his first two volumes of poetry, *The World's Flesh* (1954) and *Masters in Israel* (1961), were heavily influenced by his theology—too heavily. While these works are attracted to the authoritative, mysterious resonances or dogmatic language, they are not really at home with it, and their privacy and abstraction indicate that the dogma of Incarnation has not yet been embodied in the poetry itself. Buckley's work of this period can be said to have anticipated Vatican II (particularly *The Dogmatic Constitution on the Church in the Modern World*), working as it does with the advanced thinking of theologians like Suhard and Congar. Yet, as Vatican II was releasing its programme for renewal, Vincent Buckley was publishing *Poetry and the Sacred* (1968) and turning his investigations from dogmatic theology to anthropology. At the same time (and the process is one of reciprocated influences), the poetry of *Arcady and Other Places* (1966) and *Golden Builders* (1976) becomes more natural in its resonances and more precisely physical in its images. These volumes still employ theological terms, such as 'resurrection', but as a way of testing, rather than securing, belief.

Other Poems (Sydney, Angus & Robertson, 1976), *Late Winter Child* (Melbourne, Oxford University Press, 1979), *The Pattern* (Melbourne, Oxford University Press, 1979), *Selected Poems* (Sydney, Angus & Robertson, 1981). His prose includes: 'The World Awaiting Redemption', *The Incarnation in the University*, ed. Vincent Buckley (London, Geoffrey Chapman, 1957), *Essays in Poetry, Mainly Australian* (Melbourne, Melbourne University Press, 1957), *Poetry and Morality* (London, Chatto & Windus, 1959), *Poetry and the Sacred* (London, Chatto & Windus, 1968), 'Remembering What You Have To', *Quadrant*, Sept.–Oct., 1968, 19–27, 'The Strange Personality of Christ', *Quadrant*, Sept.–Oct., 1970, 11–25, 'Imagination's Home', *Quadrant*, March, 1979, 24–29, *Cutting Green Hay* (Melbourne, Penguin, 1983) and *Memory Ireland* (Melbourne, Penguin, 1985).

In the later poetry—*Late Winter Child* (1979), *The Pattern* (1979) and the 'New Poems' of *Selected Poems* (1981)—theological and liturgical terms, now very rare, are used to establish Catholicism as a cultural memory, rather than to indicate any formal allegiance. This could be seen simply as a movement from belief to scepticism. It can also be seen as a development consistent with an anti-ideological, indeed expatriating, intention within Buckley's work and with the poetry's growing preference for the 'idiom of sensation' (*The American Model* 143) over the language of dogma. The process is signalled in 'Places':

> Hardly thinking, in a strange church,
> A man, forgetting the common rubric, prayed
> 'O God, make me worthy of the world',
> And felt his own silence sting his tongue. (*SP* 79)

When Buckley constructs his account of the period surrounding this poem, the period of Vatican II, he shapes himself as a Catholic trying to escape the Church's 'self-enclosing formalism' (*Cutting Green Hay* 231). In *Cutting Green Hay* he presents the founding of the ecumenical Catholic magazine, *Prospect* (1958), as involving a refusal of party-line Catholicism: 'We would demonstrate the uselessness of the standard Catholic view by not applying it' (249). He contrasts the openness and pluralism of this endeavour with the wider Church's 'slightly secretive, furtive' triumphalism (253). Referring to Vatican II itself, Buckley more definitely declares a withdrawal from institutional religion:

> The Vatican Council had started, full of plans for averting the organizational and psychic disasters which had already happened inside Christianity. Fine as it was in many ways, it produced too little too late. From my point of view, it was a time to wait and possess one's soul, to move back from institutional definitions of reality, to take an anthropological approach, as it were, to institution and self alike. What was the actual state of 'belief'? What did 'belief' mean? If belief was being abandoned, what in the human psyche

was abandoning it? Something had failed deep in the Christian spirit, not to speak of other less formal spiritual traditions, in the way that something fails in the blood, or the womb, or the spinal column, and the failure needed to be realized in the present sense. Not many of my friends wanted to hear this dire message; most of them thought me wrong, and only a few wished to abandon sociology or theology in the interests of that mistress of guesswork and intuition, anthropology (250).

This shift can be seen in *Poetry and the Sacred*, where Buckley, looking for a way of discussing poetry which, though not devotional, does evidence an ultimate awareness, distinguishes between 'religion in poetry' and 'poetry as a religious act' (9). Working from the studies of Mircea Eliade, Buckley argues that poetry is a religious act inasmuch as it creates its own versions of 'sacred spaces' (9) and that doctrine and devotion have force in religious poetry 'only so long as they are seen as having a present relevance to questions of personal identity, meaningful action, and the inner structures of feeling' (11). In an attempt to counter the subjectivist tendency of this approach, Buckley then affirms, of sacred objects and poetry, 'both a movement into the world of common experience and a movement within the common experience to transcend or complete itself' (15), a movement connected to a shift in modern sensibility, 'a shift from the transcendent to the immanent, from person to process, in specifying the sacred' (58).

By the time *Late Winter Child* and *The Pattern* are published, Buckley is dissatisfied with dogmatic definitions about God, the Church, the human personality, and the soul. Such dogmatic definitions have an absolutist mode which obscures and ignores the fact that the mysteries they indicate are mysteries touched by all religions. In *Cutting Green Hay*, Buckley gives other reasons for the distant stance he more and more assumes within Catholicism. These strengthen the picture of one dissatisfied with ideological positions: it is largely an unrestrained ideological and institutional impulse within Catholicism which changes morality into moralism, turns priestly service towards priestly dominance, and sets an opposition between 'aprioristic thinking' and 'existential speculation' (231).

To appreciate how far Buckley has travelled within his Catholic context, we need to linger over a comment made in his interview with Jim Davidson:

> I should add that I'm not an ex-Catholic who hates Catholicism, or who wants to reject it or anything of that sort at all. In fact, I would go to Mass sometimes, but I am a non-believer in any sense that would be meaningful to the great majority of Catholics. On the other hand, I think that the Catholic mystical tradition and the Catholic sacramental tradition are magnificent historical developments (450).

While this seems conciliatory, Buckley, a skilled theologian, has quietly discarded the majority view by referring to the sacraments as 'historical developments', thus emphasising their temporal and changing character. Conventional Catholic theology would not give such an emphasis without qualifying it, by affirming that the sacraments are, in their origin and efficacy, of the supernatural order.

At one level, this shift in Buckley's position occurs as part of his anthropological exploration of religion. At another level, it is the expression of an imaginative need. Buckley, in *Cutting Green Hay*, is aware of this: while applauding the theological renewal of Vatican II, he notes that it may still be irrelevant to 'the needs of those whose imagination cannot entertain the presence of God' (292). There has been, he argues, over the past two centuries, a weakening of the sense of the prophetic power, the sense of nature as hierophanous, and the sense of 'the sacral possibilities in human relationships' (292). Catholic theology continues to emphasise its 'sacraments', but fails to appreciate this 'divorce in sensibility': great emphasis is placed on the cultic and liturgical celebration of the sacraments, but very little on the sacramental context, the sense of Christ's sacramental presence beyond the official enactment (292). In other words, the Catholic Church has nurtured its theology of the sacrament, but neglected that sacramental imagination which is needed if the rituals are to sacralise the heart, the subconscious, and the ordinary object. Buckley's fascination with the almost sacred particularity of sensate objects and with 'the idiom of sensation' has obviously taken him on a way different from that outlined in 'An Art of

Poetry', where James McAuley directs him to 'the Word' as the true source of language and 'universal meanings' (McAuley, *Collected Poems* 70).

This does not, however, mean that Buckley's poetics become less religious: he consistently maintains some belief in the sacralising role of poetry. In 'Imagination's Home', he suggests that, in a poet of substance, religious feeling and poetic feeling tend to be the same (28). In his interview with Elizabeth Booth, he identifies poetic perception with a rhythmic sense of life, suggesting that poetry matches the vibrations of nature with those of the psyche, and declaring: 'I think this is the key religious act: to try to experience, to understand and sometimes extend what Freud called the "oceanic feeling"' (30). In his interview with Jim Davidson, he observes that, with *Golden Builders*, he was looking for a 'locally mimetic' poetry, showing an intimate relation between the world outside the self and the language which the self has learned (454). When he calls Ireland a 'source-country' it is because it represents a religious sense of the relationship between person and place (Davidson 444). In a more recent interview, Buckley's position is even less dogmatic (Kavanagh and Kuch). Responding to questions about *Poetry and the Sacred*, he seems to retain that book's emphasis on the psychic and rhythmic nature of poetry, but to avoid any too confident reassertion of the sacralising nature of the poetic act. Speaking of his attempt to free his imagination from Catholic restraints, Buckley is concerned to reiterate his anti-ideological position:

> I was writing *Poetry and the Sacred* in order to broaden my thinking, but a lot of readers took it to be a different version of sectarianism— or a denominationalism without the determination—so I was getting my Catholic point across without using Catholic language. But I was not doing that at all. I was trying to do the opposite. I was trying to keep my Catholic base, but extend the meaning of everything I was thinking so that it did not have to have any reference at all to institutional ties (262).

Even so, he still accepts that his poetry is evoking 'the paradisal possibilities of life' (263) and that only poetry can 'use all the processes of language to

create either the depth and intensity, or the transparency, of experience'
(265). Whether he is expounding a theology of incarnation (as in the
earlier poetics) or proposing an appreciation of the hierophanous quality
of experience itself (as here), Buckley consistently locates the sacred in the
music and radiance of fact.

It is possible to discern analogies between this development in
Buckley's poetics and what emerges in his later poetry. In one sense, this
poetry becomes 'more religious' because it more transparently embodies
the deepest rhythms of sensation and language. In another sense, it is 'less
religious': not only are Catholic references very rare, but they refer more
to a cultural memory than a belief and represent the failure of imagination
which Buckley perceives in Catholicism itself.

There is a moment in 'Two Half-Languages' which registers this:

> But thoughts never stop. In the stark night
> I lie awake, inside the crackling traffic,
> insomnia, like language,
> an eighth sense, knowing
> I've lost it all, the sound
> of their blood, the nose-pitch of their voices,
> the rustle of their God, the music
> inside me, once steady as a millwheel. (*SP* 13)

If 'their God' has been lost, it is because the source, the place of
interconnected rhythms, has been lost in the transition from Irish language
to Australian situation. This is seen in the grandfather, whose Australian
context does not quite banish the language of his source-country, still
present as 'the traces in emotion of a language'. These traces, however, do
not provide a sense of completion. Whiskey does. As the poem opens,
whiskey offers a stillness 'like the land's stillness' and a 'fume of light /
we have no language for'. As the poem closes:

> You hand me the whiskey, turn it ice-bright

as the light
in a mirror: turn it
like music, and look into
the amber smokiness, turning me like music. (*SP* 13)

The music between the speaker and the whiskey is reciprocal: it is a ritual of recognition and union. Rather than conclude that God has gone to drink, we can ask whether Buckley's poetry is now more firmly taking up a new direction: searching for the 'mythic substratum' of his Irish identity, which might deepen his imaginative (and religious) life in its 'psychological substance'. These are terms Buckley uses when he describes the effect of exile on his ancestors:

> What was obviously missing from their lives was the mythic substratum of the Irish religion in which they took such a psychological interest. Because the Irish past, the reality of Irish imaginative experience, had been snipped away from their beliefs, they lived a foreshortened religious life, often intense and sometimes generous, but lacking in psychological substance. Further, they lacked all sense of themselves as having a defined and important family history, for they were the inheritors of Anonymous Man (*Cutting Green Hay* 11).

'An Easy Death' is not so confident of finding the 'mythic substratum' in a natural setting where the place does not want to know the person. Nature offers only alienating images: 'the crow's picked bones', 'dead breast bones', and 'stupid as a leaf'. The one point where Nature and speaker harmonise is at the very beginning, where a torn wing vibrates to the rhythm of a faltering heart:

> Death makes its sweep over the grass,
> wind rolled in leaves, a torn wing.
> An answering fickle beat
> flaps at the ribcage.

Indeed, the speaker is preparing for death, giving away his possessions as if he can no longer bear the feeling that the world is giving him away. He and the poem are performing a ritual of loss. When, in this context, he invokes his Catholic background, it functions more as a lost ritual than as a confirmation and elevation of the natural ritual:

> Catholics, we were trained for it,
> the maze of words, the candles
> unrolled from years of tissue paper
> for this moment, the petite firm
> forward-leaning priestly movements,
> necessary as the dying itself;
> trained to compose the soul
> for all crises: death, cancer, waste of summer,
> insolence, neglect, humiliation,
> the drying-out of friends,
> the uncouth stroke of money,
> the ordeal of homegoing,
> the rising mist of time,
> this priest packing his cold oils. (*Meanjin* 2, 1984; 218–221)

This detached catalogue does more than recall a lost Catholic world where sacramental ritual provided a pattern for death. The last line places the priest among the crises for which the soul has to compose itself. By using 'cold', the poem implies that the sacralising oils are indifferent to the suffering, perhaps impotent before them, and so it opens a gap between the world of private suffering and that of official ritual. It incorporates, therefore, the very criticism Buckley makes of Catholicism: its failure to develop a sacralising imagination as the enlivening context for the sacraments themselves. While it presents itself as an intimate, sensory memory, this perception is informed by displacement.

If 'An Easy Death' thus registers some failure in Catholicism's sacralising life, 'Purgatory' (*TP* 31) registers the profound shifts which have occurred in dogmatic and theological areas. In conventional theology, purgatory, imagined as a temporary fire, represented a real and eschatological process of purification which some souls—those marred by 'venial sins'—must undergo before entering heaven. In the poem, purgatory becomes little more than a projection of the puritanical heart. The father is praying the rosary and imagining the fires of purgatory. However, the real fires are within him, inherited from his own father's fierceness, his 'drooping' mother and 'his gangrened brother'. In contrast to this interior imprisonment the natural world is represented as glowing with new existence and freedom:

> Outside, a rising wind; objects
> in the night paddock
> lay free, gaining their new existence
> away from him: axle, hubcap, milk-can
> abandoned in the tussocks,
> in the rusty grass, glowed with moisture.

Here, as in the poetry generally, the impulse to observe details of this world breaks free of a dogmatically-expressed concern with the next world. Once again, facts are found to have a radiance—and their 'moisture' gently rebukes the fires, whether of puritanism or purgatory.

With 'Your Father's House' (*TP* 28), it is paradise that makes a faint appearance: paradise, though, as a place within sensation, where the rhythms of various noticings combine to hover 'on the edge of outcry'. Within this paradise of unified sensation, there is one perception with a specifically Catholic significance: 'Behind the door / the pale blue Child-of-Mary cape'. This momentarily conjures a time when Catholic culture offered a secure source of identity and ritual. The 'Children of Mary' sodality was a group for unmarried women, whose members wore a blue cloak and white veil, colours of the Blessed Virgin. On the third Sunday of each month, wearing their regalia, they sat together during Mass in pews marked by the sodality's banner and standards. On the same Sunday they attended Benediction and held their own meeting. Their blue and white presence also graced processions, such as those of Corpus Christi and Holy Thursday. Buckley's reference is, however, disinterested: the blue cape is simply one sensation among others, including spittle and pipe smell, which create the moment.

Catholicism, then, stays in Buckley's imagination as one of the idioms of sensation. Where its colours, smells, and patterned movements contribute a sense of the immanent sacred, a sense of origins, Catholicism keeps a place within the poetry's structures of feeling and language. Even so, that place is on the edge of sensation.

In *Late Winter Child*, Buckley does not declare of the new, late child that he has 'seen / God work in her', as he does in 'A Prayer for Brigid' (*The World's Flesh* 16). What *Late Winter Child* does is to create a voice profoundly suited to the restless sensations and changing relationships which attend the new life. The sequence subtly varies its spaces, rhythms, tonal textures, and sensate foci in order to travel the distance between surface and depth, as also between hope and dread. For instance, when VII opens, it is attuned to the speaker's pulse, 'thick, scratchy as wool'. In this cramped five-line stanza, his senses receive 'the patio-white / wall of nothing', and he himself is passive before morning's activities. Then the poem makes a lighter space: two-line stanzas, with a greater number of unstressed syllables. Becoming active, the speaker turns his eye to the woman, in whose skin the morning light is not ill-tempered, but 'at home'. Then the wall of nothing is displaced by her scarf, blown 'across the / sulphurous air'. Such shifts in rhythm occur also between poems. III, weighted with anxiety, opens 'heavy with pulse', while IV, which sets this anxiety within the promise of new life, opens with more of a 'trailing' rhythm, just as it also opens out to the external world. In XVII, at times outward and sensuous in its direction, at times withdrawn and stiff, the spaces represent the woman's flowing hands, then the man's throat 'often stiff with unshed vomit'. Similarly, the spaces which open XV embody 'a waste between us', all the things that should be said, while the closed-in shape of the final lines mimes the speaker's very private observation. Yet XXVII has no spaced lines—and there the closeness is one of shared experience and love. In this way the sequence's rhythmic character mimes the varying pulses of the situation.

If the poetry does disclose the sacred, extending the individuality of things to the threshold of deep relatedness, one of the primary characteristics of its world is a religious kind of ambivalence. Fundamental religious experience is very often associated with a limit-experience, where paradoxical feelings at once heighten and merge: feelings of finitude and infinitude, of belonging and estrangement, of desire and dread, even of despair and hope. Buckley, in the language of this poem, is achieving something similar by sounding moments until they resound with an 'ultimacy' somehow both beyond and within immediate sensation:

In your heat, my breath surrounds you.
Twelve months   the thought of lightning
glided across
your birthday   the heat
was heavy as water
low cloud
shivered with light

a waste between us

            I should have told you,
then, death was your rival
that darkened my brain
with fears, plans, the thin copper
movements of a worm on the hot stone.

            Instead, I listened for the
velvet sounds, moths, door-handles,
the rise of a footstep
the comb's kiss over the hair, its parting
tightened by summer   my eyes carried
all day their pinpoint of blood   all day
I was the object in your path
giving no echo (XV)

In its pace of language and noticing—so edgy with separateness and intimacy—this is a poem which represents much of the sequence. What it also represents, in that combination of separateness and intimacy, is the pattern of ambivalence which contributes to the religious quality of *Late Winter Child*.

The sequence tells its story very much in terms of tensions: between summer and late-winter—with the child representing both (II); between the renewed tenderness of husband and wife and the husband's obscure sense of shame (XII); between the promise and the pain of the wife's wrists 'gorged with child-veins' (V). Birth itself is strangely ambivalent: as he remembers his child's birth, the speaker suddenly deflects attention to an image which conveys the darkness beyond birth:

> (so, any second, in the clear space
> by this wall, the cat will leap
> and fill the sight completely
> as a door opening
>   open darkness beyond it) (XXI)

Here, where the beginning of life is connected to its ending, we are reminded of the sequence's fundamental tension: between the new life embodied in pregnancy and the ageing process experienced by the speaker. He tells how, during the previous summer, banks of lavender watched them walking home each night and suggested the promise of wheat. Then he finds that the banks of lavender have been cut (XVI). Driving towards his wife, he finds his movement ruled by her pulse:

>   You travelled
> fretting in my soul, as hour by hour
> distant as the moon
> the blood seeped in your body
> dangerously: (X)

Just as this anxiety seems reconciled (when the landscape offers him her face) the rhythm of seeping blood gives another image—of his ageing:

In six weeks my hands
had aged so much
they shook brushing your hair.

This ending leaves his anxiety exposed. Other poems soften it. At one point he is frightened that, after fifteen years, he might lose his wife 'distant with child', and remembers her in 'strong bright light'. Then he goes into the bedroom, where he finds her with 'cool linen on (her) shoulders' (VI). This could be ambiguous—XIX speaks of 'dead linen'—but the same line is used earlier in the poem to clothe his happy, sensuous memories of her, and linen is also explicitly associated with birth:

You called when you were sleeping
from that room   we shared, that bed
where I'd waited listening
for the birth-sounds   (so often
cool as linen   on your breast);

It is also important to note that anxiety and ambivalence are reconciled by way of the senses: not only does the 'cool linen' appeal soothingly to the tactile imagination, but the line itself has a subdued onomatopoeic quality which converts that appeal into an aural consolation. This is true of the entire sequence: its reconciling rhythms are consonant with its sensual character. Through its double-edged conception of love and existence and its breathing edges of language, the sequence conveys an obscure but profound sense of interreaching immanence.

Buckley's later poetry often uses the deeply resonant processes of sensation to suffuse immediate shapes, textures, colours, sounds, and smells with feelings of extra significance, and also to explore the imaginative origins of such feelings—feelings which, in this context, may be called religious. 'Origins' (*SP* 13) includes yet another portrait of an outwardly aggressive, inwardly defeated male ancestor:

Through the two gates, with their old rusty

tin plaques, he was cut off
as in a highrock wilderness.

He kept no line to us; he never left
his name written; he rode, or walked,
the brown hills like a severed body.

This moment is approached by way of coldly objective language, miming
the cool outwardness of the person, in which a journey becomes a grocery
list—and objects such as 'whiskey' and 'bushels of feed' are noted, but
denied the sensuous presence they achieve in other poems. What this
preparatory verse does is establish that the man's condition—walking
the land 'like a severed body'—is a result of his denying his psychic and
mythic origins. In order to heal this wound, Buckley advocates an easing
back into the deeper levels of remembered sensations, sensations which
are characterised by inwardness—the 'soft closed space'—rather than
separated objectivity. The difficulty of this task is evident in the way the
final verse struggles to locate objects within 'smells'—some remain listed
as in the first stanza; some are sensuous, with an invitatory immediacy.
The final feeling is that the poem has sounded the depths of sensation
enough to make tenuous contact with a point of origin:

Rustle of sacks, the straw-ends
crushed in, the seasoned leather,
mice, spittle, bread, dung, oats,
whiskey, old papers, the sunsmell beating down
into the halfdoor, from between round hills,
till it took a mushroom or a tuberous
density; smell of sapling in the ash.
In these smells we were begotten.

Buckley says that Ireland functions for him as a source-country 'in the sense
that the psyche grows from and in it, and remains profoundly attuned to
it' ('Imagination's Home' 24). The source-country is the rhythmic space

where psyche and Ireland are analogues, each of the other. (They are also strangers.) The source-country is also a religious source:

> Further, there is reason to think that we develop our religious feelings—our feelings of significance in life—according to what images of earth and sea (archetypes of earth and sea) dominate our psyche. Such images are cognate with our images of animal life, and, through them, with images of human life; so that, psychologically, all the living organs of the place provide one ecosystem of the imagination. Whether or not gods grow from such systems of interiorised perception, certainly they seem to be expressed in them. For me, this imaginative eco-system bears a deeper resemblance to Ireland than to anywhere else ('Imagination's Home' 24).

This notion of Ireland as a source-country might appear to be a private mythology, a substitute for Catholicism. For instance, Patrick Shivers, whose Irishness and Catholicism make him oppressed and invincible, could well represent a new version of the heroic belief once exemplified in Tarsisius and Mindszenty.[4] In addition, the place names, saints, and holy wells which are invoked still possess a memory and authoritative resonance akin to that of a dogmatic tradition. They become sacred sites of language in a way which recalls the earlier use of terms such as 'eucharist' and 'resurrection'. It may well be that some escapist elements do operate within Buckley's mythic endeavour, but to isolate them is to ignore the possibility that the primary purpose of a source-country is not to provide a substitute for the religious feelings once more obviously associated with Catholicism, but rather to penetrate the 'mythic substratum' of those feelings. At that level, Buckley's notion of a source-country is really a story of a return to paradise. His grandparents, denying their Irish origins, exile themselves from the source, with all its integrating rhythms, and so from the psychic origins of religious feeling. 'What remained was the ache of their absence...

---

4. See 'Tarsisius' (*The World's Flesh* 9) and 'In Time of the Hungarian Martyrdom' (*Masters in Israel* 50–57).

One of the possible tasks for their grandchildren is to get back as much as possible, by whatever means are available' ('Imagination's Home' 25). Since the source-country nevertheless remains unreachable (even as it moves through him), Buckley also continues to develop structures which have persistently characterised his imagination: a metaphysical tension between belonging and exile, with its corresponding emotional tension between separateness and intimacy. 'Endlessly/ you ride before it, being watched, never touching.' ('Gaeltacht', *TP* 12)

Although most clearly manifested in the emigration of Buckley's ancestors, the 'Fall' from origins is not really a geographical condition. (Nor is it an attempt to deny Australian identity.) As 'Rousings of Munster' (*TP* 16) demonstrates, the source-country is lost when these Munster people deny, not the place, but the psychological significance of the place, and so abandon their mythopoeic memory. His ancestors fail to appreciate Munster as a source, seeing it as 'a hag's country', with its gaps and black shadows imaging the hag's dribbling mouth and the stretch marks of her exhausted productivity.[5] Indeed, they utter the credo of all those ultimately displaced, declaring of Munster: 'It could be anywhere.' 'Gaeltacht' (*TP* 10–15) tells the same story:

> They were from Munster. Every part of Munster. But would not talk about it: 'No, we're Australians now.' Really, a separate kind of Irish (*TP* 14).

They banish Ireland from their speech. 'From them came no cries of "Up Tipp." or "Rebel Cork"' (*TP* 14). What remains are ruins of the imaginative eco-system: 'yet they talked occasionally in tongues, in a world-defying wife-hating babble, drank Paddy ...' (*TP* 14).[6] Buckley then begins the

---

5. 'The source had been rejected as rejecting. It was like disowning the memory of a cruel mother.' 'Imagination's Home', 25.
6. Buckley says of his father that while he was establishing his Australian identity, his existence retained its 'Irish Mode'. cf. 'Imagination's Home' 25. Also, *Cutting Green Hay* 12–15.

reversal of the story: his ancestors' place of arrival becomes for him 'a point of departure, not home' (*TP* 14), as the son takes up the burden of exile:

> Their silence was not only lock but key, to be turned sometime in the future, their sullenness a burden to be carried secretly and placed back whence it came (*TP* 14).

Clearly this is not a choice between nations, but a choice for the imagination, that it may begin a reciprocated return to the land of origins, where religion, as well as poetry, may discover the source of 'its flavour, its dimensions, its very shape and guiding concepts' ('Imagination's Home' 25). 'Gaeltacht' makes this quite explicit:

> The origin is not
> one place but ten thousand:
> not a particular but a general
> fish-web of fathers: something so ordinary
> you sit half-suffused with fear
> in front of it. (*TP* 12)

Buckley's return to the source is not, then, simply accomplished by his living in the country: it is more a matter of discovering where the country is living in him—and where it is not. Under the influence of a sea-changing rhythm, he is able to find himself being harmonised with Dublin's music:

> Ireland as usual
>
> the soft pads of hands
> blessing, or welcoming,
> till I thought the raw seawall
> floating in rain, the sea
>
> burn, and the city,
> for all its cold

willow colour, melt into it
no more than a membrane
of air between us. ('Membrane of air', *TP* 63)

Here, by way of his exact, intimate attention to sensation, to its movement made into the rhythm of the voice, Buckley arrives at his 'source-country'. If Ireland is a place of 'stones laid inside stones, / believed in fearfully as holy wells'('Gaeltacht', *TP* 10) he does not pretend he has arrived home by making surface contact with the holy wells. He arrives when he recovers the mythic perception which lies beneath belief and sees how 'further out, on the peninsula, the stones in their intricate circle seem almost to decorate the sun that pleasures them'('Gaeltacht', *TP* 13). Places function as holy spaces when the sacralising imagination can

Concentrate on the music. It trails and swells like the grain of the land itself. Lean your elbows; your teeth hum with sound entering you. ('Gaeltacht', *TP* 13)

The rhythm of place is one with human and animal in 'Membrane of air':

Throughout Autumn, the pigeons walked, using
voices soft as mucous
under moss; you'd scratch your skin
as though scraping at lichen.
The tree withered all night. Even
the gravel stepped softly
the stonewalls were
tuned with rain, the glass
incontinent, flowing.
You'd never think
the earth
could tire of its animals. (*TP* 61–62)

However, not all experiences of Ireland afford such feelings of paradisal significance. In the same poem, 'Membrane of air', Dublin is described ambiguously as 'fracturing / and clinging as an eggshell', while the speaker must approach this 'source-country' on its own terms, whether it be 'guest, foreigner, son' (*TP* 59). 'At Millstreet' (*TP* 23) shows how, even though he touches the stones of the curing well and hears 'the tree-trunks settle / in the peat, fathoms down', he is still receiving the hospitality reserved for tourists. In this sense the Ireland poems seek not so much to dispel the feelings of foreignness found in 'Sinn Fein: 1957' (*MI* 13), but to search their source, and so place them in relationship with feelings of familiarity. This is well realised in a moment when, frightened of his foreignness, the speaker begins to sweat, then finds in that a bond and so survives to see a sternly reassuring image:

> I sweated
> woodsweat
>   outside, the green mound
> soft and vulnerable as moss
> upheld its one treestump, surviving
> death by water. ('Membrane of air', *TP* 59)

Obviously he will not survive if, like the Dublin pensioner, he is 'afraid of thresholds, / hoping for nostalgias'('Membrane of air', *TP* 58). He must undergo the precise discipline of the senses, and that involves exposing the nerve-ends of the self, as well as of the world. Indeed, in this highly sensitive poetry they have become much the same: as he is edging towards the sensations and speech of Ireland, they are moving their edges further into him. While either may be happy to have the 'forelands', neither can afford to deny the 'whetted stone':

> Hence
> the need for Gaeltachts, forelands
> shouldering the common burden, where we come
> to suffer that past, that enigma,

which will visit us
in the night-patterns, jeering
at our sleeplessness, while through the wrack
of their survival the land shines
in the distance, like a whetted stone. ('Gaeltacht', *TP* 15)

It would seem, then, that the Ireland poetry is not escapist, that it is rather a discipline of sensation. Its intention is not to return to the past, but to revivify the present. Ireland itself offers no easy guarantees. Indeed, as the Buckley figure is looking for some connection with the spirit of the place and 'letting (his) mind bulb around one / image or another', he suddenly finds himself within an image of suffering:

Yet, miles inland, as I
pulled the heather from the road's
rockface, I could feel the sea
penetrate my hand. ('Gaeltacht', *TP* 10)

'Discipline in Baggott Street' (*TP* 55) is important here, as it tells how the masters of pub conversation fear and avoid what they might hear from stones. Buckley renders the pace and place of their conversation superbly: the visual textures of the bar, the way they 'drank, quiet as madmen', the inflamed conversation on pieces selected from 'a wrack of topics'. Finally, one drinker speaks of discipline, and another of Original Sin. It is a moment which concentrates a great deal of Catholic culture: discipline, will-power as the way to virtue, the power against evil; Original Sin as the somewhat comforting reminder that Irish men, at least, are only human. There is the fierceness, and then the compassion. Buckley, however, intimates that the moment has renewed force because the traditional language releases and renews the primitive religious feeling which gathers beneath their voices:

Things to be made good
in our throat and soul, some ancient
metaphor or piety come to life

in the spittle of their voices.

With their moral and doctrinal language so suddenly enlivened by its mythic substratum, the drinkers, who had 'avoided speaking freely / about freedom', hurry home—'home', that is, in its literal and comfortable sense. They leave 'a blind man / listening at the table'. To sense what it is he hears we need to return to the poem's beginning and recognise the discipline which the too eloquent drinkers avoided:

Inside this humpbacked bridge
are voices, adhering to the stone
or, at your approach, falling,
as if they tasted
the terror of something needing to be said.
We passed them: no trouble.

If the blind man has heard these voices and their terrible, necessary words, it may be because he has touched the 'unimaginable centre' feared in 'The Blind School' (*TP* 24). Certainly, if hearing is to be done on 'this humpbacked bridge', then it will be painful. And even if sight is restored, Ireland will not necessarily be any closer to the senses, as 'Write' (*TP* 22) indicates:

and when the warmth
crept into, conserving
the bared room, what you
felt was   your eyes returning.

Remember it. Forget nothing,
standing level with the cloud-eye.
Yet you have not seen, not touched,
the buds of Ireland.

Ireland invites and refuses the poet's language. In fact, Buckley's imagination has always set its search for 'home' in play with its sense of 'exile', and the poetry's images of child, source-country, and God are different versions of that persistent tension. 'In Time of the Hungarian Martyrdom' has God voyaging between the heroism of Mindszenty in Europe and the professed cowardice of the speaker in Melbourne. 'Stroke' is searching for God in the dry distances of the land and the heart. 'Golden Builders' locates its God somewhere between the city and the grave, and we do not know if the grave is meant to be empty or inhabited. The religious, then, is structured in a way which corresponds to the poetry's own central concerns and strategies—as, for example, the relationship between estrangement and belonging which characterises Buckley's treatment of Australia and Ireland, the relationship between intimacy and distance which lies beneath his evocation of love, and the liminality of a language which wants to enter deeply into sensate experience and break through to moments of deeper realization, transparency, even innocence. What the later poetry shows is the later stage of this process, whereby traditional religious symbols are more and more incorporated into Buckley's expatriating imagination.

At the same time, it shows the imagination stretching out to respond to a world which is varied and particularly immediate, a world of rural memories and international travel, of horse-racing and pubs, of gestation and ageing, of steel and sedatives, of political protest and cynicism, and in such a way that the moral and spiritual dimensions of that world are embodied in its actual condition. It may well be that Buckley's greatest achievement as a religious writer was to take the notion of 'immanence' seriously and to risk dogmas in a way that other Catholic writers like McAuley and Webb were not prepared to do. In this his poetry challenges and somewhat reconciles the separation of 'sacred' and 'secular' which so deeply characterises and confounds Western religious imagination. Corresponding to this, there is a development in language, as the poetry modifies the hierarchical strategies of its earlier forms and voices and incorporates contemporary influences which sustain its search for the 'idiom of sensation'. To communicate the depth-dimension of its sensed world, Buckley's poetry no longer needs emblematic phrases and rolling rhetoric. It speaks in an idiom which combines precision and sensuousness, as if enacting a process of sensation which is at once a work of observation and inwardness.

Works Cited

Booth, E. 'Vincent Buckley: An Interview with Elizabeth Booth'. *Quadrant*. August 1976. 27–32.

Buckley, V. 'Ease of American Language'. *The American Model*. Joan Kirkby (ed.), Sydney: Hale & Iremonger, 1982.

——. *The World's Flesh*. Melbourne: Angus & Robertson, 1954.

——. *Masters in Israel*. Sydney: Angus & Robertson, 1961.

——. *Collected Poems*. Sydney: Angus & Robertson, 1971.

——. *Selected Poems*. Sydney: Angus & Robertson, 1981.

——. *Cutting Green Hay*. Melbourne: Penguin, 1983.

——. 'Imagination's Home'. *Quadrant*. March 1979, 24–29.

——. *The Pattern*. Melbourne: Oxford University Press, 1979.

——. *Late Winter Child*. Melbourne: Oxford University Press, 1979.

Davidson, J. 'Interview: Vincent Buckley', *Meanjin* 4, 1979. 443–458.

Eliade, M. *The Sacred and the Profane*. New York: Harper Torchbook Edition, 1961.

Kavanagh, P. and Peter Kuch, 'Scored for the Voice: An Interview with Vincent Buckley'. *Southerly* 47:3, 1987. 249–266.

Windsor, G. 'Australian Literature and Catholicism'. *Australasian Catholic Record*. April 1981. 118.

James McAuley

THE POSSIBILITY OF DESPAIR

He held a small company spellbound during a whole lunchtime while he spoke of the beauty and pathos of the film [of Thomas Mann's Death in Venice*], and of 'man's search for absolute beauty'. He said that the film in its own way 'spoke the language of desire'. He said that when we are closest to grasping what we most desire we are closest to the possibility of despair.* —GWEN HARWOOD

THIS ORPHIC CONFIGURATION OF beauty, desire, and death may seem out of character to those who serve at the shrine of McAuley the conservative, anti-communist, Catholic politico-poet, but I think it uncovers the negativity that originates his writing. I want to move out from 'Because' (*CP* 200), one of McAuley's most well known poems. It was written in 1966–67 and became part of the autobiographical sequence, 'On The Western Line', that ushered in the late phase of his career. To start with the very obvious, 'Because' is a 'because' poem. It wants a final reason for human sorrow. Yet it writes fall, fault, death, belatedness, and displacement. It presents as a story of reconciliation, yet performs a series of complex, interrelated variations on 'descending'. It seems to be coming to terms with limited parents and limited love, but despair is already hidden in the opening:

My father and my mother never quarrelled.
They were united in a kind of love

As daily as the *Sydney Morning Herald*,
Rather than like the eagle or the dove.

This stanza performs a descent from linguistic and romantic purity to daily print and deceptive appearances. The central incident, of the son recoiling from his father's rejection, confirms that, because love is flawed, the son must learn a language of disguise:

Small things can pit the memory like a cyst:
Having seen other fathers greet their sons,
I put my childish face up to be kissed
After an absence. The rebuff still stuns

My blood. The poor man's curt embarrassment
At such a delicate proffer of affection
Cut like a saw. But home the lesson went:
My tenderness thenceforth escaped detection.

There is a fall figured in the line breaks: 'kissed' descends to 'absence', 'stuns' to 'blood', and 'affection' to 'Cut like a saw'. The rhyme scheme becomes, as often in McAuley's work, a means of contesting meaning: 'cyst' against 'kissed', 'sons' against 'stuns', and 'affection' against 'detection'. It is the last rhyme that sets division at the heart of communication and institutionalises this as the father's rule. This secret and separated place of non-detection will eventually emerge as the 'central deadness', which itself reprises the image of the dead heart made memorable in 'Envoi'. In other words, I do not see the final 'despair' as something which defeats the poem's attempt at hope, but something being summoned from the beginning. What brings about the poem's undoing is what brings about the poem: the fall of and from the father. The father is a (god-) figure who encourages and thwarts the son's desire to close the circle of meaning, to have a 'Because', a source and end. Because he falls from the father, and sees in that the fall of the father, and because he makes these falls irrecoverable by making them undetectable, the son falls back onto a language of separation (and disguise), which is to say that he falls into the separation within language.

The poem's final and most fundamental evasion is to shift attention from the imperfections of the father to the imperfections of a son who has yet to face judgment day:

> Judgment is simply trying to reject
> A part of what we are because it hurts.
> The living cannot call the dead collect:
> They won't accept the charge, and it reverts.
>
> It's my own judgment day that I draw near,
> Descending in the past, without a clue,
> Down to that central deadness: the despair
> Older than any hope I ever knew.

While this is one of McAuley's favourite deferrals, from history to eternity, it here unravels any theological ambition the poem might have had because it defers the fear of rejection across the grave and sees its judging God as a figure who might execute the ultimate rebuff. The father, that is, becomes God, and so the son's hiding heart arrives at its last counterpart, 'that central deadness: the despair / Older than any hope I ever knew'. What appears to be theology's answer to the pain caused by the father's rejection is also a disclosure of theology's fault. Theology is also at fault in 'Father, Mother, Son' (*CP* 181), which opens:

> From the domed head the defeated eyes peer out,
> Furtive with unsaid things of a lifetime, that now
> Cannot be said by that stiff half-stricken mouth
> Whose words come hoarse and slurred, though the mind is sound.

This is a father who, because he derives presence and power from 'unsaid things', sanctions the defeat of meaning. His 'half-stricken mouth' and slurred speech are figurative as well as physical, associating with the unsaid, the furtive, and the defeated. While it would be easy to see the defeat as psychological, this is to ignore the way in which 'defeated' and 'domed' look to each other. That glance releases the possibility that the church defeats the father, but also the possibility that the high and hollowed dome, which is both father and church, is defeated by words that come hoarse and slurred, however 'sound' its mind might be. And even as 'though the mind is sound' is used to maintain belief in some transcendent truth, 'sound', as also another version of 'words', brings such belief into question.

When the poem attempts to frame the dying father within theological discourse, it cannot get back to Paradise, to sacred word, but has to settle for a work of 'sad geometry':

For fifty years this one thread—he has held
One gold thread of the vesture: he has said
Hail, holy Queen, slightly wrong, each night in secret.
But his wife, and now a lifetime, stand between:

She guards him from his peace. Her love asks only
That in the end he must not seem to disown
Their terms of plighted troth. So he will make
For ever the same choice that he has made—

Unless that gold thread hold, invisibly.
I stand at the bed's foot, helpless like him;
Thinking of legendary Seth who made
A journey back to Paradise, to gain

The oil of mercy for his dying father.
But here three people smile, and, locked apart,
Prove by relatedness that cannot touch
Our sad geometry of family love.

The father has obviously abandoned his Catholicism in order to marry the mother. In the fifties it was not uncommon for Catholics to believe that such a man, if he died unreconciled with the Church, would be damned. Even so, I would argue that the poem, written in 1962, is not simply reflecting a particular theology, but also projecting onto that theology its own sense of the lost father, much as 'Because' projects on the divine judge its own inability to abandon the rejecting father. In this sense the father's 'unsaid things' and 'slightly wrong' prayer have their analogical counterpart in the son who cannot achieve 'the oil of mercy', and their analogical and ultimate consequence in a God who may not speak the word of mercy.

The *'Hail, holy Queen'* is a prayer to Mary, as 'mother of mercy', from the 'poor banished children of Eve' who suffer the world as a 'valley of tears'. It is the 'gold thread' that may yet lead the father through his labyrinthine 'lifetime' and restore him to eternity's cloth. However, as soon as this 'thread' is introduced it gets knotted. The father says the prayer 'slightly wrong, each night in secret': a description that turns the prayer back towards the furtive eyes and slurred words of the opening stanza and forward to the negativity in 'Unless that gold thread hold, invisibly' (especially negative in a poem where 'invisibly' is caught up with the furtive, unsaid, and secret). The son, thinking of Seth's quest for mercy, becomes a surrogate for the father threading his way through the labyrinth, but, since he has already named himself and his father as 'helpless', he might also represent the father's separation from God. This separation is then confirmed in 'But here', which disengages the 'sad geometry of family love' from the 'legendary' and the 'gold'. The theology of mercy fails, therefore, to compensate for the theology of damnation. So the poem's use of theological discourse generates not consolation but contestation, showing within itself meanings 'locked apart' and offering the historical moment, the 'But here', nothing more than a 'relatedness that cannot touch'.

A similar sense of the fault within theology is at work in 'Pieta' (*CP* 179). At first reading, it is easy to believe this poem affirms the redemptive power of the Cross. At other readings, it becomes more difficult to ignore the contest coded in the rhyme scheme, whereby 'Cross' is aligned with 'loss', 'light' with 'night', and the touch of a 'hand' with the inability to 'understand', with the more negative term, in each case, having the final say. When the 'came' of the child's birth is then associated with the 'no-one to blame' of his death, one can certainly read a statement of acceptance, but one can also say that birth and blame are drawn together. When one follows the connection between 'farewell' and 'I cannot tell', one can say that this rhyme embodies the difficulty of painful speech, even the inadequacy of language, but one cannot quite deny that it might also signal a farewell to language, a despair of making meaning. Using 'the Cross' to signify hope, the poem actually encounters 'the way of the Cross' in a dark corner of its own making: the more it wants to manufacture a theological meaning for death, the more it implicates theological meaning in loss, fault, and death. Surprising as it may seem, McAuley's poetry here reflects Mark C. Taylor's account of the origins of postmodernism:

> Postmodernism begins with a sense of irrecoverable loss and incurable fault. This wound is inflicted by the overwhelming awareness of death—a death that 'begins' with the death of God and 'ends' with the death of ourselves. We are in a time between times and a place which is no place. Here our reflection must begin (6).

This atheological bent is active in other late poems, such as 'Music Late at Night', 'Moulting Lagoon', and 'Parish Church'. While the final word of 'Music Late at Night' (K 223) is 'care', suggesting commitment and even compassion, that word still connects, by way of rhyme, to 'despair'. And this rhyme seals a moment when the speaker, waiting for 'the start of a new day', can only see a 'lighted empty street'. 'Moulting Lagoon' (K 228) sees writing as being 'always...too late', declaring: 'My marks on paper are a kind of postscript.' It wants the clear presence that might come with its final word, which is 'simple', but by the time it gets to 'simple' its voice is stained with an awareness of 'The beauty almost destroyed, or the light fading'. 'Parish Church' (K 228) also writes itself into a time of late belief. The first stanza seems still to see the vision of ceremony, but, even as it mediates the entire drama of redemption through its stained glass window, it brings together 'heavenly places' and 'bonewhite' in such a way as to hint at some death in the theological enterprise. At one level this is explained in the next stanza, which tells of the speaker's disillusionment with the liturgical reforms initiated by Vatican II. The third stanza then completes this story with its depiction of a late, stubborn belief. It is, however, worth remembering that this kind of 'I will not let you go' belief is well rehearsed in 'In a Late Hour' (*CP* 105), which was written some twenty years before 'Parish Church'. It is, therefore, possible that 'Parish Church' need not be read simply as the autobiography of a disillusioned Catholic conservative:

> I bring with me my griefs, my sins, my death,
> And sink in silence as I try to pray.
> Though in this calm no impulse stirs my breath,
> At least there's nothing that I would unsay.

The speaker's determined presence before the stained glass, the mediator of transcendence, the theological sign, is undone, not only by the fault in Vatican II, but also by the rhyming of 'death' with 'breath' and 'pray' with 'unsay'. These disempower Catholic symbolism, arresting all activity of the word with the negativity of 'there's nothing that I would unsay'. As a double negative, this final line resists scepticism in order to maintain belief. If, however, a reader allows a slight emphasis on, and a slight pause after, 'nothing', and if a reader sees that the juxtaposition of 'silence' and 'calm' also associates 'nothing' with 'griefs', 'sins' and 'death', such a reader will receive the full impact of the absence that was hidden in 'bonewhite'. For this reason anyone wanting a biographical angle on this poem would do better to forget McAuley's comments on liturgical renewal and to consider instead his assessment of the contemporary condition of religious language:

> Christianity has lost its traditional picture-language. From original Jewish sources, from the Roman world, from medieval cosmology constructed out of analogies, a symbolic language could be drawn. That language is now obsolete...I think it was partly this that made Pascal say of the new universe: "The eternal silence of those infinite spaces terrifies me" (*K* 136).

'Private Devotions' (*K* 221) can also be read as the story of a believer disillusioned by changes in his church. The speaker can be read as a 'McAuley' who felt that Pope Paul VI undermined papal authority when he hesitated over *Humanae Vitae*, that renewed liturgies had lost all sense of transcendent beauty, and that 'situation ethics' was corrupting theologians who should be defending moral absolutes (see 'A Small Testament' *K* 126–39). This is a valid reading, but it does assume that the loss of theological confidence is caused by conditions external to, even denied by, the poem itself, whereas I want to entertain the possibility that the loss of theological confidence is caused by the poem. The title positions the believer in a place analogous to the 'artesian heart' of 'Envoi' and the 'central deadness' of 'Because'. It is a place caught between the withdrawal and return of Christ, determined by his absence. 'The tabernacle open wide' is a precise liturgical reference. After the Mass of the Last Supper, on Holy Thursday evening, the Blesssed Sacrament is removed from the main altar and the tabernacle door is left open to show that Christ has been delivered into the hands of his enemies and his Passion has begun. The Blessed Sacrament is not returned to the tabernacle until the Mass of the Resurrection. The empty tabernacle is, then, a liturgical symbol for the absence and 'death' of Christ. Of course, the empty tabernacle was too dangerous to be left alone. It was, in practice, surrounded by homilies on how believers ought not imitate the sleepy Apostles, ought not leave Christ to suffer alone in Gethsemane, but should stay and pray before 'the altar of repose', where the Blessed Sacrament was secreted. So that the 'unsafe' symbol of absence was, in a manoeuvre very familiar to McAuley's poetry, redirected until it became a call to presence, a test of faith. However, no amount of such theological 'care' can suppress the way in which the empty tabernacle gives reason for 'despair':

> Floor-wax, a trace of incense lingers;
> The tabernacle open wide
> Is like an empty tomb inside.
> Beads held in reluctant fingers

Guide the murmur of the breath.
Trespasser now tread with care
Between the reasons for despair
All the way as far as death.

The poem does indeed take negativity 'All the way', naming the private god, the one at the empty heart of the poetry's theological fabrications, 'death'.

One way of reading the darkness of McAuley's late poems is to relate them to his disillusionment in the post-conciliar church, his awareness of approaching death and his alienation within cultural and political debates (particularly as the children of Ern began to take their revenge and *Quadrant* was found to have been partly funded by the CIA). In such a reading the late poetry falls away from the calm and ceremony associated with Catholic-confident poems such as 'New Guinea' and 'Celebration of Divine Love'. Another way of reading the late poetry is to see it as a manifestation of a story of despair that has been told and retold throughout the poetry, and so stress continuity.

Two poems that explicitly propose a 'Catholic' metaphysics are 'A Letter to John Dryden' (*CP* 85–95) and 'Celebration of Divine Love' (*CP* 73–76), from the post-conversion volume, *A Vision of Ceremony* (1956). Yet in each of them there is a moment when the discursive, dogmatic enterprise falters and a lyrical, mystical discourse momentarily emerges. This moment (and it is a faultline in McAuley's poetry) shows how the poetry negotiates between classical and romantic, discursive and lyrical. It also shows that the poetry's religious claims are made within (not above) that negotiation, even though the terms might sound a little different: when it is writing belief McAuley's poetry is writing between hope and despair, doctrinal and mystical, theological and atheological.

It is possible, from one angle, to describe 'Celebration of Divine Love' as an allegorical narrative that sees nature perfected by grace and expresses confidence in theological representation. It is even possible to conclude from this that the poem sees its discursive, doctrinal mode being 'perfected' as it surrenders to its lyrical, mystical moment. But such a reading, if it stands alone, is likely to leave unexamined the possibilities for negativity which emerge right at the end:

> Now is the three hours' darkness of the soul,
> The time of earthquake; now at last
> The Word speaks, and the epileptic will
> Convulsing vomits forth its demons. Then
> Full-clothed, in his right mind, the man sits still,
> Conversing with aeons in the speech of men.
>
> You gentle souls who sit contemplative
> In the walled garden where the fountain flows,
> And faint with longing have desire to live
> But the brief flowering of the single rose,
> Knowing that all you give
> Into the keeping of your tender Lord
> Shall be enriched and thousandfold restored:
> Before the herons return
> Abide the sharp frosts and the time of pruning;
> For he shall come at last for whom you yearn
> And deep and silent shall be your communing;
> And if his summer heat of love should burn
> Its victim with a sacrificial fire,
> Rejoice: who knows what wanderer may turn,
> Responsive to that fragrant hidden pyre! (*CP* 75– 76)

This seems at first to celebrate the triumph of complete signification as the Word rises above the void and casts out its demons, as 'the man' recovers 'right mind' and heavenly speech. Then it falls away from its own apocalyptic utterance, entering into a more intimate, and particular, address, forgetting what it has just named as the 'Unmeasured measure of immensity' and noticing 'the single rose', forsaking the eternal now for a moment 'Before the herons return'. In other words, having reached its theo-liturgical apotheosis in its vision of Christ as 'the bond and stay of his creation', the poem cannot hold it. Once the poem utters the phrase, 'speech of men', the 'Word' withdraws: in the final stanza Christ has returned to the future as a 'tender Lord', signifying hope rather than presence, and drawing language back into 'longing'.

The' 'mystical moment' in 'A Letter to John Dryden' is very brief and only faintly disturbs the speaker's attack on secularism, positivism, relativism, and Communism. If, however, it is read in conjunction with the self-deprecatory close (in which the past is lost, the future cancelled and the self 'gone'), it introduces the possibility that the polemic is as much an effect of mystical and poetic negativity as a response to cultural and philosophical perplexity. This is, after all, a poem addressed to a dead poet by a speaker who can no longer write the poetry he wants, a speaker who comforts himself with the thought that, should his verse fall back into oblivion, 'I don't suppose I'll care when I am gone' (*CP* 95).

In 'New Guinea' (*CP* 80) it is the missionary, the Christian hero, who is 'gone', and the poem might be described as a reading of his roadside grave. The dedication is a cue for the belief that the missionary is a sign of Christ. This is the belief that seems to conclude and complete the poem when Archbishop de Boismenu is explicitly made a sign of that 'Splendour, simplicity, joy' which comes when life, 'Configured ... in eternal mode', becomes 'authentic'. Yet, if the poem makes the missionary a sign, it also shows that the sign of the missionary is his grave, which emerges from the dash after 'Splendour, simplicity, joy'. This gap is as much making as made by the poem.

At one level the language is being used to convey the ideal of a Christian society founded on justice and peace and the reality of cultural and political corruption. At another level the language is being used to say the unsayable. The first stanza reads the island according to the word 'apocalypse', so that there is as much breaking as making of meaning, concealing as well as revealing: the 'doors of the spirit' may 'open' but the island still guards a knowledge that is 'secretive' and 'obscure'. If 'bird-shaped island' is a quiet pun on Holy Spirit, Bird of Paradise (see 'To the Holy Spirit' *CP* 69), it is hardly a pentecostal tongue that the poem finds, but a convulsive speech, a language of volcano, earthquake, and shaking trance. In the second stanza the land is called the figure of 'inmost dream'. That dream is, however, so inmost that it cannot quite countenance the fair periphery of words, obscuring itself in phrases like 'untellable recognition' and 'wordless revelation'. Such paradoxes are, of course, readings of 'apocalypse' and, as such, they support the poem's theological enterprise, but they also gesture towards a silence that may and may not accept the protectorate of words. If the terms for the knowledge of mystery are 'untenable' and 'wordless', these also remember 'secretive' and 'obscure', and so cannot entirely ensure that the unknown is a positive space. This ambiguity is given its fullest expression in the third stanza:

> The stranger is engulfed in those high valleys,
> Where mists of morning linger like a breath
> Of Wisdom moving on our specular darkness.
> Regions of prayer, of solitude, and of death!

While 'specular darkness', coming out of St Paul's 'we see now through a mirror darkly' (I Cor. 13:12), extends the *via negativa* of 'untellable recognition' and 'wordless revelation', it does other things as well. If the phrase wants to say there is a wisdom which is dark, it cannot not say as well that darkness lies behind the reflecting surface of language. As the stanza then moves to recognise the Wisdom who is companion to the Creator breathing over the void and talking up creation (Proverbs 8: 22–31), it is also re/members and so re/embodies the void it wants to keep beneath the breath of God. So 'breath' is rhymed with 'death', and the final stress on death jeopardises the appeal to prayer and solitude. The fourth stanza then shifts into 'Life holds its shape', as if a slightly more discursive, straightforward tone will teach unruly words their place, and the following stanzas preserve this tone until the last image of the missionary's roadside grave. This image is carefully controlled: although splendour, simplicity and joy go into the past with de Boismenu (in whom they 'were seen'), the perspective may be opening into the future since the final emphasis falls on 'road' (rhymed with 'eternal mode'). 'New Guinea' is, then, confident in its belief, but this does not mean it is denying the spaces it opens between history and eternity, words and revelations, prayer and death.

There is also evidence of profound and constitutive negativity in poems which predate the use of mystical theology, and this adds weight to the argument that the negativity is not just an indication of spiritual disappointment, nor of mystical inclination, but also an effect of the fall within language. In other words, the poetry's atheological activity comes before and may even count on its commitment to theological symbolism. McAuley's early love poetry, for example, predicts the McAuley who will tell Harwood that desire and despair are on intimate terms. 'Monologue' (*CP* 3) intends 'To speak of love' but also knows that 'talk / Corrupts imagining.' 'When Shall the Fair' (*CP* 3) ends by rhyming 'unfulfilled' with 'build'. 'She Like the Moon Arises' (*CP* 4) comes to rest on a contrary combination of 'infinite' with 'nevermore'. Even 'Celebration of Love' (*CP* 34–37) finally assumes the status of a non-epithalamion, coming 'too late', bearing a meaning which is indiscernible, promising and witholding its praises.

Something similar happens in McAuley's early use of Greek mythology. 'The Hero and the Hydra' (*CP* 45–59) uses the goddess Ceremony to embody ritual in a way that anticipates the later use of New Guinea and Catholicism. Yet Ceremony enters through a story of 'Fall'. Summoned as a way of saying that history has abandoned myth, she abandons history to the knowledge that 'The myths are void'. Following her disappearance, the poem offers the death of a god. 'The Death of Chiron' is a narrative of kenosis: 'The year sinks underground, and with it I / Put off divinity and learn to die.' The hero also dies. 'The Tomb of Heracles' then seals the poem's concerns:

Look, cranes still know their path through empty air;
For them their world is neither soon nor late;
But ours is eaten hollow with despair. (*CP* 59)

Yet it is not simply the world that is 'hollow': the poem's opening image, of 'A dry tree with an empty honeycomb', implies that poetry too is somehow empty, unknowing, always too soon and too late. This may help explain why the fall from the ceremonial order to the divided human occurs also in McAuley's 'landscape' poems: from an early poem like 'At Bungendore' (*CP* 5) through to the late Tasmanian scenes, McAuley's landscapes function as much to displace as to place their speakers, throwing them back from the consolations of order to the dilemmas of will. They allow McAuley to continue to use his favourite myth, which is the myth of the Fall. To quote 'At Bungendore':

> The blossoms have their will;
> I would that I had mine:
>
> That earth no more might seem,
> When spring shall clot the bough,
> Irised by the gleam
> Of tears, as it does now.

What I am suggesting is that the poetry's involvement in this myth of fall also implicates it in the fall of myth.

Of course someone may object that this is a warped reading of McAuley's poetry, and clearly it is, or, rather, it is a reading of a warp within his poetry. It is a reading designed to show the degree to which, the manner in which, the poetry admits that theology is not immune to the dangers of speech. It is particularly signficant that when the speech of Christ first enters McAuley's poetry it enters as a sword, and no doubt a double-edged sword.[7] 'Jesus' (*CP* 20) opens by touching the book of Ezekiel. Although the 'thick and thorny' script intimates that prophecy may involve some share of pain, the book of revelation is seen in terms of power, judgment and light. The book of nature is not so bright:

> Then turning from the book he rose and walked

---

7. 'The word of God is something alive and active: it cuts like any double-edged sword but more finely: it can slip through the place where the soul is divided from the spirit, or joints from the marrow; it can judge the secret emotions and thoughts. No created thing can hide from him; everything is uncovered and open to the eyes of the one to whom we must give account of ourselves.' (Hebrews 3: 12–13)

Among the stones and beasts and flowers of earth;
They turned their muted faces to their Lord,
Their real faces, seen by God alone;
And people moved before him undisguised;
He thrust his speech among them like a sword.

This makes the faces 'real' by making them also secret, hidden, private, and invisible. If, in the same movement, it also makes them faces 'seen by God alone', this is not entirely consoling. Rather, it appears as if they are seen by God because they cannot not be seen. Truth is not so much a triumph of presence as a failure of pretence. Divine speech may have the power to make things transparent, at least to God, but it also leaves them 'muted' and 'undisguised' (which could be taken to insinuate that speech and disguise are related). Speech as a sword opens a wound between word and recognition. It is easy to say that this wound is a painful truth, but such an interpretation cannot quite control the dangerous surplus in 'sword', such as the possibility that reality is somehow resistant to and defeated by revelation. The final image continues the poem's concern with speech:

Spoke to the dust, the fishes and the twelve
As if they understood him equally,
And told them nothing that they wished to know.

The speech of Jesus promises community among its hearers, community based on equality of hearing. That is, it promises an answer to theological desire because the one truth will be heard by all and all will become the one truth. But just as it seems about to fulfil its promise, the speech of Jesus denies them the peace of meaning, telling them 'nothing that they wished to know'. If a reader allows a slight pause between the shock of 'nothing' and the disappointed, falling cadence of 'they wished to know', then Christ's speech has placed his listeners, not at the axis of metaphysical vision, but within the (supreme?) cycle of emptiness and desire. The hearers of the words of 'Jesus' have been set up for a fall.

Works Cited

Harwood, G. 'Gentleness'. *Quadrant,* March, 1977, 16.

Kramer, L. (ed.) *James McAuley: Poetry, essays and personal commentary.* St Lucia: University of Queensland Press, 1988.

McAuley, J. *Collected Poems 1936–1970.* Sydney: Angus & Roberstson, 1971.

Taylor, Mark C. *Erring: A Postmodern A/theology.* Chicago: University of Chicago Press, 1984.

Francis Webb's 'Harry'

CAN IMBECILITY BE MADE INNOCENT?

FRANCIS WEBB (1925–1973) is an Australian poet who was diagnosed a paranoid schizophrenic and spent much of his later life in institutions such as Winson Green, Callan Park, Plenty Hospital and Rydalmere Hospital. Some readers are encouraged, therefore, to think of his work as embodying the myth of the mad poet, heart blasted by vision, rationality more liminal than limited. They might be called the 'believers'. Others, the 'sceptics', will not accept that Webb's well-known obscurities are oracular and see only confusion.

Douglas Stewart was among the first to claim that Webb's poetry had greatness and others—David Campbell, Vincent Buckley, Bruce Beaver—have since supported his view (*Poetry Australia* 56, 4). James McAuley, preferring coherence, was more cautious: 'That the powers of a remarkable poet were present in Webb one cannot doubt: that they were used effectively is open to considerable doubt' (273). All agree that Webb's work is densely metaphoric, but disagree as to where its associative energies gather and where they scatter. This argument can only conclude that Webb's work is sometimes great, sometimes not, then degenerate into a numbers-game. What is more interesting is to consider whether the poetry's successes and failures are equally due to its own attempt to make a partnership of scepticism and belief.

In imagining suffering, particularly mental suffering, Webb's poetry wants to avoid sentimentalism and factualism. It does not want its symbolic readings to escape immediate experience, nor does it want experience to become alienated by empiricism. As belief, the poetry wants to transfigure the sick, dying, and insane, making them agents of Christ, the sign of contradiction. So the poetry tries to claim a paradox: there is a kind of suffering which is glory. As scepticism, Webb's poetry rarely succeeds in converting its raw experiences into sure belief. It keeps struggling for a descriptive simplicity, an attentive physicality, to counterbalance its own 'Huge symbols featuring strangeness' ('A Drum for Ben Boyd', *CP* 20). It is as if the poetry recognises that its belief in paradoxical suffering is effective only to the degree that its language itself suffers reality. This is particularly true of the sequence, *Ward Two*, where Webb tries to write Christian meanings into the everyday emptiness of a psychiatric ward.

Ward Two suspects its own belief. While this work is often enough described as a record of fragmented experience or even an effect of breaking words, its religious language is often presumed to signify a state of desired wholeness. Yet the poetry is breaking the very theology by which it hopes to transfigure the ward and its occupants. 'Pneumo-Encephalograph' (*CP* 223), wanting to see the Holy Spirit in a bubble of oxygen travelling towards the brain, still claims its right and need to 'confess the power / To loathe suffering . . .'. Before attempting its final transfiguration, the poem concentrates on the 'only', the alienated fact of suffering:

> Only your suffering.
> Of pain's amalgam with gold let some man sing
> While, pale and fluent and rare
> As the Holy Spirit, travels the bubble of air.

Even the way the Holy Spirit is so precariously present signals a struggle, one which places amalgam and poem between desire and defeat, as if aware that sacralising intentions can easily become sanitising ones.

One of the guiding anxieties in Webb's poetry is its awareness that words can build walls, attitudes which want to isolate, objectify, evaluate, even exile experience. Like a leper outside the walls ('A Leper' 70), the poetry puts its faith in 'sacred dishevelment'('Wild Honey' 232), and this condition is seen to incorporate even divinity, as when 'A Man' (*CP* 229) dismantles the idea of the 'First Cause', that principle of Catholic philosophy, whereby all is guaranteed as ultimately ordered:

> Canaries silent as spiders, caged in laws,
> Shuffle and teeter, begging a First Cause
> That they may tear It open with their claws
> And have It hanging in pain from solid wall.

In a sense, both belief and scepticism are being put aside, since the poetry wants to make, not coherence, but companionship, particularly the companionship of a God who knows how the mind can peel away from solid logic.

With 'Harry' (224), *Ward Two* tests a belief that imbecility can embody the most primitive wisdom, indeed innocence. Andrew Taylor argues that the insane are, in Webb's poetry, innocent of language and its division between signifier and signified (98–111). 'Harry', he says, wants (but cannot quite manage) to be 'filled with the Word unwritten', the transcendental signified, the Word of God which has not fallen into human language. Certainly there are many moments in Webb's poetry when the subject seems to slide out to the edge, trying to surrender to some empty space or mystical silence. Taylor's reading illuminates these shimmering absences which often occupy the centre of Webb's work. However, Taylor underestimates the poetry's refusal of silence, its persistent fidelity to battered words. He also keeps belief and scepticism separate, appropriating the theology of creation but ignoring that of incarnation, confining God to other-worldly terms in some meta-linguistic realm of mystical elisions. Yet 'Harry' is not really trying to elevate experience so that it is divinised; it is trying to break 'God' and bring divinity down into the immediate and vulnerable moment.

The poem proposes an imbecile's attempt to write a letter as a sacrament of the Word. Although Harry's action is 'painstaking' and inarticulate, it may be one with original wisdom. Although endangered by institutionalised forces, it may terrify the 'giddy alphabet' which constructs the conventional world. It may even transfigure that world with its own 'retarded and infantile Light'. Yet Harry's action is finally unsure: his letter is sent 'to the House of no known address'.

Theological terms ('Sacrifice? Propition?')[8] and liturgical references ('vestments' and 'cruets') are used to open the possibility that Harry's act, like Christ's, has a representative and redemptive character, and is the work of a sacred fool. However, this possibility does not develop easily. The poem derives its dynamism from the interaction between the speaker's use of high, sacramental language and Harry's own 'mongol mouth'. As it shifts between symbolic and literal intentions (and both are fragile), the poem is enticing the reader to mediate between a conventionally scientific assessment of Harry and its own more paradoxical belief.

Harry's language has been 'Shaped' by 'our' memories of 'the world of commonsense':

But it is no goddess of ours guiding the fingers and the thumb.

She cries: *Ab aeterno ordinata sum.*
He writes to the woman, this lad who will never marry.
One vowel and the thousand laborious serifs will come
To this pudgy Christ, and the old shape of Mary.
Before seasonal pelts and the thin
Soft tactile underskin
Of air were stretched across the earth, they have sported and are one
   (224–25).

He is sporting with the feminine personification of Wisdom—'no goddess of ours', but God's everlasting companion, active in creation. *'Ab aeterno ordinata sum'* is her cry:

Yahweh created me when his purpose first unfolded, before the oldest
   of his works.
From everlasting I was firmly set,
   from the beginning, before earth came into being (Proverbs 8:22–23).[9]

---

8. Catholic theology refers to the Mass as a 'propitiatory sacrifice'.
9. This is the Jerusalem Bible translation: 'From everything I was firmly set'.

Harry's imbecile wisdom, because it is original and outcast, now threatens the walled power of conventional learning:

> Was it then at this altar-stone the mind was begun?
> The image besieges our Troy. Consider the sick
> Convulsions of movement, and the featureless baldy sun
> Insensible—sparing that compulsive nervous tic.
> Before life, the fantastic succession,
> An imbecile makes his confession,
> Is filled with the Word unwritten, has almost genuflected (225).

The rhyming of 'succession' and 'confession' locates a tension which runs through the entire poem, between empiricist and theological evaluations, between the 'fantastic succession' and the Word. Here the language of 'fantastic succession' creates a central focus in which Harry is simply described: convulsions, nervous tic, and a head which is shiningly bald, but featureless and insensible. Around this is woven the symbolic language of altar and Word. This language has a reverberating quality: the altar-stone remembers and makes present earlier references to sacrifice and the eucharist. The 'Word' recalls the references to Wisdom. So that the symbolic perspective is reverberating more deeply even as the physical description becomes more direct.

This strategy is maintained in the final stanza. We are given two heart-rending images: children screaming 'at the sight / Of his mongol mouth stained with food'; Harry licking 'the soiled envelope with lover's caress'. Around these we discover words of resurrection and transfiguration. The intention of the poem is made explicit: it is 'because' of the two realistic images that Harry may be seen transfigured:

> Because the wise world has for ever and ever rejected
> Him and because your children would scream at the sight
> Of his mongol mouth stained with food, he has resurrected
> The spontaneous thought retarded and infantile Light.
> Transfigured with him we stand

Among walls of the no-man's-land
While he licks the soiled envelope with lover's caress

Directing it to the House of no known address.

Right down to the fact that the envelope is soiled, this is a portrait of a suffering servant (Isaiah 51: 14–15) whose writing transfigures others, especially those it confronts, those who think themselves wiser and more beautiful than he—and confronts them precisely from a position of weakness. With the final ambiguity, the servant is denied consolation. His letter will be read by no woman. The poem, however, is there, besieging Troy, yet containing its belief and scepticism: the person or place addressed may be more reliable because not 'known', or the letter may have arrived at that innocence which is no more than emptiness.

Obviously, it is not uncommon for the poet to be depicted as one who suffers on behalf of humanity, one with prophetic gifts, one whose word is ignored, even one who performs a Christ-like role. It is important, however, to hear the variations Webb sounds within that theme. His poetry is a vision of both terror and love. If the poet's neglected vision is vindicated, it is not so much because he or she sees life entire and whole, as because her or his speech is riddled with compassion. Struggling between complex symbolic utterance and simple statement, between dramatising the (often complex) subject and focusing the (often simple) object, Webb's poetry stays with the suffering of language.

Works Cited

McAuley, J. *A Map of Australian Verse*. Melbourne: Oxford University Press, 1975.
Perry, G. (ed.) *Poetry Australia 56. Francis Webb (1925–1973) Commemorative Issue*. Five Dock, NSW: South Head Press, 1975.
Taylor, A. *Reading Australian Poetry*. St Lucia: University of Queensland Press, 1987.
Webb, F. *Collected Poems*. Sydney: Angus & Robertson, 1977.

Francis Webb and the Will of the Poem

When I write, I do, not my own will, but the will of my poems—that is, I try to serve most scrupulously some spiritual event which my life proposes to me, of which the shape is not yet defined—but whether this is also the will of God I cannot know on earth. —James K. Baxter

When a poet is described as 'Catholic', the hardened reader quite often begins to work from a particular interpretative expectation: either belief will be censoring imagination, or imagination will be subverting belief. On the one hand, the poet is quite often viewed with some suspicion. Since he gives allegiance to the Catholic belief-system, then his imaginative independence must be surrendered to a dogmatic authority, and his writing must be falsifying experience for the sake of theology. On the other hand, the poet is quite often regarded with rueful sympathy. No matter how hard he tries to be loyal to Catholic dogmas, he will find himself lost within the distinction between 'faith' and 'sensibility', will find his imagination always returning to experience—and experience, of course, will not reveal the order, certitude and consolation which (apparently) Catholicism holds in store for those who love it. (The softened reader may well operate differently: giving sympathy where the imagination is elevated by grace and illuminated by belief, suspicion where it falls away to express unredeemed experience.) What this exposes is a general failure to appreciate the way in which belief is an act of imagination, and imagination an act of belief.

This is, of course, a strategic generalization which, when it is so expressed, sounds simplistic. Nevertheless, there is I would wager, sufficient evidence to argue that the interpretation of religious poetry has too often assumed a distinction (not to say 'dichotomy') between 'dogma' and 'experience', where dogma was almost exclusively associated with belief and experience with imagination. This distinction was persuasive largely because it was supported by a long fellowship of similar distinctions: between the sacred and the secular, between the abstract and the concrete, between the transcendent and the immanent, between the essential and the existential, between the spiritual and the material, between the supernatural and the natural. It was also, at least in Catholic culture, supported by a prevailing assumption that the imagination was very much a secondary way of knowing God, not at all as reliable as the rational, theological way associated with dogma.

At present the situation seems to be changing. There is a growing appreciation that 'religious' cannot be so tightly associated with 'dogmatic', that it is a dynamic complex in which various other dimensions interact.[10] We have become more aware of religion as a dimension within ordinary experience, not just a separate category. We are now more accustomed

---

10. Among the works which have influenced and exemplified this changing appreciation are: Ian Barbour, *Myths, Models and Paradigms* (Harper & Row, New York, 1974), Peter Berger, *A Rumour of Angels* (Penguin, 1969), Vincent Buckley, *Poetry and the Sacred* (Chatto & Windus, London, 1968), John Coulson, *Religion and Imagination* (Clarendon Press, Oxford, 1981), John Drury, *The Pot and the Knife* (SCM Press, London, 1979), Avery Dulles, *Models of Revelation* (Doubleday & Company, New York, 1983), Mircea Eliade, *The Sacred and the Profane* (Harcourt, Brace & World, New York, 1959), Andrew Greeley, *Religion: A Secular Theory* (The Free Press, Macmillan, New York, 1982), Giles Gunn, *The Interpretation of Otherness* (OUP, New York, 1979), David Hay, *Exploring Inner Space* (Penguin, 1982), William James, *The Varities of Religious Experience* (Fontana, 1960), Sallie McFague, *Metaphorical Theology* (SCM Press, London, 1983), Rudolf Otto, *The Idea of the Holy* (London, 1959), Ian Ramsey, *Religious Language* (SCM Press, London, 1957), John Shea, *Stories of God* (The Thomas More Press, Chicago, 1978), David Tracy, *Blessed Rage For Order* (The Seabury Press, New York, 1975), *The Analogical Imagination* (Crossroad, New York, 1981), Ninian Smart, *The Phenomenon of Religion* (Herder & Herder, New York, 1973).

to speaking of a dimension of 'otherness', or 'ultimacy', or 'oneness' or 'mystery'. We are more sensitive to the tensive character within religious experience and language: the Mystery both conceals and reveals, frightens and fascinates, alienates and gives identity, delimits and unlimits, destroys and renews. Studies in comparative religion have shown that, although religions may display differences at the level of dogma, they have many striking similarities at the level of myth. More recently, studies in narrative and metaphorical theology have acknowledged the primary role of metaphor, myth and symbol within religious experience and language and have challenged the supreme position afforded the propositional and dogmatic mode of religious language. Dogmas are more and more seen as derivative, as providing a more precise, analytical, and propositional formulation of truths primarily expressed in metaphor, myth and symbol. Indeed, some theologians are now arguing that dogmas become lifeless, even enslaving, when they lose contact with their roots in metaphor, myth and symbol. At the same time, critics such as Coulson and Gunn, considering the relation between religion and literature, have shifted the ground of comparison: somewhat away from metaphysical and moral ideas expressed by both, more towards the processes of imaginative articulation and assent.

While this means that the religious character of poetry is now not so likely to be confused with its doctrinal component, there are indications of a reactive impulse to name as religious any experience articulated in language which faintly resembles a 'language of ultimate concern'. This impulse can have an effect which is, in general, positive. It can signify a re-earthing of the religious imagination. (I am not primarily suggesting that imagination needs to be earthed because attention to 'earth' gives a greater guarantee of truth than attention to 'heaven'—rather, that the imagination, because of its integrative and mediatory impulses, enjoys best a close and equal conversation between the two.) It can challenge any over-confident application of distinctions such as those between sacred and secular, transcendent and immanent. It can enliven appreciation of the profound analogies to be discovered in religious and poetic processes. It can redirect our sense of mystery, associating it more with immediate presence than with remote reality.

Given that dogma has often played too dominant a role in religiously interpreted experience, this attempt to return some power to what we imagine as 'raw experience' is beneficial. However, while I agree that there is a religious dimension within experience, I am not yet convinced that we ought assume such a dimension is always, or easily, active. It seems to be a dimension which is quite often present less as an actual element and more as a potential one. There is often a religions sense in poets, but this is not the same as a religious vision. To confuse the two is to reduce vision to deeply felt experience, to weaken its cognitive claims, and so to weaken appreciation of and response to its symbolic character. [11] If the religio-experiential element is to have a more actual power within religiously interpreted experience and language, then it needs to exhibit a more defined and defining direction towards other integral elements of the religious complex—towards images and stories at least, if not towards particular dogmas. This is not to say that the stories and/or dogmas should determine the shape of uttered experience—only that where all the dimensions are in dialogue (each determining each), there is a different, more defined religiousness operating than where the cry of the real is still in search of myth and belief.

Yet those who identify religion too liberally with a kind of depth-experience could easily repeat the very error made by those who identify religion with a belief-system: they could assume that the imagination is less active in our (interpretation of) experience than it usually is, and so underrate its creative, integrative and mediatory functions. My own conviction is that the key to interpreting religious poetry is a renewed appreciation of how, in the case of certain poets, the imagination has a shaping role in and between religiously interpreted experience, myth, and dogma.

For the moment, I want to leave that as another in my list of generalizations, and turn to Francis Webb's poem, 'Five Days Old'. I would

---

11. Paul Ricoeur shows a fine appreciation of how the symbol performs a critical function in 'The Symbol Gives Rise to Thought', Giles Gunn (ed.), *Literature and Religion* (SCM Press, London, 1971), 211-20.

argue that it is not appropriate to interpret this poem's religious character as originating in Webb's belief in the doctrine of redemption (even though the poem does express such belief). Nor is it appropriate to locate the poem's religiousness in an experience of sacred dread, as the small moment of light is surrounded by great darkness—not because that is not very much what the poem is 'about', but because that is more an imaginative structuring—than 'raw experience'. What is appropriate is to see the way both 'doctrine' and 'experience' are determined by an underlying imaginative structure which informs, integrates and enlivens both. The religious quality of the poem is to be discovered (as it reveals itself) in the structural relationships within Webb's imagination.

In that sense, the poem's imaginative foundation rests not so much in Webb's theology of redeeming grace, nor in his personal devotion to Christmas, but more in the tensive structure of the situation from which the poem arose:

> This poem was written by Frank in response to the experience of holding a five-day-old baby, named Christopher John. His kindly doctor had provided this experience in the hope that Frank would begin to write poetry again after a time of silence and protested barrenness (Sister Francisca Fitzwalter 75).[12]

The imaginative sympathy between Sister Francisca's narrative and Webb's poem is instructive. In both a saving power is centred in one who is very vulnerable. In both the structuring tension is that between the tiny, simple moment of peace and the large, surrounding world of complex pain. Simplicity is achieved within suffered complexity:

> To shrive my thought for perfection
> I must breathe old tempests of action

---

12. Sister Francisca is now known as Sister Pauline, but I refer to her still as Francisca so as to be consistent with bibliographical information.

For the snowflake and face of love,
Windfall and word of truth,
Honour close to death.

Webb is here recognizing that he must discover the proper, if paradoxical relationship between weakness and strength if he is to see the mystery of the child. If he is to cleanse (and heal?) his understanding, and so be able to appreciate the child's perfection (its existence as utter act), then he must struggle along the breath, must live though his tormented history, and hope in that way to achieve, not so much a state of resolution, as a state of sacred tension between the weak and tiny snowflake and the strong and strengthening face of love. The phrase, 'face of love', incorporates a reference to Christ, who is the often unrecognized but ever revealing face of God's love.[13] So does the phrase, 'word of truth',[14] but the absolute, steady presence of this phrase is set in play with 'windfall', which can connote fragility (and so recapitulate earlier references to 'trembling' and 'blown straw'), yet can also suggest unexpected good fortune (and that could have its theological correlative in the notion of redeeming grace). From within this structure, Webb indicates that the way to appreciate the birth is to enter the paradox of death.

This becomes clearer as we find comparable tensive structures throughout the poem. The title has a sound which is as solid as an immediate fact, yet also as fragile as the awed perception of mystery. 'Christmas is in the air' operates as a statement of fact, yet lifts itself, with 'in the air', towards some presence which is insubstantial, yet possibly transcendent. The poet's own presence is similarly complex: 'You are given into my hands.' This conjures power, something of the independence of the ego, but it is also receptive and relational. When the child is described as coming from 'quietest, loneliest lands' and when 'lands' is rhymed with 'hands', Webb creates a complex interaction between transcendence and vulnerability.

---

13. cf. John 1:1–18, 6:46, 12:44–46, 14:1–21.
14. In Johanine theology, Christ is the Word (John, 1:1–18) and the Truth (John, 14:1–21).

His own response is both inarticulate and eloquent—'My trembling is all my prayer', where 'all' can mean both 'merely' and 'completely'. He follows this with: 'To blown straw was given / All the fullness of Heaven'. What is clear at this point is that Webb's imagination is in conversation, not with the entire Christmas story, but with that aspect of it which emphasizes Christ's kenosis or self-emptying (Philippians 2:6–11) and which reflects on how the Creator became subject to the very world he had made. Here he finds an analogy between the structure he sees in Christopher and the structure he sees in Christ. Webb next utters what is effectively his religio-poetic creed: 'The tiny, not the immense, / Will teach our groping eyes.' There is a gentle interplay here between the active and the receptive self, which represents a coming together of spiritual journeying and unearned epiphany, of effort and grace. Yet the centering impulse is directed always toward the tiny, just as in other poems it is towards the broken, the ugly, the leper, the idiot, the dead.

It is possible, I would argue, to describe the religious character of Webb's work in this way: by apprehending its structural relationships, by perceiving the root-metaphor or model through which his predominant imaginative and tensive framework is made present.

It is not too difficult to indicate some of the significant tensions which constitute and are constituted by Webb's model. There is the spiritual paradox in his preferred vision: 'All beauty, all joy? / Yes, and all pain and disfigurement.' There is the drama of recognition, in which the tiny, pitiable, rare, often the rejected, are unexpectedly found to contain a saving revelation and power. This vision, however, is most often attained at the centre of very immediate suffering, where the centre of reality and perception appears almost as a redeeming wound: 'Light is the centre of our darkness. I am to tell you / Of all light, all love, fast to the Cross and bleeding . . .'. (Webb so often applies the word 'all' to a broken situation.) There is the constant combination of words evoking strength with those evoking weakness. There is the preoccupation with failure as somehow a sanctifying influence—Webb's vision here is eucharistic (as Eyre is finally transformed into an Emmaus traveller). Even Webb's metaphoric density shows the presence of his model: the usual individuality of words suffers a breakdown and thereby enters a new fellowship of meaning. The model is also seen in the way Webb creates dramatic absences which are then surrounded by diverse and partial perspectives, so that truth is always breaking towards wholeness and speech. Truth, for Webb, seems to lie at the heart of a secret, wounded sanctity, rather than in public statements which are clear and coherent. The imbecile Harry speaks a Word deeper than all acquired learning.

These correspond to a classic model in the Judeo-Christian tradition: that of the 'Suffering Servant'. This model has its classic formulation in the four 'Servant Songs' of Isaiah. The first song (Isaiah, 42: 1–9) contrasts the great and final justice which the servant will accomplish with the unassuming, delicate way he will go about it. So too, the servant's call is described in terms which are at once intimate and awesome, and his mission identifies him with those we would today describe as marginalised. In the second song (Isaiah, 49:1–6), the servant, now in exile, is reminded that God's saving design is secretly at work in failure. In the third song (Isaiah, 50: 4–9), the servant recalls his ministry to 'the wearied', his vocation to suffer and so cooperate in God's redemptive purpose. In the fourth song (Isaiah, 52:13–53:12), the servant's ugliness and disfigurement, almost inhuman, breaks open as revelation: it is his very suffering which brings peace—and peace to those who neglected, even despised, his truth.

Webb's religious imagination, then, is strongly attracted to this 'Suffering Servant' model, particularly because it structures a close, causal, and ironic bond between glory and suffering, as well as a corresponding drama of recognition where the 'least' will hold the revelation. (Of course, the attraction operates more through an atmosphere of influence than through a consciousness as explicit as this overview might make it seem.)

There are definite advantages in using this 'Suffering Servant' model as a (flexible) frame for interpreting the religious character of Webb's poetry. The model helps articulate the reciprocity which exists between the vision and the strategy of the poems, names Webb's vision of suffering in a precise yet subtle manner, and opens up a complex relationship between the poet and his Catholic culture.

The way in which the model determines a reciprocity between vision and strategy can be illustrated by 'A Death At Winson Green'. It is possible to find in the poem evidence of a theology which claims that death gives way to eternal life and, therefore, that the dying man moves towards the core of triumph won by Christ's redemptive suffering and death. This is not, however, quite the movement which the poem enacts. Its religio-poetic strategy says the dying man is himself the core of triumph. If Christ is anywhere in the poem, he is at that core, in the man's woundedness.

Our groping eyes are continually being directed towards the single word, 'dead', and each time we see it we move closer to the core reality. It is here that Webb locates the gaping truth which is the poem's centre or core: 'a man is dying–at the core / Of triumph won' (*CP* 153). As the man is dying the sun is rising, but Webb restrains the possibilities for transcendence within that standard image of resurrection, and contains the sunrise within his repetition of 'dead'. Whereas those who assume redemption is an unambiguous process would expect to follow sunrise all the way to resurrection, Webb insists on holding the focus on 'dead', so increasing the tension between dying and rising. At the end, the dying man does achieve a Webbean style of transcendence: he becomes 'all life'. Yet this state, as much one of wounded fellowship as of triumph, is never separated from his broken fact, which has the last word: 'thrown on the gaping bed, / Blind, silent, in a trance, and shortly, dead.' This is not because his belief in resurrection is in conflict with his experience of suffering. It is because his imagination wants to speak the moment where power and weakness converge.

Webb introduces his characteristic tension at the very beginning of the poem, when he describes Winson Green as 'a green spell stolen from Birmingham'. Is Winson Green a thief, deserving the general world's suspicion and judgment? Is it a place of rest rescued from the city's movement? Or is it a restorative space of almost magical potency? It may even be that the 'green spell' is effective for Birmingham, as well as for the patients of Winson Green.

Birmingham does not seem to recognize Winson Green as its saving wound, Visitors' Day is succinctly and starkly represented: 'the graven perpetual smile, / String-bags agape, and pity's laundered glove'. It is important to examine the effect of 'agape'. It is a word which might easily be passed by, but it is deeply informed by Webb's 'Suffering Servant' model. It does more than describe a visitor fumbling through a bag. It tells how the visitors are afraid of the patients, how they stare in discomfort and, precisely, disbelief. In this way it encodes the attitude which would make Winson Green a space to be peered at from outside. Yet it also encodes the opposite attitude: by linking itself with 'one gaping bed', the word implies that the visitors' helplessness, discomfort and fear might yet constitute their saving wound. It is a little word which invites us to share in the poem's drama of recognition and to consider, from within the poem's correspondences, where we might discover the truth.

Webb continually reminds us that recognition is possible only if we keep our attention on the core:

> Two orderlies are whistling-in the spring;
> Doors slam; and a man is dying at the core
> Of triumph won. As a tattered, powerful wing
> The screen bears out his face against the bed,
> Silver, derelict, rapt, and almost dead.

This is superb writing. The casualness of spring contrasts powerfully with the laboriousness of dying. The end-of-line pause on 'dying at the core' creates its own 'core' in the text, and this passes into the notion of triumph, a triumph itself absorbed, in the same line, by the image of a wing which is at once 'tattered' and 'powerful'. This tension between strength and weakness is then heightened by the final line, which yokes glory with dereliction and death. All the while, the core of the perspective, the space which might repel as easily as attract belief, is the dying. Webb's language never fades upwards towards the effect of transcendence. Mystery will be found in the close presence of suffering. Webb's religious imagination can only respond to the rapture of death while simultaneously and rigorously regarding its waste and ugliness.

In the final stanza, Webb makes a characteristic shift of power. The one in power, the one with narrative power, is rendered helpless and must rely on the paradoxical power of the dying man. As the speaker decreases, this man, disfigured and disregarded, begins to increase and to assume, first of all, the condition of the speaker, and then of all humanity. He finds fellowship with all the broken and, at the core of the despicable, the 'all':

> I cannot pray; that fine lip prays for me
> With every gasp at breath; his burden grows
> Heavier as all earth lightens, and all sea.
> Time crouches, watching, near his face of snows.
> He is all life, thrown on the gaping bed,
> Blind, silent, in a trance, and shortly, dead.

Even here, the universalizing, transcendent effect of 'He is all life' is firmly placed at the centre of 'the gaping bed'. If the man has achieved representative status, he has done so surrounded by commas, by the fragments of his suffering.

What begins to emerge here is that Webb has a particular vision of suffering, and that the 'Suffering Servant' model helps clarify that. To say that Webb's vision of suffering is Christian is accurate, but it is not yet sufficiently precise. In Christian belief, suffering is more than brute fact and disorder. It is an opportunity for incorporation in Christ's own redemptive purpose and activity. However, there can be different emphases within this general belief, different theological models. One way of describing these differences is to talk of an eschatalogical model of suffering and an historical one.

The more eschatalogical model hopes to find the meaning of suffering beyond this world, in a place (or state) of eternal happiness where every tear will be wiped away. Suffering is a test which is passed by endurance. There is, then, a strong emphasis on self-discipline and willpower, while, at the same time, the person has little creativity, has primarily to submit to the 'will of God'. While the 'will of God' guarantees the relationship between suffering and glory, it implies that the connection is an extrinsic design ultimately established in a transcendent realm, in the 'otherworld'. Passing through pain and into the glory of Christ (who, in this model, seems to be on the other side of suffering), the person then achieves a victory over suffering.

In the more historical model, the victory is a victory of suffering. Christ is more an immediate presence within suffering. Rather than have the human figures struggle to a point beyond pain, this model has Christ move into the pain and be discovered among them. This model encourages the kind of fellowship Webb himself valued: the community of compassion and consolation. In this it also challenges the presumptions of power, as suffering is more intrinsically connected with redemptive power and becomes a 'sign of contradiction'. This model also affords the sufferers, in collaboration with (rather than in submission to) Christ, a more creative role: whether their suffering is destructive or recreative depends largely on their shaping imaginations. The purpose of suffering is discovered (and created) not so much without, in the divine understanding, as within the barely articulate fellowship and humanity it can constitute:

> At this ruthless curve
> We are driven to live. O sudden, the rags of our pity
> Come back to us as a portrait of pain, a city
> Of glory and torment—human. ('The Stations', *CP* 94)

Webb's vision of suffering is, surely, most informed by the historical model (which is itself sympathetically attuned to the 'Suffering Servant' model). His sense of its mystery rarely displaces his feel for its actuality, and he locates the mystery within the fact, just as he finds saving power within the wound. The sacralizing effect of suffering is that it can create humanity as fellowship, as it does for the dying man at Winson Green, who becomes through brokenness 'all life.' Yet Webb's vision of suffering is also a critical one. His sufferers have more than a submissive role: they witness a contradictory and challenging truth in their very weakness. It has become a conventional piety to claim that the poor are especially identified with Christ, but Webb takes this view beyond sentimentality and into experience. His vision of suffering has an extraordinary and spiritual realism. There is not too much promise, nor too much blame. There is a meeting of mercy and justice. His imagery closely critiques the oppressive structures which help create and sustain some suffering, yet these structures are overturned not by power, but by poverty of heart.

As a way of further suggesting the complex and shifting character of the term 'Catholic', let me illustrate two qualities in Webb's vision of suffering: its capacity for compassion, and its capacity for criticism.

To illustrate the compassion, I take an unlikely poem, 'The Father' (from *The Canticle*). At first sight, this seems to express stern disapproval of materialism and secularism, those dread enemies of religion and Catholicism. Bernadone is the object of some disapproval: he treats his son as if he were a piece of cloth, thinks his wife a sentimental nuisance, and is incapable of seeing God's purpose operating in his son's life of poverty. Yet Bernadone speaks within a metaphor of weaving—a metaphor over which he presumes total control, yet a metaphor which assumes an independent and ironic power.

Everything is centred towards his ego and power as he controls the metaphor through which he tells the story of Francis. Francis is born from his 'clean fibres' and his birth happily coincides with financial success which 'wove continents'. (Bernadone certainly opts for the large at the expense of the small.) Love is a matter of 'Obedient threads'. When the mother seems to devise 'some wicked warm design / For [his] son to tread the unruly way', Bernadone not only thwarts such a sentimental design, but greatly enjoys his own authoritarian display. Yet when his son reaches adolescence and uses women to experiment with manhood, Bernadone is happy with his liberal craftsmanship and blesses 'Whatever is carefully profligate'. Even war fails to hinder the father's weaving hand. Then:

> But within him was born this contravention
> And wilful swerve from the one true shape.
> Now from his absolute dimension
> A man of my fibres would escape
>
> Floorwards, displaying for a badge
> Mere snippets, formless. Thrown outside,
> He renders the final sacrilege—
> Almsgiving of my hard-won pride.

I say, as a man: what was of me
Is offal. Can a last obstinate
Thread get past the double eye
And tinsmith's beauty of my hate? (*CP* 72)

While Bernadone is here employing words with his habitual, unthinking authoritarianism, the relationship between his use of biblical images and their more usual association becomes ironic. At the very point where he thinks he is using language to display his power, the language itself, out of its own memory and integrity of reference, initiates an independent judgment against that use of power. In order to describe how Francis denied his wealthy lifestyle and adopted the dress of poverty, Bernadone, still seeing himself as an absolute creator, invokes a parodic image of the Fall, directing it towards Francis's fault, fall from favour, and expulsion. This does not, as intended, justify Bernadone's position—rather, it contrasts his intransigence with the redemptive inclination attributed to the other creator in Genesis. When he celebrates his capacity for hate and asks whether 'a last obstinate / Thread' can get past its 'double eye' he judges himself as that rich person whose passage to glory will be more difficult than a camel's passage through the needle's eye (cf Matthew, 19:23–26).

However, since Bernadone draws this irony down upon himself and since it evolves organically from his own metaphor, the moral judgment is muted. This does not mean that Webb softens his attitude towards Bernadone's kind of suffering, which remains self-induced and unnecessary. Indeed, Webb underlines this by giving Bernadone such a gratingly self-congratulatory tone. The biblical references also underline Bernadone's culpability. Yet they also cooperate in another, more redeeming irony: at the point where Bernadone declares his determination to keep his son's fault an unhappy one, he has introduced biblical language which reminds us that Adam's fault is traditionally seen as 'happy', since it occasioned the Incarnation and Redemption. This leaves Bernadone in a state which he would be the last to recognize: subject to the design of the divine weaver.

When next he speaks (in the second of the poems entitled 'The Father'), Bernadone confesses his own responsibility for the break. He even appreciates the divine irony, seeing himself as 'Creator declared journeyman of undoing'. Now when he refers to his fabric—'the needle-prows of a schism / Tormented my fabric'—he is wanting to possess his own, vulnerable self. Yet he has not replaced his metaphor. That remains, drawing him into the 'Suffering Servant' model, showing him other liberating possibilities which emerge as he abandons his control of the metaphor. While still within his metaphor of weaving, Bernadone acknowledges his failure ('the cerecloth's moth-eaten pallor', which acknowledges both the fact of failure and the spiritual significance), and recognizes a paradoxical design in the 'one obstinate loitering thread' which 'From dead twilight fibres coaxes a sun'. Then he is able to name his fellowship with and surrender of his son:

A continent is unbound,
Still of my fibres, but of countless fibres,
Still of my limits, but not of the mapping-pen's,
Still of my trademark—but of daylight and vine (*CP* 79).

This marvellous fulfilment of Bernadone's metaphor encourages a compassionate sense that redemptive possibilities, though unrecognized and even rejected, were at work in the imaginative pattern of his suffering.

With 'A Leper' (also from *The Canticle*) we are faced with suffering which originates in external factors beyond the leper's own control. Webb does not take the opportunity for a devout meditation on the mysterious ways and permissive will of God. Instead, he exploits the confrontative capacity which such suffering can have and attacks the values which lie behind oppression. Even as he does so, he continually emphasizes that it is the leper's very deterioration which so powerfully contradicts the presumptions of power.

The image of the 'high wall', expressing both 'inclusion' and 'exclusion', shows how much oppression is motivated by self-preservation and fear. As the passing crowds and passing seasons conspire to marginalize the leper, they betray the essential cowardice of the oppressive power structure: the group subjugating the individual to its own needs. The priest 'Whose discreet senses dare not linger upon [him]' signals an indictment of cosmetic charity, where 'a halfpenny's smug bandage' is used as a substitute for real engagement with suffering. Interestingly, the leper does not make a direct attack on such injustice and oppression. He is always on the edge, struggling to utter himself into some more secure and acceptable reality. He never achieves that kind of power. It is the leper's act of being (or just-being) which remains his most potent and frightening word. It is not just that Webb sees the act of existence as the most articulate speech. It is that he finds such speech where the act of existence has been so disfigured that it seems no longer human (cf Isaiah, 52:14). Therefore, almost because people find his existence disgusting, the leper's broken fact of being enters their mind (as it does the reader's) as an irrefutable speech:

> There is always *this* question, *this* something, in its yellow
> Rags which prefigure the almost living ulcer
> Beneath them, whose words are the filthy vivid trickling
> Never quite congealed by a halfpenny's smug bandage.
> [...]
> Look aside, look aside. Yet this non-human thought
> Cannot furl its bewildering pennon, must utter itself.
> I am the graceless utterance, the question, the thought (CP 70–71).

In allowing the leper such an activity, Webb is also challenging fatalistic, stoical attitudes towards suffering (strongly present in mainstream Australian culture), which assign the sufferer a role which is basically one of passive resistance. Webb implies that suffering needs a more active response: the creative and sympathetic response of mercy. This is subtly and ironically conveyed when the leper describes how he is assigned a church:

> God's mercy upon all, then: a church is assigned me,
> Of Santa Maria Maddelena—so there are stones, eyes
> To contain my grossness without the blink of ruin?

> For Santa Maria there was mercy; for me only vengeance,
> An effigy sour as my body, and a scampering priest
> Whose discreet senses dare not linger upon me.
> Nor can I credit the Love aloft in those hands.

The leper questions whether the church and people use charity so that their walls/eyes may house his ugliness without their having to become him, to discover in their strong eyes 'the blink of ruin'. This is enough to expose their hypocrisy. Webb, however, is doing more: the association of 'church' and 'ruin' reminds us that, in Franciscan lore, Francis found his mission when he dreamed he had to restore a ruined church. Here, the devout ones, refusing the ruin, refuse the Franciscan vision. They also effectively deny the eucharist (as bread that is broken). For all their well established structures of devotion, they lack the brokenness needed for mission and for such love as is symbolized in the eucharist. The leper, however, is drawn by his words more deeply and more barely into the true meaning of 'the Love'.

If it is not yet clear that the term 'Catholic' cannot be applied to Webb's religious poetry as if it were a label with a single, fixed meaning, that it should be used to indicate a dynamic environment of interacting experiences, metaphors and dogmas, then it may help to consider one of the *Ward Two* poems: 'Homosexual'. In this poem we find Webb's model offering a searching critique of conventional Catholicism, saying that the homosexual embodies Christ's love more deeply than his virtuous judges do. This should not be all that surprising: Webb's model encourages a model of authority which is horizontal and centric, whereas Catholic sexual morality derives mainly from a model of authority which is vertical and hierarchical. In this way, Webb can be said to have confronted the central tension in contemporary Catholicism. This is often described as a conflict between vertical and horizontal models of authority, though it is more deeply a crisis of imagination or symbolism. Webb's whole work implies that a vital religious symbolism requires the imaginative reintegration of vertical and horizontal poles, but also that, at the level of imaginative process, preference must be given to a non-judgmental and empathetic engagement with the real.

He begins the poem:

To watch may be deadly. There is not judgment, compulsion,
And the object becomes ourselves. That is the terror: (*CP* 227).

This effectively disowns a distinction at the very heart of the official
Catholic teaching on homosexuality: the distinction between objective and
subjective moral states. The official position has been (and remains) that,
in the objective order, homosexual actions are sinful because intrinsically
disordered, but that, in the subjective order, a prudent assessment should
be made in regard to the degree of freedom, and hence the degree of
moral responsibility, involved in such actions. This distinction has been
used to create a space, sometimes benign, often patronizing, between
theological and pastoral approaches to homosexuality. Webb's imaginative
eye, focusing on the personal rather than the natural order, sees this
objective/subjective mentality in a different way: he implies that what
really operates in such situations is a wall between 'them' and 'us', a fear of
becoming one through imaginative sympathy. Ironically, this wall excludes,
not the homosexual, but those who oppress him: they are excluded from
the elemental and sacred fellowship of suffering, from the visionary space
created by knowledge of the saving wound. Those who reject or condemn
him are then either condemned or saved by his suffering. They are saved,
as the speaker is, if they follow the direction of the 'Suffering Servant'
model and acknowledge that his movement, his thought, his being, his
dying, even his sin, are no longer 'his' but 'ours'—'ours were the sufferings
he bore, ours the sorrows he carried' (Isaiah, 53:4). They are condemned
if they persecute him and fail to see his Christ-like and representative
humanity. Webb indicates this as he depicts the homosexual's entry into
oppressive experience:

Now the God,
The Beginning, the joy, give way to boots and footmarks.
Pale glass faces contorted in hate or merriment
Embody him; and words and arbitrary laws.

He is embodied, he weeps—and all mankind,
Which is the face, the glass even, weeps with him (*CP* 228).

In its Catholic context, this is more subversive than we might at first realize. Webb is so informed by his model, his vision that the broken reveals God, that he is not only affording the dying homosexual a representative and radical humanity, not only arguing that he may be specially loved by God, but also arguing that repressive and righteous attitudes have not, as would presumably be intended, preserved God, but have actually expelled him (or her). Further, he says that the actuality and sympathy of experience is replaced by pharasaic 'words' and that personal freedom is destroyed by 'arbitrary laws'. Webb's position is not precisely a theological one (except inasmuch as his imagination might anticipate and attract a theology consistent with its meaning-intention). What we see here is the degree to which the 'Suffering Servant' model informs Webb's vision, and it is at the end of this poem that we find one of the most beautiful expressions of that vision:

> Again I am tempted, with the Great,
> To see in ugliness and agony a way to God:
> Worse, I am tempted to say he has found God
> Because we cannot contort our faces in merriment,
> And we are one of the Twelve Tribes—he our king.
> He has dictated silence, a kind of peace
> To all within these four unambiguous walls,
> Almost I can say with no answering scuffle of rejection,
> He is loving us now, he is loving all (*CP* 229).

If the speaker uses 'Almost', it is not because he is unsure of what he says, but that what he says must keep its own shape close to suffering.

Using the 'Suffering Servant' model, it is thus possible to approach Webb's religious poetry in a way which encourages appreciation of the interacting dimensions within the religious complex, which reveals the reciprocity between its religious and literary dynamics, and which provides a precise description of the intricate and varied relations between that poetry and its Catholic context. The balance to be established is the one implicit in Baxter's comment. The will of the poem has its own kind of religiousness, operating between the 'spiritual' and 'life'. It has its own authority, which must be obeyed even though it cannot be identified with that more formally religious authority, 'the will of God'. Indeed, it has almost to resist the will of God: when Baxter begins, 'I do, not my own will', he is quoting Christ, who continues, 'but the will of the one who sent me' (cf John, 6:38). Baxter disrupts the expectation within his text, thus planting in his own text a tension between where the words were expected to lead, to 'the will of God', and where they actually arrived, at 'the will of the poem'. As I read him, he is suggesting that the important and creative authority is neither the somewhat shapeless will of life, nor the all-shaping will of God, but his own imagination—or, the will of the poem.

Works Cited

Baxter, J.K. 'Literature and Belief.' *The Man on the Horse*. Dunedin: University of Otago Press, 1967.

Fitzwalter, Sister Francisca. 'From Word to Wonder', *Poetry Australia* 56 (1975), 75.

Webb, F. *Collected Poems*. Sydney: Angus & Robertson, 1977.

'Are you from the Void?'

A READING OF WEBB'S 'STURT AND THE VULTURES'

IN THIS ESSAY I want to attempt a negatively theological reading of 'Sturt and the Vultures'. That is to say, I want to trace a bent in Webb's poetry, an inclination to say of God neither yes nor no, to see divinity as an outline hanging in the void, and hanging in the void with divinity: language, meaning, even the order and hope of redemption. I want also to acknowledge that I am invoking negative theology largely because of an ongoing dissatisfaction with my own reading of Webb's poetry. I have been reading Webb's poetry for some fifteen years now and I have never felt that I have found a way of criticism that keeps fidelity with the tattered eloquence of the poetry itself. When I began reading Webb's poetry I was impressed by its sacramentality, particularly its capacity to see in Australian culture and history signs of Christ. I was persuaded by the way in which 'Poet' reconciles heaven and earth as well as Christ and sinner, and, like Jim Tulip before me, by the way in which 'Banksia' (from *Eyre All Alone*) crosses Australian history with sacred story to allow epiphany (Tulip 36–39). Then I became dissatisfied with this reading: it seemed, simply, too redemptive a reading, too comforting and comfortable. The reading was being taken up into Christ as Word and Sign of God, into plenitude and presence, but the poetry itself was staying with the broken. I noticed, for instance, how 'A Death At Winson Green' disciplines its own possibilities for transcendence, resurrection, directing them back to the unknown address, the word which ends each stanza, 'dead', a word which creates, as it were, a wound where the eye would be. So I began another reading, one in which Webb's poetry became an enactment of confrontative compassion, a sign of contradiction. In this reading I wagered that Webb's poetry was dangerously Catholic. When most Australian literary critics, and many Catholics, imagine Catholicism, they see a system of doctrines, they see Catholicism under the guise of its ideology. They see its logos as distinct from its mythos. Then they perform what I would be tempted to call a Vatican reading: they read down from the ideas to the poetry. The problem with such a criticism, and such a Catholicism, is that it assumes that poetic imagination is obedient to theological reason, and forgets that theological reason is also a work of poetic imagination.

When I think of Webb as a Catholic poet, I am not inclined to think of Augustine, Aquinas, and Ignatius (Ashcroft). I am more inclined to think of popular devotions such as the Stations of the Cross and the Novena to Our Lady of Perpetual Succour, of the Good Friday service with its empty tabernacle, its story of Isaiah's suffering servant, its great drama of redemption which also became a personal dilemma of faith and betrayal. I am more inclined to think of Chesterton on St Francis, and Francis's stigmata, which becomes in Webb's poetry an image of the saving wound, but also an analogue of the eucharist and even the sun. Webb's poetry is dangerously Catholic, then, because it is a poetry in which Catholic doctrines are made to serve the image of the suffering servant, the servant who saves because he is unrecognised, the image which establishes a causal connection between dereliction and glory. Webb's poetry is dangerously Catholic because it continually enacts, in its procedures as well as in its concerns, the kenosis of Christ. In the same move, the poetry becomes subversive, naming in Catholicism a temptation to dogmatism, a temptation to construct pharisaic, almost fascist walls of meaning, but committing itself to a more compassionate, and more Franciscan, Catholicism, wanting 'To see in ugliness and agony a way to God' ('Homosexual', *CB* 222). Or, as Michael Griffith has shown, Webb's poetry challenges institutionalised understanding with the paradoxical power of God's Fool. But even this reading left me dissatisfied: because the word 'God' continued to operate in the reading as a sign of coherence and transcendence. It was, in other words, a reading in which the poetry suffered but the theology did not.

This is to read Webb's poetry as if it were James McAuley's, where Catholic doctrines clarify and elevate images and vertical hierarchies support a hope than can transcend despair. However, Webb's poetry is more horizontal in the way it imagines its own authority, its own world. It is always taking that journey to Emmaus, to the recognition of Christ, but in the broken bread. And, once I began looking at how theological references actually operate in the poems, I noticed that Webb does not allow them to stay clean and tidy. He breaks, scatters and abandons them to the giddy yarn fumbling in 'the moron's painstaking fingers' ('Harry', *CB* 217). Webb's, in other words, is not just a poetry about the kenosis or self-emptying of Christ: it is a poetry which empties Christ. Because of this I want to do a negatively theological reading of 'Sturt and the Vultures', taking my cue from Carl Raschke's point that, after the death of God, a theology of crucifixion has also to be a crucifixion of theology (27).

'Sturt and the Vultures' (*CB* 236–238) is based on Charles Sturt's 1844–46 expedition into the central Australian desert in search of an inland sea. Sturt discovered instead the kind of sandblasted experience the poem relates and he and his men may well have perished had they not found permanent water at Depot Glen on Preservation Creek. There they were trapped from 27 January to 16 July 1845, when heavy rain brought relief and, using Depot Glen as a base camp, Sturt was able to make further forays into the interior. Robert Sellick argues that the poem has its source in one of these trips, when Sturt set out to seek the assistance of some Aborigines who had been seen in the area. He was accompanied by Browne, the surgeon, as well as a stockman and servant. It was during this trip that the incident with the birds occurred. Sellick cites Sturt's journal to show how Webb is using Sturt's own description of the harsh terrain and the wind:

> The morning we started to pay a visit to the blacks was more than usually oppressive, even at daybreak, and about 9 it blew a hot wind from the N.E. As we rode across the stony plain lying between us and the hills, the heated and parching blasts that came upon us were more than we could bear. We were in the centre of the plain, when

Mr. Browne drew my attention to a number of small black specks in the upper air. These spots increasing momentarily in size, were evidently approaching us rapidly. In an incredible short time we were surrounded by several hundreds of the common kite, stooping down to within a few feet of us, and then turning away, after having eyed us steadily. Several approached us so closely, that they threw themselves back to avoid contact, opening their beaks and spreading out their talons. The long flight of these birds, reaching from the ground into the heavens, put me strongly in mind of one of Martin's beautiful designs, in which he produces the effect of distance by a multitude of objects gradually vanishing from view. Whatever the reader may think, these birds had a most formidable aspect, and were too numerous for us to have overpowered, if they had really attacked us. That they came down to see what unusual object was wandering across the lonely deserts over which they soar, in the hope of prey, there can be no doubt; but seeing that we were likely to prove formidable antagonists, they wheeled from us in extensive sweeps, and were soon lost to view in the lofty region from whence they had descended (Sturt Narrative 265, qtd. in Sellick 311).

Sellick also points to significant differences between the journal and the poem. While both describe a desert landscape in which the wind dominates, the poem makes the wind 'not so much hostile as malicious: it appears rather as an expression of a childish irritability, with its testiness and its "little hot tantrums" fitting evidence of a God who has shrunk to senile ineffectualness' (313–14). Sturt's birds are a menace, even a threat of death, but Webb's are made intensely ambivalent: 'The birds are vultures, emissaries of a terrible God, but at the same time their descent is a vision of the Paraclete, the Comforter, filled with the promise of Pentecost' (314). Sellick allows the literal correspondence between the two accounts of the birds to convince him that the poem is also referring to this one, same trip, yet the poem is making its own exploration of the 'interior' of the journal, collecting pieces of cadence, mood, and imagery from various stages of the expedition in order to transform it all into another journey into the dry interior of meaning itself. Here is a passage, recording Sunday August 31st, 1845 and dealing with a later journey, which provides the poem with a Browne who is ill and a Sturt who is losing faith in the inland sea:

> We have now penetrated direct into the interior from the Depot 347 miles, but we have seen no change in this fearful and unparalleled desert. I have now lost all hope of finding any body of water or of making my discovery, and I feel that I am subjecting myself and others to all this exposure and privation solely to discharge my duty conscientiously. It is a service I sought with how different anticipations. But I may not shrink for it under the circumstances. Poor Mr Browne attends me *malgre soi*, and is heartily sick of traversing such a wilderness. How much more then, Dearest, must I yearn to turn my back on so dreary a region to fly to you and to my home once more, but weeks have yet to transpire ere I can feel myself justified in giving up this most difficult and most anxious task (Sturt, *Journal* 71).

Such a passage is, I would suggest, at least as relevant as that dealing with the birds, even though it is not as easy to establish a literal and obvious correspondence. And the passage which seems to me to come closest in mood to the poem is that recording Sunday, October 5th 1845, when Sturt, after a final, futile excursion, had to relinquish all hope of ever finding his inland sea:

> Thus, my Dearest Charlotte, terminated an excursion that was to decide the success or failure of the expedition. A second time had we been forced back from the interior, conquered alike by the difficulties of the country, the severity of the season and the scarcity of water, and I had the painful reflection before me that whatever my exertions had been, I had made no discovery to entitle me to credit or reward, and that therefore I should fail in the only object for which I sought and undertook this tremendous and anxious task. Providence had denied that success to me with which it had

been pleased to crown my former efforts, and I felt that instead of benefitting those for whose happiness and welfare I had made such sacrifices, I should only have inflicted an injury on them. In vain had I prayed to the Almighty for success on this to me all important occasion. In vain had I implored for a blessing on you and on my children, if not on myself. But my prayer had been rejected, my petition refused, and so far from any ray of hope having ever crossed my path I felt that I had been contending against the very powers of Heaven, in the desperate show I had made against the seasons, and I now stood blighted and a blasted man over whose head the darkest destiny had settled (*Journal* 79).

Yet this also shows the great difference between the journal and the poem. Even though Sturt sees himself as someone who had contended with God and been blighted, he can still derive a grim consolation from words like 'destiny' and 'Providence' which allow him to write his failure off to the will of God. Nor is this just a last cry from the depths; it is a major theological feature of Sturt's journal. While the landscape is variously described as miserable, gloomy, desolate, and the expedition as a 'severe trial' and 'punishment' which might result in death, God is always invoked as a figure of providence and mercy. This theology would seem to provide the poem with a basis for its parody of Calvin's God. Calvin places great emphasis on the absolute sovereignty of God: his will is the ground of all that exists; his will is known through Scripture; Scripture is only known through the secret testimony of the Spirit; humanity can do nothing about its fallen state, though some souls are undeservedly rescued by the mercy of God. (The rescued ones are 'the elect' to whom the poem refers and the undeserved choice is known as 'predestination'.) In Calvin's theology predestination is not as irrational and oppressive as the poem imagines: God's mercy comes through Christ in whom, by the secret efficacy of the Holy Spirit (but not by any human act), the elect have faith. The poem is not so much referring to this theology as using it as a metaphor for sovereign and ultimate purpose, so that its effect is not so much to expose the shortcomings of Calvinist theology, as to disassemble the very idea of theological exploration when the Void annuls so sovereign a God. In the Institutes Calvin writes:

> The will of God is the supreme rule of righteousness, so that everything which He wills must be held to be righteous by the mere fact of His willing it. Therefore, when it is asked why the Lord did so, we must answer, Because He pleased. But if you proceed further to ask why He pleased, you ask for something greater and more sublime than the will of God, and nothing such can be found (417).

In a sense 'Sturt and the Vultures' takes Calvin, and Sturt, that one journey further, distorting the 'will of God' into a supreme fiction for an irrational universe and finding that 'nothing'.

In other words, whereas Sturt can see himself as failure and God as power, 'Sturt and the Vultures' is not so sure. The poem is keyed by its opening word, 'MINCING'. While the obvious assumption is that this is spoken by Sturt, rewriting the heroic trek as clownish stumbling, I want also to wager that there is another, more shadowy figure hiding in Sturt's voice, a figure somewhat like a pantomime director. This figure is hinting that anyone who goes into the poem will enter a process of shredding. Other hints follow immediately. The use of 'follows' is familiar to readers of Francis Thompson's 'The Hound of Heaven': it is something Christ does in pursuit of the soul that wants to escape his love. It is not Christ who is following here, but 'This hot nor'-easter'. Whatever its literal function, this is another hidden sign of disintegrative intention, a sign by which 'easter' is annulled (for the poem is fundamentally concerned with words being annulled). The wind is also likened to a wobbling wheel and the horses its sprockets, as if the expedition is a movement into derangement. The sense of a 'journey of the mind' going amiss is intensified as wind and mind are associated when the image of tiny, annulling pebbles in the 'tantrum' wind make their way into 'My thoughts skip among the stones'. In what is probably the most important foreshadowing undertaken by this opening stanza, the 'nor'-easter' also cancels any words thrown at death:

> Browne may be dying.
> Little hot tantrums of wind and tiny pebbles
> Dessicate and annul the words I toss to him (*CB* 236).

Browne functions in the poem as both a figure dying and a dying figure and words cannot make contact with him. The 'nor'-easter', irritable and inevitable, moves in to complete the first stanza.

The next five stanzas, leading up to the appearance of the grotesque paracletes, are dominated by an image of a Grandsire God which has supported patriarchal and imperial aspirations, but which is now rendered ludicrous by the mincing activity of 'the Void, the sand, the pebbles'. This Grandsire God is manifested in the poem as the speaker's consciousness shifts back to the Depot, the place of water, and also back to a time when his military father exacted obedience to the 'old bearded Predestinator'. Although he exacts the duty of Scripture—'I give Him His text early'—this figure is 'old', 'misunderstood', 'moping', sobbing, and tired of working the bellows which drive the hot nor'-easter, all of which supports Sellick's view that this is a God 'shrunk to senile ineffectualness'. Nevertheless I think the poem is doing more than suggest that its Sturt has lost faith in his father's Predestinator. This is a God who is a victim of his own ambition for total control (an older, feebler version of the walled, pharisaic God):

> Feel for Him, there, old bearded Predestinator
> Trying to look kind ... it's the plan He's tied to:
> The elect and the—the—*wind, stones, pebbles.*
> Browne may be dying (*CB* 237).

He is a God whose presence disintegrates before the fragmented awareness that 'Browne may be dying' (a phrase that slices the poem like a fatal(ist) antiphon) and before the 'words' tossed out by the desert wind. The word that disappears beneath the wind, stones and pebbles, the other of 'elect', is 'damned', and this is what the speaker fears may be his destination, a space unWordable and without God, an absolute 'Void'.

The poem comes close to implying that the Void is created by so absolute a God. The Predestinator is an oppressive figure of judgment who guards the 'father's fireplace', like St Michael hurling the fallen angels into hell and like an angel guarding the gates of paradise. I take the 'father's fireplace' to be a symbol of security and beginning, another version of 'the lighted house, the security, the Beginning' and 'the God,/The Beginning, the joy' which are denied the protagonist of 'Homosexual' (*CB* 220). The Predestinator exercises such control over human happiness that he takes away hope. He seems to know this in the moment when 'prankful vermilion' (a mischievous and perhaps Holy spirit) plays up to his face:

> Yes, I saw that prankful vermilion
> Frisk up almost to His face. At the Search it was
> —*Wind, Stones*—for an instant the Old'un looked hopeful
> And about my own age (*CB* 237).

Yet the Predestinator is an absolutely sovereign God who once suited the imperial certainties of one who 'was solidly in the army': the poem is implying that the theological text and the imperial text corroborate each other. At the same time both these 'solid' texts start to unravel. The address to the dying figure twice interferes, dissatisfaction and desire intrude under guise of 'the Search for something', Old Father Predestinator is shown as unhappy as his fated children. As the wind, stones and pebbles begin again to shred memory's image, the stories of God and heroes are swallowed by the desert, subjected to its crumbling of images.

The poem clearly depicts a God who sees predestination as 'the dear sacred scheme of His dotage', a God tilting under the burden of his own role 'Dispositioning the just and the damned'. As this schematic God breaks up entirely and the desert reoccupies the writing, the hope of salvation recedes to the fragmentary mention of *'Water back at the Depot'* and 'the Void' is finally admitted. It would be easy to say that the poem is merely displacing what it sees as a distorted image of God, but the text does more than lose its God: it takes what is its most absolute and death-defying word and tosses it at the 'hot nor'-easter' only to have it scattered in 'the Void, the sand, the pebbles'. God is not simply lost in the past: God is subjected to a writing which dismantles sovereign schemes, whether of gods, fathers, soldiers or explorers. As in 'Melville At Wood's Hole' (*CB* 77), where a storm does the dismantling, it is when mind and language are undone that vision is possible, though it is, in both poems, a vision of 'terror and love'. Like the Chinese sailor falling from the maintop and knowing 'In what he had sought and loved destruction calling', Sturt is falling through his theological scheme of providence into that uneasy marriage of desire and death which the birds represent:

> —The birds, the birds! Crying like children,
> Closer, wheeling, wheeling, descending, closer!
> They come in ecstatic flight, rapturous as the Paraclete,
> Tongues of fire—it's a well of voices. Crying like children.
> My horse props, makes to rear, shivers, and cannot move.
> They come at us, begging, menacing, at eye level, above.
> I lash at them with my hands, filled with terror and love (*CB* 238).

It is unwise to give too much credibility to 'rapturous as the Paraclete' and conclude that the poem is now replacing the Predestinator with its own more ambivalent theology. The poem is not as confident as Sellick that 'their descent is a vision of the Paraclete, the Comforter, filled with the promise of Pentecost'. It uses the word 'Paraclete', but as if it is a theological word thrown into the contest for meaning. Then, seeming to support it with three other comparisons, the poem rapidly distends the theological concept of the paraclete. If the birds are signs of the Holy Spirit, albeit a Holy Spirit who is more ambiguous than usual, they are also signs of death. The theological enterprise is still very much in question, and 'terror and love' is not so much a consoling paradox as a space where two words may cancel each other out and open up the Void.

Another theological distention occurs as the birds/paracletes become poets who 'wheel away' from the explorers. Like the camels of 'Poet', they too are figures of unknown origin and destiny:

Fire a shot, Mr Browne. And, poets you wheel away.
You are lost, gone. Where do you come from? (Feel the caressing
     nor'-easter
Following, following, chanting.) Are you from the Void?
Poets of dry upper nothingness, you are hunger, we are hunger,
You are thirst, we are thirst (*CB* 238).

Up until this point the desert has been largely working at the edges of awareness, but as the birds become poets the desert shifts to the centre and lies contained, secreted within the possibility of 'the Void'. Given that the birds have just been likened to the Paraclete, the question 'Are you from the Void?' might also release the possibility that the Holy Spirit comes, not from the Predestinator, but the Void, or at least betoken that it is precisely an awareness of this possibility which makes the comparison of vultures and Holy Spirit self-consciously feeble. As this comparison is more and more distended into the comparison of vultures and poets, the Paraclete is also dismantled, until he bears little resemblance to the Christian Muse. As the explorers identify their own 'hunger' and 'thirst' in that of the poets/birds, they are also nearer to becoming themselves 'Poets of dry upper nothingness' and they may also be admitting that the Paraclete, the Comforter, is as 'lost, gone' as the birds.

The Paraclete cannot claim special exemption from the analogical process which admitted him into the poem. Having been uttered in relation to the vultures, he cannot then pretend to be an absolute and immaculate reference. He is implicated, and in this case implicated in the torturous comparisons by which 'Sturt and the Vultures' discloses its hidden purpose: to establish that Sturt's venture into the central desert is the poet's journey into words. This might have been the opportunity for Webb's typically fractured theology to make another appearance, but the perspective has now become acutely negative:

We go mincing along followed by the hot nor'-easter
—But sometimes we stray towards Sacrament, creek-bed, Virgin —
You stray, poets. But you ride neither high Heaven

Nor the earth of statuesque stones. Something lures you down,
Quartz, slate, limestone, an eyeball, an opal, a prisoner,
Till hunger and thirst wheel into madness within you,
Your immaculate Words, cryings (O hear the sweet nor'-easter)
Piping to us, see the lovely Madonna-faces in the gilt
Frameways of pure sand and pebbles! (*CB* 238)

It is easy to see that the desire for water might tempt the desert travellers
to 'stray' towards a 'creek-bed', but the temptations to 'Sacrament' and
especially the Virgin Mary are temptations to spiritual consolation of a kind
denied those who venture across the forsaken territory of predestination in
search of inner water. The poets, however, are drawn down into an interior
landscape where, as the earlier images of the wheel are reworked, their
journey becomes a descent into the deregulation, not just of the senses,
but of meaning itself. There is a thread connecting 'immaculate Words' to
'lovely Madonna-faces' which might be said to encircle the poet's desire for
a pure and elevated tongue with a vision of Mary. Yet Mary herself encircles
'cryings (O hear the sweet nor'-easter) / Piping to us', which means that
the desert has taken up position within her image and that Mary is being
herself evaporated. This passage is framed by the desert, appearing first as
'the hot nor'-easter' then transforming into 'Frameways of pure sand and
pebbles' (and the way 'immaculate Words' are framed by 'sand and pebbles'
is a trope for the defeated eloquence of poetry). The desert also occupies the
centre of this and all exploration: the descent is motivated by a desire for
the landscape of 'Quartz, slate, limestone', but also by a desire to remember
the father who searched for 'an opal, a prisoner', and even by a desire to see
again the 'eyeball' of the deadly paraclete. At the same time, the poem tries,
finally, to expel these poets ('Are you from the Void?'), driving them 'out
of sight and mind like exhausted breath'. But even this attempt to exhaust
the breath is undone: by a subtle use of placement and cadence the birds
are brought back, bearing a name the poem has been avoiding:

                                        Only something far beneath
Cowers away when you come.

And its name is Death (*CB* 238).

Had the last two lines been reversed, their intelligible content would remain the same, but their meaning would be more positive. This ending gives enormous force to the presence of Death, by hiding its name until now and giving it, so to speak, the last word. The reader, meanwhile, is abandoned to a desert of questions. Is Death another face of the Void? Why does Death cower from the Paraclete when the Paraclete has already been associated with the vulture, itself an image of Death? Is Death afraid of poetry? Or another name for that original void over which the Spirit of God (and also of poetry?) breathed? But now that breath is 'exhausted', is poetry just a wind-wheel turning madly? Is Death the speaker, the one who drives the birds away? Whatever the answers different readers will give to such questions, one thing seems clear: if Death does cower away from the poets/ birds, Death is still there after they have become exhausted breath.

So: that is my reading for today. Next time I will, I guess, have a different reading, and one of the best things about reading Webb's poetry is that it reminds, me at least, of the partial and transitory nature of reading. Next time round I am likely to think that Webb's poetry is like an interpretation of Maria Goretti, that it is an innocent space on the edge of a textuality which invites and resists penetration. One of the Webbean subtexts is concerned to occupy the space of innocence (and the victim is a way of doing this) in order to displace anxiety about something pharisaic and fascist in the phallus. Where the poetry most nearly approaches such innocence it is least convincing: it finds in the figure of Mary, Mother of God, a woman who is beyond the phallus and mother of all peace, and, in order to have her, exchanges ambiguity for sentimentality. Where the poetry forsakes innocence for 'sin', entering a subjectivity in sympathy with diseased sexuality, it gains an extraordinary and subversive power. Next time I might argue that the desire for the innocent woman and mother, so obvious in the Mary poems, is the other side of the identification with the male victim-priest in 'Homosexual'. But that's another reading.

Works Cited

Ashcroft, B. *The Gimbals of Unease*. Nedlands: The Centre for Studies in Australian Literature, UWA, 1996.

Calvin, J. *Institutes*, III, xxii.11; xxiii.2, cited Williston Walker. *John Calvin*. New York: Schocken Books, 1969. 417.

Griffith, M. *God's Fool*. Sydney: Angus & Robertson, 1991.

Griffith, M. & J.A. McGlade (eds.). *Caps and Bells: The Poetry of Francis Webb*. Sydney: CollinsAngus & Robertson, 1991.

Raschke, C. 'The Deconstruction of God.' Thomas Altizer et al (eds.), *Deconstruction and Theology*. New York: Crossroads, 1982.

Sellick, R. 'Francis Webb's "Sturt and the Vultures": a Note on Sources'. *Australian Literary Studies*. 6:3 May 1974. 310–314.

Sturt, C. *Narrative of an Expedition into Central Australia*. London, 1849. Cited Sellick.

——. *Journal of the Central Australian Expedition 1844–45*. Jill Waterhouse (ed.). London: Caliban Books, 1984.

Thompson, F. 'The Hound of Heaven.' *Complete Poetical Works*. New York: The Modern Library, 1913. 88–93.

Tulip, J. '"Banksia"—An Australian Epiphany.' *Poetry Australia* 56, September 1975. 36–39.

Patience and Surprise

THE POETRY OF VIVIAN SMITH

IT WOULD BE EASY, but misleading, to praise (or bury) Vivian Smith's poetry on account of its composure and serenity. While it quite often concerns itself with things that can still or cannot any longer be put in place, his poetry does not indulge a nostalgic belief in order at the expense of experience. At its best, it recognizes and respects the 'savage' as well as the 'serene': those forces which might easily invade and fragment the achieved 'centre of stillness', the artistic will.

Of course, his poetry is, in its formal aspects, tightly and persistently controlled. But this discipline mostly serves an expressive rather than repressive purpose. It concentrates the quiet power of his poetic voice and it indicates the epistemological, moral and aesthetic implications of his work. His poetry wants to render the disparate particularities of experience, but also to search for the unifying pattern: detail and design. His poetry records feelings of failure, disbelief, and 'such final bareness', but, by an act of will, resists these and gives faith to a precise, patient attention to beauty and life's strange elation. While it is grounded in accurate observation, his poetry is more than rhythmical reportage: Smith believes the imagination has an ability and responsibility to shape the truths of art from the facts of experience. Throughout his poetry, then, control functions as a means to freedom—particularly the freedom to appreciate the 'moment that catches us still unprepared'.

In his preface to *Selected Poems*, Smith writes:

And I have become more conscious than ever of the centrality and polarity of the two places in which I have spent most of my life: Hobart and Sydney. They seem to represent the two extreme points between which my poems move (v).

What we find in Smith's Hobart poems is an attempt to reconcile the paradoxical qualities of the Tasmanian landscape,[15] as if this strenuous dialogue between the shaping imagination and the observing object might advance some understanding of and between the forces of personal will and those of an outside, obscure, possibly malign fate. The landscape does not simply allow itself to be absorbed and contained by the meditating consciousness. It resists:

> Something in the landscape
> attentive, stares at me:
> nothing's shape or shape of fear
> it watches discreetly. ('The Shadow' 22)

If we admit as well that 'No image can ever be deserted' ('Deserted Bandstand, Kingston Beach' 14), we see the anxiety which works beneath the lyric surface of Smith's Hobart poems. For this reason I doubt that it is very useful to treat these poems as a kind of 'pastoral', if that implies more external order and interior simplicity than the poems themselves evidence. Tasmania is not for Smith a symbol of original harmony in the way that Bunyah is for Les Murray. It is more question than answer. The question, to do with the relationship between chance and purpose, is clearly voiced in a recent, non-Tasmanian, poem:

> Such threads and lines that link our different lives,

---

15. Smith has said that Tasmanian poets 'have brought a peculiar concentration to the fashioning of images which can reconcile their own humanity with the paradoxical qualities of an enduring yet changeful landscape'. ('The Poetry of Tasmania', with Margaret Scott, *Quadrant*, November 1985, 87.)

coincidence or miracle, who knows
what random purpose conjures and contrives?
('Chance Meeting' 94)

In 'Bedlam Hills' a landscape 'as empty / as a blindman's stare' refuses the imaginative construct which would contain it within a Wordsworthian story of Mad Clare, displaces the personal force, and threatens the mind with an image of madness. While 'Bird Sanctuary' depicts yet again a poet's self-defining appeal to swans and silence, it does include weed as well as silence in its 'centre of surprise', and it does have its swans seek a shade curiously described as 'cautious lengthened', as if it slides from their search even as it submits to it. In 'The Other Meaning' the 'hard incisive light' of the Tasmanian landscape destroys the 'standing shade' and any hope that joy and pain might be emblematically reconciled through 'those simple trees that hold / their brief and formal birds' gives way: 'I have failed: finding the world alive / with pain, and without its other meaning' (20).

The failure must have been instructive. 'The Other Meaning' struggles between a way of speaking which is emblematic and one which is more attuned to immediate experience. 'Return to Hobart', from Smith's second volume, speaks with a new, a surer voice. There is a selective description of detail as 'we' travel from the airport to the family home. These details suggest randomness, even vacancy, as the image of vacant streets confirms the need for style, then, in a manner typical of Smith's moral insight, turns back and questions whether 'style' can become 'façades'. Appreciating the 'precise labour' with which the Salvation Army play their hymns, the poet shifts into himself ('we' disappear), remembering his childhood. Then:

My taxi swerves into a dug-up street
with half a road unfinished. Home again.
Challenged by change, the sense of the incomplete (40).

This poem does not simply praise the past. It suggests that the real continuity between the present and the past is their incompletion. What is left behind at the airport is 'the tall unfinished bridge'. What is arrived at is 'half a road unfinished'. Smith's metaphysical intuition of 'the steady incompletion of our days' ('Il Convento, Batignano') informs his use of the journey metaphor, just as it informs so much of his meditation on the process of change.

'Revisiting' is more obviously to do with what has gone and how this might still be kept intact by memory's art. Remembering his youth, the poet describes contemporary experience (in a generalized fashion) as 'a concrete path with weeds'. While this image may imply a moral judgment about the depersonalizing influence of an advancing technological society, the poem also recognizes that art itself can become depersonalized: 'We can't rewrite the past to suit our needs / though some will fake their lives to fit their poems.' But these anxieties are firmly contained: 'everywhere the sky, the mountain range'. This affirms the possibility of permanent meaning in a world of change. Yet the final image escapes the composure of this meditation. Sitting 'on the new steps in the cold sun', the poet notices how

> Against the hard step a patch of sun
> dries unblown seeds on dandelion clocks
> swaying the way the breeze moves as it passes (84).

The sense of corruptibility released here is worthy of *Ecclesiastes*. The brave old world of human initiative, but lately blessed by the sky, is now regarded indifferently by time itself, as sun and breeze conspire to corrupt the promise of the 'dandelion clocks'.

Smith does not always manage, in such a composed way, to discomfort the mind. In 'Late April: Hobart' (56) he perhaps intends to write a poem which enacts Autumn's 'sense of balance between rot and bloom'. However, the tone becomes depressive as the rhymes which support the 'rot' half of the balance (with their harder consonants and longer vowels) have the edge on those which hold the bloom. The repetition of key concepts also introduces a heaviness, as does the tendency to overstate the theme of balance. While the poem claims that 'All points of stillness hover out of range', it is itself strangely static and its asserted balance between depression and elation is tipped in favour of the former as its music takes a dying fall. This may be the proper way to reach the final, autumnal note: 'Beneath it all such final bareness waits.' But I doubt the poem does what it says it will do: catch the peculiar, intermediate beauty of Autumn, tell how 'sustained by filth, fertility survives', celebrate how 'In time each shifting harmony arrives'. Since there is too much harmony and not enough shifting, this poem, despite itself, becomes a lament for 'the statements of the summer dawn / when love grew more abundant with excess'.

'Warmth in July: Hobart' is more successful. The observation is more precise, less patterned. The weight within the rhymes is more equally distributed. The July Tasmanian light seems to catch change in the act, between beginning and end, incomplete. While this reminds the poet of death and makes him ask, 'could I bear such clarity while dying?', it also reminds him that 'meanings start / in detail that may never reach design'. Meaning is humbler than certitude: it is an effect of discipline, of 'strict repose' and 'hard precision'. And this precision yields not precisely an intellectual recognition of life's strange relation, but a sensuous apprehension of life's elation. In Smith's poetry, precision is the way to sensual ease, and sensual ease the condition for appreciating beauty. Precision, therefore, prepares for feelings of surprise, elation, wonder and promise. (It also at times prepares for feelings of quiet horror.) These feelings (more than intellectual resolutions) reveal the continuities within a changing world, as the incomplete turns into the unexpected:

> The light is caught: no shadow overflows.
> And nothing's yet begun. No season's ended.
> All buds are merely knowledge in the mind.
> Implicit in the twig are hip and rose;
> but waiting, waiting too is still intended.
>
> We seek too soon the end, the final things:
> we try to grasp the whole where meanings start
> in detail that may never reach design.
> But feel the light and how it soaks and stings

and taste the blue where branches fall apart

till all your knowledge is mere warmth and glow,
all apprehension—as of sensual ease:
a sense of sure precision deep in things.
The year has still its separate months to go
but change is promised and awakenings (57).

Smith's is poetry of and about the will—the will's capacity to discern
and decide, but, more importantly, its capacity to desire, and be surprised.
In 'View From the Domain, Hobart', a sudden apprehension catches the
will moving between caution and courage:

I catch the way the bridge divides the harbour
and wonder what it is my future fears:
the small anonymous life of love and labour,
or growing coarse and cautious with the years? (61).

Yet this unexpected apprehension is also an effect of patience and discipline.
The poet has been viewing Hobart from above, noting details in such a way
that the poem's underlying concern appears as if from the place itself, with
its composed, yet uncontained, features ('jagged cape', 'smooth hills'), its
city creeping past its own orderliness. As the speaker attempts to block the
city out with his hands, the place extends its influence and his attempt fails
because 'something of the uncontained persists'. As he then surrenders
more and more to the undesigned detail of the scene, remembering by
association how childhood promises could not be contained as life went on,
wondering how his poetry will change, he summons his own surprise: the
sight of the bridge, an image of the transition process. The poet then moves
into the image, completing the poem's transition from outer to inner scene,
yet finding that the image leaves the question of his future open.

One of the questions asked in this poem is: 'Could other places now
mean other styles?' Does his style change when he moves from Hobart to
Sydney? His awareness changes: the Sydney poems are more conscious

of humid summers, night lights and human bodies. But his favourite structure persists: the relationship between what is finished and what is unfulfilled, what is composed and what is uncontained. If there is a change in style, it is that Sydney encourages in Smith's poetry a distancing technique which is self-critical and even self-mocking. It encourages a quality of compassionate irony.

'Summer Sketches: Sydney' acknowledges a different precision in Sydney's lights and colours. It also sees the uncontained possibilities in sensuality. Here sexuality is a drifting thing, at odds with the preferred precision:

> At night the cool precision of the stars,
> the neon glitter and the sexy cars,
> the easy pick-up in the close green bars (39).

In the fourth of these sketches Smith signals that his response to Sydney will seek much the same pattern as his response to Hobart. Considering how art both contains and uncontains, he suspends this tension in order to validate meaning through a moment of joy (a quiet joy, somewhat withdrawn from commercial city-life):

> A holiday like some smooth magazine;
> how photos can improve the simplest scene.
> They isolate the image that endures;
> beyond the margins is the life that cures.
> But when the surface gloss is thought away
> some images survive through common day
> and linger with a touch of tenderness:
> the way you brushed your hair, your summer dress.

Sydney's summer weighs restlessly on Smith's senses. Creeping over him in a hazy flow of sound and colour, summer carries with it shrill noises, bad news, and nearly naked bodies ('Balmoral Summer,'66'). This is not his season. It gives the mind no relief, but 'presses on [his] ageing bones' with its sweaty ripeness until growth becomes a matter of what survives its corruption: hair, nails and teeth. It is a season which resists meaning:

> Dead Summer will not yield. Green stones
> are all the garden has to show and they
> will not solve all our problems of decay. ('Summer Notes' 63)

Such alienation increases his anxiety about his future as a poet. In a
Mosman room, continuing his 'small anonymous life', he compares himself
to 'Chardin in Mongolia / and Nolan at the South Pole with a brush'. In
a 'time of crude effects', he is failing to write a poem about a storm. The
storm has its own crude effects—its violence shakes his sense of harmony,
until the moment of greatness flickers, cracks and shows nothing more
than an ordinary and disordered world:

> Beneath transfigurations the inane
> waits like a broken fence beneath a vine,
> a horde of leaves, an overflowing drain.
>
> And what to make of this, and where begin?
> Must this too still be sung, this inert slush? ('A Room in Mosman' 65).

The storm image is still worrying him in 'Twenty Years of Sydney'.
Has it come to signify the violence inherent in his change of city, as well
as some sense of being threatened by Sydney? There is still a reserve about
Sydney. There is still a question as to whether he will change his poetic
style—just as there is, in the tone, an implied commitment to discretion,
tenacity and quietness as his poetic values. However, there does seem to be
a change. It is difficult to tell because it is difficult to catch the tone of the
last line and to decide how much Smith is speaking with irony, how much
with simplicity. After recalling a night of storm and chaos, he continues:

> That was the week I met Slessor alone
> walking down Phillip Street smoking his cigar,
> his pink scrubbed skin never touched by the sun.

> Fastidious, bow tie, he smiled like the Cheshire cat:
> "If you change your city you are sure to change your style."
> A kind man, he always praised the young (73).

There is, surely, a throw-away effect in this last line? It could be an unaffected acknowledgement of Slessor's critical support for Smith. But it also seems to sound a note of irony—irony directed more at Smith than Slessor, as the older (Sydney) poet in Smith meets the younger (Hobart) one (the inner scene paralleling the outer), and wonders whimsically what has become of him. Perhaps both notes are sounded, with Smith returning praise to Slessor and taking now for himself the smile.

'Late May: Sydney' shows this ironic detachment at work within his more usual poetic pattern. As the poem opens, he is still comparing Sydney to Hobart ('even here'), but finds—at last—that Sydney light reveals the preferred paradox:

> Autumn in the tropics: even here
> the first touch of winter clears the air
> making the light astringent and serene (86).

The poem then takes a familiar path: the evocation of a landscape delicate in detail but incomplete in design; the introduction of human figures, who find their place in the landscape not so much because they perceive relatedness, but more because they feel elatedness. Their contentment is derived from the joy of an interrelational moment, and it is this joy which vindicates an implied belief in the interpersonal nature of meaning:

> The spider lifts its way beneath the leaf
> and we find our contentment talking here
> of people and the games words like to play.

This small moment of serenity is then apparently disregarded in favour of a larger question: whether Sydney has finally lost the innocence D. H. Lawrence saw in it. While the name of Lawrence lends the question some authority, Smith's own subtly ironic tone is taking the poem in another direction, intimating that simple joy is preferable to metropolitan cynicism.

This self-regarding irony, which seems to have been nurtured by 'the exactness of a foreign place' as well as by a more assured use of conversational tones and rhythms, allows him to locate his own work more easily within his more general vision of art as a discipline which holds and releases meaning. Smith makes his own a kind of wry meditation—as in 'Sparrows: Mosman', where he ruefully regards sparrows creating their world, then compares his own descriptive effort to the art of Japan:

> An artist from Japan would get this right
> in two ticks showing nature's life
> simply doesn't need us to go on:
> a stone wall, a clutter of bamboo—
> a few lines that gather up the whole
> the way a tendril speaks for the full vine,
> a brushstroke sparrow for a thousand birds.
>
> And here I sit and listen to their din
> and how they turn the garden to a room (95).

The tone is carefully balanced between confession and self-mockery. It is this quality which allows Smith to respect the differences between the three artistic efforts at the same time as he reconciles them in the notion that any art may make the world a place of habitation.

This is not to say that Smith's poems about not writing poetry are exercises in convention. I think there is a genuine anxiety operating, an anxiety he has himself diagnosed, in describing himself as 'afraid of chaos, and of order, too' ('Reflections' 33). This is no doubt why the tension between containment and release is so central to his work. It reflects the drama of his will, resisting both composure and shapelessness.

Since it does so truthfully reflect the drama of will, Vivian Smith's is a moral poetry—in the sense that it embodies a fineness of feeling and perception, a recognition of some difficult relation—patient, strict—between beauty and truth. This is most evident where he adapts Wallace Stevens:

> We neither live by dogma nor by theory:
> still even without orders there's relation.
> I cannot grasp the whole my heart believes.
> But watch that sparrow hunt that butterfly:
> life's nonsense pierces too with strange elation
>
> and through what's most absurd my heart is riven
> and out of sight both bird and butterfly...
> and still and still my sense of joy persists ('For a New Year' 55).

Three of Smith's most well known meditative poems show how feeling evokes and vindicates its own perceptions: 'An Effect of Light', 'At An Exhibition of Historical Paintings, Hobart', and 'Still Life'.

'An Effect of Light' has the poet retreating to a 'tranquil park', hoping it may help him regain his composure, which has been disturbed not only by the day's work, but by years of half-realized projects. What he finally receives is this image of swans:

> I watch the fussing wings across the pool
> and wonder what it means, regeneration;
> and see within the circles ruffling out,
> the waterlily's simple revelation (51).

This absorption into a healing landscape may seem to replace the mind's complexities with the heart's simplicities. This is true inasmuch as Vivian Smith does suggest that a fine appreciative experience has a truth which does not need to explain itself. ('Love is the totally unexpected view / and being, need prove nothing to the world.' For A New Year' 55) But the poem has a cyclic as well as a linear design. It attempts a 'centre of surprise'—moving between inner and outer moments, blending the two, finding but an instant's beauty and joy within the circle of ruffled experience.

It opens with an image of indignant swans and disturbed water, then switches to a moment of inner agitation as the poet doubts his life's direction. Now the landscape is seen as something more than a soothing force—it has revelatory potential, and Smith searches it for an image which might effectively contain and convey his sense of disarray. Images from academic life, art, and nature are tested, but found inadequate. However, as we move from one image to the other, there is a curious development: whereas the image of life as 'a discarded scratched-out note / one cannot read' is easily contained by the mind's questioning and is inadequate because it does not say enough, the third image is discarded because it says more than can be contained:

I would ask this as clearly if I could
as that white dove that's tumbling in the sky:
how can a sense of meaning still persist
so intertwined with sense of no reply?

His imaginative responses are gradually freed from his conceptual difficulties. Objects exist more to show beauty than to illustrate relation. The poem's technique, then, is to describe an area of potential meaninglessness and pierce it with an unexpected apprehension of beauty. This is done with full knowledge that it may be an evasion. As the swans re-enter the poem, their image unifying and concentrating its linear and cyclic directions, Smith voices the very accusation which might be levelled at the poem's apparently evasive structure:

I turn towards the sight of paddling swans.
What is confusion but no attitude;
or is tranquillity a touch of light
that merely lingers till the mind's subdued?

I do not think the poem constitutes an evasive manoeuvre since I do not think Smith sets out to provide the 'Meaning of Life'. There is a search for meaning going on, but this is guided by an all-important recognition that what may make the search valuable is not so much the truth that is patiently uncovered, but the beauty that is unexpectedly 'there'.

In 'At An Exhibition of Historical Paintings, Hobart', moral feeling is found breaking the frame of mediocre art. Having too little talent and too great a taste for tidiness, the artists in the exhibition have betrayed reality (where things 'more themselves' are also 'less accurate'). Smith implies that this is a serious betrayal because he links their aesthetic responsibility with Tasmania's moral responsibility toward the Aborigines:

The last natives. Here that silent slaughter

is really not prefigured or avoided.
One merely sees a profile, a full face,
a body sitting stiffly in a chair:
the soon-forgotten absence of a race ... (29)

But he also claims that history is an artist: 'History has made artists of all these / painters who lacked energy and feature.' (In 'Old Men Are Facts' he claimed: 'old men are part of what they make and what is made.' 5) This suggests the need for the artist to develop an imagination which is receptive as well as active—but receptive to some uncontained potency of life which breaks through despite the facts (in this case, the mediocre paintings). Submitting to these paintings, an astringent sensibility can still, precisely because they do embody a failure of intention, feel the truth behind the incompletion: 'Around the hall / the pathos of the past, the human creature.'

'Still Life' has art and life again exert power, each on the other, to frame and release the truth within beauty. The opening line is beautifully balanced. While it can be playful in tone, it centres a meditative attention and delicately implies that life is more life where there is a focus and stillness. By repeating the demonstrative, Smith quietly insists that we do follow his focus, yet once he has us fixed on 'These massed hydrangeas standing near the wall', he allows his instinct for analogies to break the frame. Just as the flowers 'bring such fullness to the room', their meaning expands (through a broadening, deepening line of imagery): from the domestic world of 'cushions puffed up on a chair', to the more simply joyful 'pink clowns in the air / who just perform and do not need to know', to the remembered Tasmanian landscape—'They bloom with blue like heaped-up mountain snow'. Finally they image 'resurrections from the tomb' (82).

In that moment within appreciation there has been knowledge, understood as 'all apprehension'. Smith then tries to debrief as well as describe: 'There are colours with a flower's name'. Here he both affirms the naming ritual within his poem and favours the appreciative engagement. The hydrangeas carry his belief that art draws meaning and throws it off, and so is always, but wonderfully, incomplete, always increasing desire:

> We sit and watch their clouds of pink, their sheen,
> the way they look both savage and serene
> drawing the light and holding it at bay:
> a storm inside a storm that has been stilled
> with something finished, something unfulfilled.

I think, though, that this concern for 'how things change and how they hold' is in danger of being overstated, I also think there is in Vivian Smith's poetry a much greater range than might be implied by his image as a lyric poet affirming continuity within change.[16] There are poems which indicate surrealist, satiric and religious aspects of his imagination.

In some of the very early poems, there is a surrealist impulse which then seems to be discarded in favour of more controlled poetry ('Bedlam Hills', 'Winter Foreshore', 'Aloes and Sea', 'The Last Summer'). But the impulse cannot be deserted and Smith's poetry returns to images which seem to

---

16. In his review of *Selected Poems*, Michael Haig doubts the accuracy of the term 'lyrical' in relation to Smith's poetry. (*The Age Monthly Review*, November 1985, 13.) James McAuley also argued that we should not confine our attention to the lyrical poems, and noted comic, ironic, satiric and surrealist elements in the poetry (*A Map of Australian Verse*, 299).

reach out and threaten to take the mind over. This awareness of the object's power informs two very fine poems: 'Bus Ride' and 'The Man Fern Near the Bus Stop'. 'Bus Ride' is a peeping monologue in which a character 'always troubled by sex' enters what seems to be a close and entire busload world of women. Smith uses a surrealist touch in order to let the fantasy inflate itself. While this accurately renders a character whose desires outpace his performance, it also creates a space for judgment. The discrepancy between the willed and the realized is used to generate an unobtrusive moral restraint. It is also used as a space for compassion. The poem closes with a wonderful blend of moral sensibility, irony and compassion. As the male agent becomes more receptive within the network of images, the girl who was the object of his fantasies becomes the agent of an epiphany, and his lonely yearnings are suddenly pierced with a moment's elation:

And staring at your face
and through your summer dress,
the dry mouth of lust
flows with tenderness (48).

'The Man Fern Near the Bus Stop' defies any easy explanation. Its dramatic base is simple: the speaker, about to catch a bus, has his attention caught by the swaying frond of a man fern and is then drawn into a web of associations. Yet what emerges is an extraordinarily potent sense of existential contingency, reaching out at him, capturing his mind with darkness. This is offset only at the very end by two lines which might suggest new life. The man fern, with 'one scaly feather swaying out of the dark', seems to represent an active universe which may be menacing (mainly because of its ambiguity): 'slightly drunk with rain and freckled with old spores / it touches me with its slow question mark.' Its question is presumably the one familiar to Smith: the ultimate value of choice and will given the disintegration at the heart of life. As the speaker recognizes and resists the power of this questions-in-image, Smith, in a superb succession of surrealist imagery, releases his full sense of life's decay:

Something in the shadows catches at the throat,
smelling like old slippers, drying like a skin,
scraped like an emu or a gumboot stuck with fur,
straining all the time to take me in.

Cellophane crinkles in the fern's pineapple heart.
The fur parts slowly showing a crumpled horn.
A ruffled seahorse stands in swaying weed,
and held in cotton wool, a mouse unborn (76).

The conclusion barely resists this image of disintegration. As if the word 'unborn' half-reveals an underside of promise, the final lines turn towards a more positive possibility: 'the buds of fingers breaking into power / and long fibres breaking in the voice.' It is only a possibility, though: 'breaking' could connote disintegration as well as emergence.

There is a satiric impulse, but it is difficult to describe as it is closely related to a self-deprecating wit. If Smith wants to make a point about standards or values, he makes it best by criticizing himself. He is not really a full-frontal satirist. 'Deathbed Sketch', a portrait of one who creates himself as a writer, has moments of thrust, such as:

His first book made him known to a small band:
it passed in the antipodes for Art.
with verses full of God and sex and wars.
It proved he had no ear and far less heart (44).

Here there is the poise which indicates good aim, and the rhymed lines hit their mark precisely and deftly. At other moments—where the impulse is deflected into narration or self-criticism—it takes a little too long to extract the rhyme from the target. Smith's attack is weakened by his underlying sense of ambiguity, revealed when he abandons confrontation in favour of confession: 'Of course we all agreed we would be kind, / haunted by our own sense of deeper failure.'

Yet this same instinct for self-criticism, coupled with a more general awareness that only the inhuman is accurate, gives other poems a smilingly shrewd character. The Prufrockian speaker of 'Quiet Evening', having survived the horrors of coming home on a bus and in a storm, is looking forward to a quiet evening with a bath and a book. In tones which are discreet and civilized he tells how 'The shapes of simple and coherent life / surround [him] and define [him] from without.' However, coherence and definition soon come under threat:

> a furtive slips his key in Madam Y's:
> I hear him enter. And for all I know
>
> someone enters Cyril's round the back (43).

Though the speaker declares, 'O my dear I'm too / broadminded to be horrified', there is a feeling that horror and broadmindedness here confront each other. The horror springs not from moral indignation, but from the way 'The moment loosens and the doorways glide / Pandora's monsters ...'. The broadmindedness comes from a somewhat comic recognition of self:

> And reading how I dream I might have been
> a golden youth with narrow hips and thighs
> adored on beaches by wet girls and queens,
> Pandora's monsters or her butterflies:
>
> I'm too controlled. I make them fly away.
> It floods outside as if disaster's near.
> I light a cigarette. I'm glad my mind's
> so elegant, so various and clear.

Behind the self-mocking poise there is a brittleness, as if the poem doubts whether its own urbanity will have sufficient force to avert disaster. The deluge is at hand and Vivian Smith has brought centre stage, not Noah and his ark, but Noel Coward and his cigarette.

'My Morning Dip', so unassuming and conversational within its slightly more relaxed frame, could easily float by unnoticed. Yet it makes some hard-hitting points as it blends satiric and confessional impulses and allows a glimpse at the quiet integrity of this poet. At one level it is another poem about the poet's mid-life crisis. He swims in a context of change:

> These are the years when some will change their style
> and others cease to write to build a garden,
> when the academic starts to grow stiff joints
> and the hack's arteries begin to harden
>
> when marriages break up or settle down
> some at last embrace their long-lost cause,
> while others change their sex or flounder through
> the menopause (80).

It is clear that Smith himself will not plot such unlikely wonders. He is 'trying just to keep afloat'. His way of doing so is to disown idealistic enthusiasms— '(I can't believe the weather will get finer)'—and to own the past—he has 'much to remember, nothing to forget'. Sustaining its self-mockery, the poem yet concludes by attacking the idea that poetic development presupposes immersion in every tide or trend of experience:

> Arthur Waley never went to China
>
> and I'll not grow a pony tail
> or join a commune yet.

Though the ending is somewhat 'open", this mild-mannered piece is a strong plea for individuality and pluralism within the poetic community.

With its balance of iambic and conversational rhythms, of long and short lines, 'Looking Back' hovers between a desire to tell the whole truth and a need for reticence. Having already disapproved of those who 'fake their lives to fit their poems', he gives away his own childhood-confessional poem with an almost fastidious honesty. Not that it is a simple record of the facts. As well as depicting life on the peripheries, he incorporates a battler humour ('we had no background past a weekly pay'), a comment on the link between poverty and surprise ('we knew the gifts that still arise unplanned'), and moral realism ('and though things were not right we were not wronged'). It is therefore possible to read the poem as an astringent re-presentation of family struggle—until the last line: 'we were what you call the urban poor'. The throwaway tone and the use of the label suggest that the poem may have been looking back at itself with a degree of irony.[17] While the formal restraints of 'Looking Back' do mimic the restraint needed to tell the truth about the past, they also help the poem raise a smile, which seems to be saying that it is a little too easy to empty the family diaries and call the record art.

There are also poems where the last line destroys an illusory serenity and shocks us with an image of inexpressible possibilities, approaching at times epiphany, whether of light or dark forces. This indicates a religious dimension in Smith's work: a conscious world which is unable to hold belief and unable to let it go is suddenly pierced by 'this / moment that catches us still unprepared' ('The Traveller Returns'). Again, Smith does not espouse any formal resolutions for the problem of belief. He merely intimates that the capacity to be deeply surprised by life may be a religious capacity.

'Il Convento, Batignano' promises to be familiar Smith territory. We have the landscape attracting the observer and helping him reflect on the relation between what one makes and what is made. We have the slightly self-deprecating assessment of personal-poetic achievement. We have the concern about 'something unfulfilled'—here it is expressed dynamically as 'the steady incompletion of our days'. Yet on this meditative lyric base is grafted a piece of casual dialogue which creates in the poem two contrasting points of view, personalities and places. And the beauty of

17. Smith has admitted, in conversation, that his piece was partly a reaction to the way certain poets were, at the time, continually making claims about the size and importance of their respective ancestries.

the poem is the way the two viewpoints, achievements, personalities and places are so gently respected and reconciled when Smith compares the bees of this foreign-but-present pond with the cattle of his familiar-but-absent landscape and brings them together:

> You stretch and realign a damaged frond
> and as we talk the chirr and whirr begin
> and bees come down like cattle to the pond (74).

The tone is peaceful, but the effect of the image is to break open the poem and reorder its story of two artists who made different choices and took different paths towards incompletion. That story was an invitatory ritual, preparing them for this shared moment of misapprehension. It is more than a damaged frond that has been realigned.

'The Edge of Winter' opens with images which highlight the predatory character of parrots driven down from the mountain by snow and hunger. I am not sure that this opening is successful: the parrots are presented abstractly and seem to freeze on the line, and the too-familiar rhyme of 'bay' with 'day' drains ferocity from the scene. And ferocity is what is wanted as the parrots next become a frightening image of wanton destruction:

> Such images of hunger strike our lives
> the way that summer lightning rips the sky;
> they scream and swoop and scatter flowers among
> the other flowers they break with swivelled tongue —
> like green velvet with unbuttoned eye (81).

The simile is very effective: familiar, but unusually menacing. Smith then risks the poem's focus with a conversational line, which, while it introduces a memory central to the poem's narrative and logic, also distracts us with the sense of someone standing just to one side of where we are being asked to concentrate our attention. The ending, however, is superb, as the poem moves from an enclosed, bored world out into one wide with summer promise and sudden, quiet horror:

Our lives were kept indoors like animals
while boredom ate the protein in the brain.

And then one day the rain began to lift.
We went outside recalling summer skies.
The letterbox half hanging from its hinge
was full of drowned and broken butterflies.

This last verse can serve as a closing image of Vivian Smith's poetry:
the muted struggle between hope and mortal awareness; the hanging
letterbox like the tightrope of the will; the broken butterflies some
defeated, yet persistent promise of being—still surviving because their
very unexpectedness somehow lifts them into a moment of apprehension
where, if only for a brief and broken instant, meaning becomes what
beauty might be.

Works Cited

Smith, V. *Selected Poems*. Sydney: Angus & Robertson, 1985.

Justice, Sacrifice and the Mother's Poem

Must I guess human sacrifice is at the heart of literature
—THE BOYS WHO STOLE THE FUNERAL 29

IN 1999, WHEN PETER ALEXANDER'S *Les Murray: A Life In Progress* almost appeared,[18] literature did seem ready to take a few human sacrifices. Murray and his first biographer were about to be burnt on the altar of single truth and irreducible fact by people who normally (I mean more than usually) keep faith with de-centred subjectivity and the textuality of all things. If Murray felt he was again under attack from Narrowspeak fascist intellectuals who never praise Auschwitz, his alleged persecutors, picking through Alexander's one-sided account of scheming envy, faithless friends and unkind reviews, felt that their Otherspeak had been well but not truly sacrificed to Murrayspeak. It was like a scene from a Murray poem, with creatures circling in deep conflict and clamour about the place of blood, brought together in a victim narrative. Their circling at times made it difficult to disentangle the narrative of victim from the victims of narrative, from narrative as victim. Now that the dust has settled a little (and the blood?), it is clear that many see *Les Murray: A Life In Progress* as too sympathetic to Murray and, therefore, unreliable. Many, that is, read

---

18. The publication of Alexander's biography was delayed for a year because of threats of legal action.

biography as history. Others find it useful as evidence of what Cotter calls Murray's 'emergent self' (37), especially in the way it illuminates the autobiographical basis of *Fredy Neptune*. Certainly it is possible to make more of Alexander's book if it is read as Murray's story, since it then becomes a fascinating account of how the figure known as 'Les Murray' makes and is made of narrative. In particular, it reveals how stories of the sacrificial victim bleed through Murray's life and work.

Alexander also shows that Murray's originary victim narrative, his story of his mother's death, is wrong. Whereas 'The Steel' (*The People's Otherworld* 32–6) represents the mother as the victim of a city-bred doctor's snobbish indifference, the biography shows her to be the victim of her husband's puritanical inhibition and stubborn clan antipathies (Alexander 34–40). It would appear that Murray's belief in sacrifice has made a victim of the facts. This could mean that, in one of those retaliatory moves that sustain sacrificial economies, the poem will now be handed over to history for punishment and crucified between ethics and literature. Ivor Indyk seems to want to prevent this, maintaining that, although the poem is 'unjust in its accusations' against the doctor, it contains a deeper truth in its 'tolerance, its breadth of sympathy, its ability to absorb perspectives larger, or later, than the poet's own' (55–56). Indyk does, however, seem prepared to sacrifice the poet in order to save the poem. When he finds blame and accusation in the poem, he is as likely to attribute such behaviour to 'Murray' as to 'The Steel'. When, however, he recognises tolerance, sympathy, and 'complex psychology', he writes as if the poem is the moral agent responsible for such behaviour. Accordingly, when he remarks that the poem 'knows more than the poet', the effect is somewhat mischievous: it sounds as if he means the poem is more tolerant than the poet. For Indyk the main question raised by Alexander's disclosure is: 'How are we to read a poem that makes so much of "being just, seeking justice", when, as we now see, it is itself unjust in its accusations?' (Indyk 55). This takes us into ethico-literary territory and, before following,[19] I want to make two

---

19. When I say 'following', I do not mean to give the impression that this piece was conceived in response to Ivor Indyk's column. I first raised questions about sacrifice

points. The first point is that the metonymic habit of speaking of a poem's knowing, willing and acting can be unhelpful in discussions of ethics and literature. At a fundamental level, ethics involves and revolves discussion of responsibility for real acts, such as eating someone else's fruit, which is something poems do not usually do, even though Adam would, no doubt, have loved the chance to tell the God of Genesis, 'It wasn't me. It was the Writing you put me in'. Readers have, individually and communally, to take responsibility for their own actions. Poems, inasmuch as they can convey ideas and model how to act may have effects in ethical contexts, but they are, in terms of accountability, effects made by readers (and writers). The second point is that to talk about ethics in writing is (should be) to give attention to the ethics of reading. Reading, as Gadamer observes, is an effect of horizons meeting, and one implication of this is that 'my' reading is often a work of autobiography, happening when the horizon of 'my' story approaches or intersects the horizon of 'your' story. This also means that reading is more like a conversation than an analysis and, like any good conversation, requires some respect for the truth and authority of the other. Reading, that is, involves me in 'an ethics of dialogue: not knowledge-extraction from words but the ongoing, in-folding, recursive attempt to do justice to the Other in words' (Branch West 192).

Even so, I do not think Alexander's disclosure need radically alter how we are to read 'The Steel', although it may alter how we value it. What 'we now see' simply gives greater emphasis to a component of doubt that would normally be part of reading (reminding us that even 'now' we still do not see). It also gives greater emphasis to a question that usually operates in reading works that present as autobiographical, the question of how to relate historical, fictive and fictional. Readers of 'The Steel' still need to

---

and the mother's blood in 'Les Murray and the Unseen Opponent' (*Southerly* 51:2, 1991. 319–30) and in 'Intending Wholeness' (*Southerly* 52:2, 1992.165–74). I should also note that 'ethico-literary' is not meant to refer only to criticism that discusses literature in explicitly ethical terms. As the discussion of Helen Garner's *The First Stone* and Helen Darville's *The Hand That Signed the Paper* demonstrated, ethical assumptions inform literary criticism more often than we might want to admit. They often disguise themselves as 'political', and can sometimes be identified in words like 'should', 'ought', 'must'.

allow poetry and history to test each other. They still need to keep deciding how to balance the various obligations to fact, imagination, emotion, and the unknown that come together to constitute their responsibility to truth. And they still need to watch and weigh the differences that play within the poem's complex perspective, since it is not at all self-evident that the poem finds satisfaction in blaming the doctor. An ethico-critical reading of 'The Steel' needs to allow that justice is not a single quality that goes by the name of accuracy, but a constant measuring of and by different interests inclined to community. Justice, that is, is not solitary; it always appears in company, and sometimes in the company of injustice (since it has to live in time, space and difference). If such a dialogic notion of justice is transferred, analogically, into reading, whether the poem is 'just' and/or 'unjust' depends on its factuality, but also its tone and structure, its ways of relating images, and particularly its use of perspective to give attention, respect, judgment to the other. It also depends on how this particular poem embodies what might be celled the 'fundamental option' of the poetry. The 'fundamental option' was a term some moral theologians used in the late 60s and early 70s to encourage a relational understanding of moral acts and to alleviate a tendency to depersonalise moral acts and judge their worth in an isolated, objective, and dogmatic manner. Individual choices were to be evaluated (not necessarily excused) in terms of a person's 'basic intention' and 'basic freedom' (Häring 168). For similar reasons, I want to suggest that 'The Steel' reveals more of its truth, more than its truth, when read as part of a larger narrative of the victim in search of justice, a narrative that keeps getting written into Murray's poems because none of them does it justice.

'The Steel' can easily be read, and often is read, as a poem in search of someone to blame. In this reading, the writing is still coming out of a long-held grief. Thirty years after the event, Murray is still feeling so victimised by his mother's death that he has himself to find a scapegoat. So the poem appears as an act of judgment. Its gaze moves along a line of suspect causes (as if a reason might make death less absolute): the mother herself, the induced baby, the lost baby that brought on the blood, the 'Cheers child' who was the reason for the induction, even the out-of-order Dodge. Each is innocent. Finally, judgment settles on the doctor who is portrayed as one whose city-bred and university educated prejudices caused him to underestimate the hillbilly's call for help and refuse the ambulance that might have saved Miriam Murray née Arnall. So ferocious is this judgment that the moment in which the doctor's story is told threatens to undo the poem: the turn from grief to accusation shatters the mood; the exercise of vengeance cancels the final appeal to divine justice even before it appears. It was always possible to argue that the poem does exactly what it admits to doing: it makes a scapegoat of the doctor. Now that we know it also makes a mistake of him, the first problem confronting the reader remains what it always was. The first problem is not whether we now excuse the poem its injustice on account of its grief. The first problem is whether this reading itself does an injustice to the poem. In my view, it does because it affords insufficient attention and respect to tone, theology, and the way in which the poem (or is it Murray?) has grasped that the scapegoat is a figure at once guilty and innocent.

It is a mistake to identify the tone of 'The Steel' with the different feelings dramatised by the poem. Tone then becomes simply a contest of grief, self-pity, bewilderment and anger, a contest that pulls the poem apart. Tone can be more than an effect of feeling. It can emerge when feeling begins to look at itself, to think about itself, as it does in 'The Steel'. In this case, tone is layered, as it often is when the narrator is also a character in the story. The character's different feelings are under/stood by another tone that emerges from the combined pressure of grief and theology. Tone is, of course, sometimes difficult to establish, and most readers look to rhythm, diction and perspective to provide the clues. Sometimes, however, images provide clues, inasmuch as poetry can encode the emotional in the visual. In 'Midsummer Ice', the second of the three poems in memory of Miriam Murray, the speaker looks across 'A doorstep of numbed creek water the colour of tears'. The image of arrested liminality might be said to locate feeling as well as perspective (and perspective often is as much a matter of feeling as of seeing). The image of the doorstep opens up a space between this and the otherworld. It also opens up a distance within feeling, a distance that might, for the moment, be called detachment, since it sounds as if the speaker is not simply expressing his feelings, but is also examining (perhaps cross-examining) them. In this sense, the image can act as a way into 'The Steel'. Here too the speaker sounds as if he is both in and above his feelings. This helps explain why the release of an anger that wants someone to blame is always being checked by questions, questions that, even as they deflect blame, attract uncertainty (which is sometimes a manifestation of the otherworld). It helps explain the short, caught breaths with which the poem barely moves. It does not quite surrender to the various rhythms that might embody anger, guilt, or accusation, but holds them all within another rhythm. It also helps explain the sense one gets of a mind moving through unsteady feelings, playing with words as a way of holding things together. A striking instance of this is the moment when the speaker takes the blame on himself. Remembering how he had been induced to make way for another delivery that was expected to be difficult, he reveals:

> In the event, his coming gave no trouble
> but it might have, I agree;
> nothing you agreed to harmed me.
> I didn't mean to harm you
> I was a baby.

> For a long time, my father
> himself became a baby
> being perhaps wiser than me . . .

This is no simple confession of guilt. What might have been unprotected feeling is held in check by the way Murray multiplies dimensions around it, playing with 'agree', 'harm', and 'baby'. The turn between 'nothing you agreed to harmed me' and 'I didn't mean to harm you' is itself a moment balanced over steel. Such conversions of one into the other also have the effect of creating a community, even complicity, among those considered for sacrifice. For reasons such as these, I think the tone of 'The Steel' cannot be simply identified with the emotions it describes, but that these are held in and by another tone. This tone connects the kind of introverted ennervation signalled in 'our family world / went inside itself forever' to the glance of equanimity, which sees that divine justice is incommensurable and only therefore possible ('Equanimity'). This tone implies that 'The Steel' has always known that clan vengeance is not the justice it wants (much as it has always known that the father's stubborn search for 'justice from his / dead father' is 'His only weakness').

In the story told by the poem, the Murray clan drives the doctor out of town. Inasmuch as he is a character in the story, the speaker clearly derives some satisfaction from remembering this, even to the point of claiming a kind of land rights ('We came to the river early; /it gives us some protection.'). Inasmuch as he is also the narrator of the story, the speaker takes a longer view. He measures the various persons who might be made into reasons for his mother's death. While he discovers that the doctor is the safest bet, he also discovers that it is not so easy to keep victims and agents apart. What is really interesting about this poem is the way in which it finds in those who might be to blame some sign of their being sacrificial victims. As already noted, there is a moment when the speaker appears ready to offer himself as the one who has to take blame for his mother's death, as well as for the deaths of later brothers and sisters who were never born. Yet the speaker also appears as one who was born without a star and has no witness to his birth:

> I am older than my mother.
> Cold steel hurried me from her womb.
> I haven't got a star.
>
> What hour I followed
> the waters into this world
> no one living can now say.
> My zodiac got washed away.

This is not the birth of Christ (who had a star), just as the waters that wash away the zodiac are not the waters of baptism, but a substitute sign of the mother's blood, a sign even of a desire to substitute for the mother's blood. (In its half-disguised use of Christian reference and its disturbance of temporal/eternal and absent/present relationships—'I am older than my mother'—the opening is already incorporating the perspective of the otherworld and refusing just the judgment of time.) Nor is this ambiguity reserved for the speaker. As a victim of 'the steel of [his] induction', the 'Little blood brother, blood sister' (there's a grim play with 'blood', but then the poem is an intricate exploration of blood relations) is in turn interrogated to ascertain if he or she might be held responsible for the death. Even the mother is interrogated ('were you being the nurse / when you let them hurry me?'). And, as already suggested, the very move which finds her innocent (she is unselfish, he is proud of her, any virtue can be fatal, and nothing she agreed to harmed him) is the move which puts him in range of guilt ('nothing you agreed to harmed me. / I didn't mean to harm you.'). There are also brief references to victims of war and to 'spilt children' (miscarriages? abortions?), as well as con/fusions of the 'steel' of induction with the 'steel' of clan vengeance, with the 'steel' that 'grows from our mother's grace'. 'The Steel', that is, plays variations on a theme of sacrifice in the manner of the earlier sequence, *The Boys Who Stole the Funeral*. The moment in which the doctor becomes victim should not, therefore, be read as an isolated case. While it is clear that he was blamed and victimised, it is also clear that this story is being remembered into a more complex exploration of the meaning of such sacrifices. He is still one among the blood relations, the chief example of how victim and persecutor breed each other in a retaliatory economy (this is, after all, a poet who can face the blood-poem of Hitler off against the blood-poem of Christ). For this reason I think that 'Perhaps we wrong you, / make a scapegoat of you' has to be read as at once a strategic confession aimed at outmanoeuvering moral objections and a sign of the poem's other purpose. Similarly, the word 'Clan' betrays a primitive satisfaction, but cannot quite disguise that a clan is first cousin to a mob, and 'Nothing a mob does is clean' ('Demo', *New Selected Poems* 197). To hear only satisfaction in 'scapegoat' and 'Clan' is to discredit the speaker's insight into the scapegoat mechanism. As the analogies show, the speaker understands that scapegoating is an attempt to make a justifying sacrifice, one that purifies the group from the stain of 'evil'. He understands that scapegoating is more than vengeance. As René Girard has shown, scapegoating has in a sense to involve the 'innocent' in the 'guilty' (who, as a surrogate victim, is not actually guilty) in order to break the cycle of violence and guarantee peace and protection. But the question that drives the poem and shapes its feelings into tone and perspective is: 'How could that be justice?'

By introducing the concept of the 'scapegoat' into a poem whose first line refuses the measure (the justice?) of time, Murray would seem to be signalling that 'The Steel' is not just a poem in search of justice, but also a poem in search of a truly justifying sacrifice. Immediately after recounting the fate of the doctor, the speaker observes:

> Thirty-five-years on earth:
> that's short. That's short, Mother,
> as the lives cut off by war
>
> and the lives of spilt children are short.
> Justice wholly in this world
> would bring them no rebirth
> nor restore your latter birthdays.
> How could that be justice?

This is where I begin to doubt whether the speaker does endorse clan vengeance, which is precisely the kind of justice that activates cycles of retaliation and wants its satisfactions 'wholly in this world'. It is the kind of justice that wants to pay back death and so it is a time-bound calculation that cannot ultimately satisfy. The revenge taken on the doctor is, then, judged from the speaker's theological perspective: justice to be wholly justice has to 'move in measured space', it has to embody the otherworld poem. In establishing his theological perspective, the speaker might almost be said to move close to Derrida's 'Justice and gift should go beyond calculation' (Caputo 19). He is, however, more dogmatic, casting out humanism and activism on the grounds that their denial of the otherworld means they cannot advocate a last and lasting justice:

There is justice, there is death,
humanist: you can't have both.
Activist, you can't serve both.
You do not move in measured space.

The poor man's anger is a prayer
for equities Time cannot hold
and steel grows from our mother's grace.
Justice is the people's otherworld.

This ending is not as redneck as it at first appears (there is still a playfulness in the use of 'grace' to turn the vernacular towards the sacred). It is in part provocative (and/or defensive), but fundamentally it is an attempt to protect the mother from explanations that would leave her only dead and ensure that justice is forever denied her. In this regard, the ending of 'The Steel' corresponds exactly to the ending of 'The Last Hellos', the poem of the father's death:

Snobs mind us off religion
nowadays, if they can.
Fuck them. I wish you God. (*New Selected Poems* 189)

To protect the mother he has also to protect death and keep it on side with justice, so humanism and activism become the scapegoats that take absurdity away. Humanism (at least as it exists in this poem) can only have its justice now, which is no justice because it does not participate in the *Nunc Stans*, the stilled, eternal Now that liberates the desire for justice from its temporal cycle of dissatisfaction. Activism (at least as it exists in this poem) cannot serve both since it too wants its satisfactions now. This is consistent with the theological view that only God's justice can strike the balance that provides, for each and all, the 'equities Time cannot hold'. Of course, there is no a priori reason to give extra authority to the theology in the poem. In this case, however, it does seem to me to be consistent with the tone, the atemporal perspective established in the opening line, and those confusions of the innocent with the guilty that arrive at 'steel grows from our mother's grace' and so prevent the speaker achieving satisfaction.

This poem is also consistent with and central to Murray's preoccupation with blood sacrifice. Indeed it is, arguably, the imaginative source of that preoccupation. Describing the scene where his mother collapses, Murray introduces an image that may, like his broad beans, move across several dimensions:

> I was in the town at school
> the afternoon my mother
> collapsed, and was carried from the dairy.
> The car was out of order.
>
> The ambulance was available
> but it took a doctor's say-so
> to come. This was refused.
> My father pleaded. Was refused.
>
> The local teacher's car was got finally.
> The time all this took didn't pass.
>   it spread through sheets, unstoppable.

Something happens here that is more than a repetition of Cecil Murray's account of his wife soaking up her bleeding with sheets (Alexander 35). The blood also spreads, is always spreading, through the sheets of poetry Murray writes. And it does so in a way that ignores time, so that pieces written before the mother's poem can now be seen to be, indeed, pieces written before the mother's poem. Rather than explain 'I didn't mean to harm you' as unfounded guilt, I would interpret it is a sign of the narrator's desire to make reparation. In the final line of 'Midsummer Ice' the speaker offers himself as the sacrifice that will free his mother from death: 'I will have to die before you remember' (*The People's Otherworld* 31). 'Blood' (*The Vernacular Republic* 16) and 'The Abomination' (*The Vernacular Republic*

17) are early examples of how the mother's blood demands some kind of secret fidelity from the poet. Taken together, they show sacrifice to be a release of both violence and the sacred: in 'Blood' the pig-killing knife is an instrument of holiness, but in 'The Abomination' the burnt rabbit has to be stamped into the stumphole fire because of the speaker's fear of 'all the things [his] sacrifice might mean, / so hastily performed past all repair'. 'The Burning Truck' (*New Selected Poems* 1) might be read as an allegory in which the poetry warns itself about the ambiguities that attend its interest in liberating sacrifices. 'Death Words' (*The Vernacular Republic* 52), from 'Walking to the Cattle Place', describes cows bunching above a puddle of blood and trying 'to horn to death Death', comparing this to the sacrifice of the Mass. While the word uttered by the cows, however terrible, must stop in time, the sacramental words have the capacity to 'ramify still'. *The Boys Who Stole the Funeral* examines Anzac, Eucharist, abortion, and initiation ritual as variously true and false versions of blood sacrifice. Given space, other poems could be called into this discussion: 'Dog Fox Field', 'The Instrument', 'Beneficiaries', 'Demo', and 'Cotton Flannelette', and *Fredy Neptune*, with its 'How good's your poem? / Can it make them alive again after dancing in the kerosene?' (263). However the point I want to pursue is that Murray's interest in blood sacrifice is informed by a theological position.

This position is outlined in sonnet 57 of *The Boys Who Stole the Funeral* (although the poetry does not quite close the issue down as firmly as the priest does):

> *But wouldn't you agree, Father, that the First World War*
> *was in part a post-Christian en-masse human sacrifice?*
>
> *No. It was warfare. Don't make it an even worse thing.*
>
> *But surely you believe, Father, in the efficacy of sacrifice:*
> *'Without shedding of blood there is no forgiveness of sins?'*
>
> *That is completed in Christ's blood, comes the answer.*

Isn't sacrifice still though, the great guarantor of sincerity?
Doesn't it seal and commit, transform spirits, involve godhead?

Murder can do all that, snaps Mulherin at the journalist.

So the slaughters of this age are in vain, the revolutions,
the wars—the abortions too, which you would condemn—

Murder makes glamour, at most. It can never sanctify.
But what you're talking's literature. All flash and frisson.
Must I guess human sacrifice is at the heart of literature? (29)

As is often the case with Murray, some of his essays provide a useful commentary on his poetry. In 'Some Religious Stuff I Know About Australia' (*A Working Forest* 130–47), the essay in which he fuses the Eucharist and 'the common dish', Murray reflects on ways in which Australians 'feed' the 'spiritual dimension' of their lives. Distinguishing between ways which are 'wholesome' and those that are 'insidious' (although 'our fairly orderly social polity protects us from their more obviously horrifying implications'), he offers 'human sacrifice' as an example of the unwholesome. Murray continues:

Wait on! Human sacrifice? Surely that's an archaic horror that survives only very marginally in a few Third World groups that anthropologists write about? Surely the holocausts of this century in what we call 'our' civilization can only be called human sacrifices in a very metaphoric sort of way? Surely there's a distinction to be made here between the literal and the metaphorical? My answer is, there may be, but I don't know of one water-tight enough to prevent the blood from seeping through it. When I hear someone say, as I did yet again the other day, that this country needs a war to restore and cement its sense of community, I recognize that as a call to literal human sacrifice, to be performed for one of the classic archaic reasons. When I am told that thousands of Australian men died in the First World War so as to prove their country's worth to the world and make it 'come of age', I don't know whether that was in fact their motive (I strongly doubt it), but I see the assertion as one which makes their death into a post facto human sacrifice, and accepts it as such. And this despite not only the Enlightenment we used to praise as our deliverance from such archaic nonsenses, but also despite the much earlier action of Christ in consciously taking the whole deeply ancient human motif of sacrifice on Himself and as it were completing and sealing it, so that henceforth we might refer the whole complex impulse to His action and never again enact it literally on a living victim ... A much harder implication of Jesus' action, of course, is that sacrifice, including human sacrifice, is as it were wrong but not erroneous. It suggests that it is an inherent tendency in human behaviour, as universal as we observe, say, ritual to be. It could not be dismissed, as rationalism would later attempt to dismiss it; it had to be resolved, and the very act of its resolution then kept alive (*A Working Forest* 131–32).

In 'Embodiment and incarnation' (*A Working Forest* 309–25), Murray remarks on how the Eucharist 'confirms that even our most primitive, dream-impelled rituals of taking on the power of a god or an awesome animal by eating it were in their way good, because they were on the right track'. Since Christ has incorporated this 'poem' into his own, he has 'sanctified it and made it both harmless and salutary for all time to come'. Accordingly, '[t]he impulse need never again be savage, for it is redeemed, and transposed into a life-giving thing like the calm eating of ordinary food' (325). Distinguishing between those poems that are embodied as art and those that are embodied as, for example, 'Hitler's poem', Murray claims:

A poem which stays within the realm of literature completes the trinity of forebrain consciousness, dream wisdom and bodily sympathy—of reason, dream and the dance, really—without needing to embody itself in actual suffering or action, and without the need to demand blood sacrifice from us. It is thus like Christ's

Crucifixion, both effectual and vicarious (*A Working Forest* 321–22).

Passages such as these provide a theological gloss on the final line of 'The Steel' and make it reasonable to argue that the speaker does not believe in the scapegoating of the doctor. He sympathises with it, possibly participated in it once, but he now judges it as what it is, a human sacrifice that does not sanctify. For this reason, readers who might want to talk about the ethico-literary issues that now surround 'The Steel' need to, ought to, recognise that Murray has contributed to the discussion, not simply evaded it.

In 1998 Murray decided to withdraw 'The Steel' from publication. It did not appear with 'Weights' and 'Midsummer Ice' in the 1998 *New Selected Poems*, so that a new reader might be left wondering what is the story behind the mother's death, and why there is such emphasis on 'carry' in 'Weights'. In conversation with Michael Cotter, who is working on a critical biography, Murray explained that his initial reason for doing this was that he now saw the poem as a work of personal therapy that was too long to succeed as art. His decision was then confirmed when he learned what Alexander had discovered about his father's part in his mother's death.[20] Murray it seems has already sacrificed it to literature. (But it is the mother's poem, not the doctor's, and it will find its way back.)

One other thing: it is true, as Indyk remarks, that the father, the one most responsible, is the only one not considered for blame. There maybe an imaginative reason for this. In Murray's poetry, the father is identified with the land. One of the purposes of a scapegoat ritual is to expel pollution and purify the group (in this case, father and son). The poem may want to load sin onto the doctor and drive him out in order to cleanse the father's land of the mother's blood and death. It may itself want 'to horn to death Death'. If it is to achieve this, it cannot afford to see the father as guilty, for that is to see the land as again defiled. For the scapegoat ritual to work,

---

20. I am grateful to Michael Cotter for allowing me to use this information and to Les Murray for giving his permission. Given that some might now describe 'The Steel' as unjust, it seemed to me important to acknowledge Murray's action.

blame has to be transferred and the beneficiaries must pretend not to see it done (otherwise they will call back the sin). In a sense, this essay has been a meditation on why such a ritual must fail to satisfy. It is also one way of understanding why even the very early 'Evening Alone at Bunyah' (*The Vernacular Republic* 10–13) cannot imagine the father's place without talking about ghosts, without remembering how the father shot a snake, and seeing the blood.

Works Cited

Alexander, Peter. *Les Murray: A Life in Progress*. Melbourne: Oxford University Press, 2000.

Branch West, Lori. 'The Benfit of Doubt: The Ethics of Reading.' *Critical Ethics: Text, Theory and Responsibility*. Ed. Dominic Rainsford and Tim Woods. London: Macmillan, 1999.187–202.

Caputo, J.D. *Deconstruction in a Nutshell: A Conversation with Jacques Derrida*. New York: Fordham University Press, 1997.

Cotter, Michael. 'The Emergent Self in Les Murray's Poetry'. *Counterbalancing Light: Essays on the Poetry of Les Murray*. Carmel Gaffney (ed.). Armidale: Kardoorair Press, 1997. 37–53.

Girard, René. *Violence and the Sacred*. Trans. Patrick Gregory. Baltimore: Johns Hopkins University Press, 1977.

Häring, Bernard. *Free and Faithful in Christ*. Volume I. Middlegreen: St Paul Publications, 1978.

Indyk, Ivor. 'The Doctor Didn't Do It', *Australian Book Review* 227 (Dec 2000–Jan 2001): 55–56.

Murray, Les. *The Boys Who Stole the Funeral*. Sydney: Angus & Robertson, 1980.

——.*Fredy Neptune*. Potts Point, NSW: Duffy & Snellgrove, 1998.

——. *New Selected Poems*. Potts Point, NSW: Duffy & Snellgrove, 1998.

——. *The People's Otherworld*. Sydney: Angus & Robertson, 1981.

——.*The Vernacular Republic*. Sydney: Collins/Angus & Robertson, 1990.

——.*A Working Forest*. Potts Point, NSW: Duffy & Snellgrove, 1997.

Just Poetry

He who takes his stand in relation shares in a reality, that is, in a being that neither merely belongs to him nor merely lies outside him. All reality is an activity in which I share without being able to appropriate for myself. Where there is no sharing there is no reality. The more direct the contact with the Thou, the fuller is the sharing. —MARTIN BUBER

WHEN *BRINGING THEM HOME* was being discussed in Federal Parliament and politicians were deciding whether or not the nation could or should make an apology, I kept thinking about a poem. I even gave way to fantasy, imagining what would happen if that poem were taken into the House and read. Would it help anyone feel and understand that justice involves more than abstract notions of equity and debt, and much, much more than the economics of reparation? Would it help anyone appreciate that, whatever their strict legal status, emotions, bodies and stories contribute to our moral imaginations and are all part of the poetics of justice?

The poem I had in mind was Eva Johnson's 'A Letter to My Mother', which begins:

I not see you long time now, I not see you long time now
White fulla bin take me from you, I don't know why
Give me to Missionary to be God's child.
Give me new language, give me new name

All time I cry, they say—'that shame'
I go to city down south, real cold
I forget all them stories, my Mother you told
Gone is my spirit, my dreaming, my name
Gone to these people, our country to claim
They gave me white mother, she give me new name
All time I cry, she say—'that shame'
I not see you long time now, I not see you long time now. (24)

Lamenting how for its speaker 'A culture […] was replaced by a mission', the poem holds to a belief that 'One day your dancing, your dreaming, your song / Will take me your Spirit back where I belong'. It demands that the 'aliens who rule' will protect what they do not understand; it longs for that moment 'When I hear you my Mother give me my Name'. So it expresses a difficult ambiguity: at one level it tells a stolen generations story; at another level it says that such a story remains untold until mother and daughter find each other.

How does this poem incorporate a poetic of justice? To answer this question in such a way as to give credit to both poetry and justice, it is necessary to do more than ascertain whether or not it is a factual account of a child taken, legally if immorally, from her mother, to do more than assess, as if this can be done empirically, what amount of emotional damage has been done. It is necessary to enter the separation that is embodied in the poem's address, as we feel the space opening between the speaker's feelings, so definite and so intensely present, and her uncertainty about where her mother is. This is keyed in the opening line, which acts as a refrain throughout the poem. 'I not see you long time now' is, in its effect, more complex than first impressions might suggest. The I–you address provides a fundamental understanding of the relational self, and with that a relational understanding of justice. This is picked up when the speaker acknowledges that she remains incomplete until she hears her mother name her. The 'not see you' establishes the absence of the relational and reciprocal, but it also echoes the institutional imperative, the way in which policy said to mother and daughter 'you will not see each other'. Without necessarily conceptualising what the poem is doing, many listeners will hear how it turns 'long time' into the time of longing and respond with something like moral sympathy. In these ways, standing somewhere between elegy and protest, using a separated address that embodies the spiritual, emotional and physical experience of dislocation, the poem asks for justice. Anyone who responds to what the poem is doing (and it is doing more than what it is saying) is unlikely to start adding up how much 'sorry' might cost the government in compensation, unlikely to dispute whether stories and their feelings constitute admissible evidence. Anyone who responds is more likely to see that justice needs to be capable of doing much more than pronounce 'that shame'. Justice is not as simple as some isolable arithmetical calculation of what is due to and what is adequate for an individual who has wronged or been wronged. Justice needs to be responsible for the ways in which it is itself involved in activities analogous to giving and naming. Justice is as much an act of reciprocated respect as of retribution, and respect ought not be calculated. But the poem was never read in the House on the hill.

One Australian poet who did more than most to nurture respect for Indigenous history was Judith Wright. Her commitment to Indigenous rights is well known, as is her expression of this in poems such as 'Bora Ring', 'At Cooloolah', 'Nigger's Leap, New England', 'Two Dreamtimes' and 'For a Pastoral Family'. These poems make it clear that she was troubled by the ambiguities of her own family's history, in particular the way in which pastoral settlement depended on dispossession. In 'Bora Ring', 'Nigger's Leap, New England' and 'At Cooloolah' she addresses repressed memories of Aboriginal deaths, employing an image of something shameful buried under the white narration of land, waiting to shipwreck history and its claims. In 'Bora Ring' she also uses line-endings to ensure that the repressed resurfaces; as she names those aspects of Indigenous culture that have been lost, she positions them just before the end-of-line pause, so that for a moment they are strongly present in the reader's breath and mind. This is evident in the poem's opening stanza:

The song is gone; the dance

is secret with the dancers in the earth,
the ritual useless, and the tribal story
lost in an alien tale. (8)

Whatever the state of Indigenous ritual, the poem's ritual is not as useless as it pretends. Wright subtly turns absence into presence and enacts the haunted memory she is talking about. This technique is then used at the end of the poem to express 'an unsaid word'. Telling of how a white settler rides over his subdued landscape, the poem records a ghostly and accusatory apparition:

Only the rider's heart
halts at a sightless shadow, an unsaid word
that fastens in the blood the ancient curse,
the fear as old as Cain. (8)

In 'At Cooloolah', naming herself 'a stranger, come of a conquering people', the speaker confesses she is 'made uneasy, for an old murder's sake' (140). She also unsettles assumptions about ownership of land:

Those dark-skinned people who once named Cooloolah
knew that no land is lost or won by wars,
for earth is spirit: the invader's feet will tangle
in nets there and his blood be thinned by fears. (140)

Ambitious, fast designs on land and history are undercut from the beginning: the poem opens with the image of a blue crane that has fished at Cooloolah 'longer than our centuries' and is 'the certain heir' of the place. Wright's relational understanding of justice is then made explicit in the way the poem ends: even as she establishes a fundamental choice between justified possession and the 'arrogant guilt' and 'fear' that underpin illegitimate possession, she connects justice and love:

White shores of sand, plumed reed and paperbark,

clear heavenly levels frequented by crane and swan—
I know that we are justified only by love,
but oppressed by arrogant guilt, have room for none.

And walking on clean sand among the prints
of bird and animal, I am challenged by a driftwood spear
thrust from the water; and, like my grandfather,
must quiet a heart accused by its own fear. (141)

This ending initiates a critique of *terra nullius*: her prints are not the first, the sand is not 'clean' in the way a blank page might be; rather than assume ownership she has to learn to walk with bird and animal, in particular with the blue crane who does not so much own as belong in the place. Wright believed Australians would only belong in and to the land when they learned to love it. In 'For a Pastoral Family' (406), dealing more directly with her own family's claims to ownership of land, Wright evokes a melancholy irony in describing how her forerunners:

[…] took over as if by right a century and a half
in an ancient difficult bush. And after all
the previous owners put up little fight,
did not believe in ownership, and so were scarcely human. (406)

She goes on to confess how her generation did not know or did not want to know the 'really deplorable deeds' that 'happened out of our sight, allowing us innocence.' She then exposes the way in which law was used to protect this fiction of innocence, allowing the conquerors to 'enter a plea: Not Guilty'. A decade later, this plea was often entered by those who argued against the Howard government saying sorry to the stolen generations (as if one were not responsible unless one were to blame).

All this is familiar to most readers of Wright's poetry. But these poetic statements about injustices are not what constitute her poetic of justice and reconciliation. Her poetic of justice is grounded in images, tones, speaking positions that create a relational ethic. In 'Two Dreamtimes' she occupies an uncertain position: she is troubled by a childhood in which she seemed innocent of, ignorant of, the racism going on around her; she revisits an ambiguity fundamental to her life (and) writing, that between possession and dispossession, by confessing that 'they hadn't told me the land I loved / was taken out of your hands' (315); she acknowledges the loss of country, culture and dreaming, comparing this to (though not equating it with) the loss of country caused by anti-environmental practices and policies. The poem, however, does more than state its case; it enacts a relationship. All that is said is said as a conversation, a sister-to-sister talk, incorporating stories Kath Walker (later Oodgeroo of the tribe Noonuccal) has told her and giving back Wright's troubled stories of settlement. And it opens with thanks for story:

> Kathy my sister with the torn heart,
> I don't know how to thank you
> for your dreamtime stories of joy and grief
> written on paperbark. (315)

The entire poem sustains this I–you attitude. This in turn is reinforced by an image, in the fourth stanza, of the two women talking at a kitchen table. The address that is the poem depends on memories of stories that Walker told Wright. These stories have nurtured understanding between the two women, even though understanding cannot exist for Wright without guilt and grief:

> you brought me to you some of the way
> and came the rest to meet me,
>
> over the desert of red sand
> came from your lost country
> to where I stand with all my fathers,
> their guilt and righteousness. (316)

At one level, then, the poem reminds us that justice occurs within story and within community. Even so, those who do not agree with its propositions might happily dismiss it as the work of a greenie indulging in a self-satisfying show of guilt. Poems are always vulnerable to this kind of dismissal, much as peace and reconciliation are always vulnerable to power play. This poem is, however, too ambiguous for such an unfair dismissal. Even as it conjures the image of two women sharing at the kitchen table, it acknowledges a knife between them: 'I am born of the conquerors, / you of the persecuted' (317). That fundamental inequity cannot be undone by soft intention, nor by recognising 'If we are sisters, it's in this—our grief for a lost country' (316). So the speaker turns the knife, reversing power as if somehow to reverse history. The women have, finally, to relate in the space between the knife and the poem. The sister–sister relationship has to acknowledge and perhaps negotiate the conqueror–persecuted relationship. The round-table conversation may be a model for justice, but this does not mean the knotty legacies of history are easily untied:

My shadow-sister, I sing to you
from my place with my righteous kin,
to where you stand with the Koori dead,
'Trust none—not even poets.'

The knife's between us, I turn it round,
the handle to your side,
the weapon made from your country's bones.
I have no right to take it.

But both of us die as our dreamtime dies.
I don't know what to give you
for your gay stories, your sad eyes,
but that, and a poem, sister. (318)

Which is, finally, more effective: the knife or the poem? Wright does not quite resolve the problem she raises. While 'sister' gets the last word, it is no guarantee of justice. Similarly, the gift of the poem is presented as an inadequate response to Walker's stories. Nevertheless, this ending does shift their relationship from the economy of rights to the economy of gift. It is as if the poem realises that, while it is absolutely necessary to recognise rights, such recognition needs also a final generosity of spirit if it is to summon the just heart. If it is to have efficacy, the recognition of human rights depends on the capacity to give what is due.

Another poem to use a table as metaphor is Rosemary Dobson's 'Cultural Meeting'. The poem deals with two meetings: a meeting of some committee addressed by a writer in exile who 'speaks for those forgotten in camps and prisons' (*CP* 162) and a cross-cultural meeting which occurs when the speaker, entering the writer's story, recognises and sympathises with his hunger for home. This sympathy is partly evoked by Dobson's poetic, her awareness that words will never satisfy, and partly by the way that poetic plays out politically. The speaker may have a moment of cross-cultural sympathy, but it is 'Afterwards', over a meal, and it is unlikely to make any difference to a committee full of people. Dobson will elsewhere call 'bystanders' those who miss the moment. Although her writing often deals with what she calls 'fugitive annunciations' (*SP* preface), Dobson's poetic is also relational. In her sequence 'The Continuance of Poetry', she celebrates poetry's capacity to move between cultures. In one of the poems from the sequence, 'Translations under the Trees', she suggests that arts such as painting and poetry can cross borders and change imaginations, can make another language:

> Poems blow away like pollen,
> Find distant destinations,
> Can seed new songs
> In another language. (*CP* 185)

Poetry moves between words, between languages, between peoples. It does not hold meaning; it releases it.

There is, then, an uncertainty, or unknowing, always waiting at the borders of Dobson's writing. It makes for discretion. It also makes for humility. There is no room for imperialist epistemology, because meaning is never made entirely present, never entirely subdued to the mind. There is always a sense of something like an active horizon that separates and joins what is brought into a poem and what stays beyond it. One of the strongest expressions of this is found in 'Over the Frontier', a poem about how poetry and art emerge between being and non-being and carry with them a memory of, which is also a hope for, that place on the other side of existence, that desire that keeps poetry and art always next to nothingness.

> And the poem that exists
> will never equal the poem that does not exist.
> Trembling, it crosses the frontier at dawn
> from non-being to being
> carrying a small banner,
> bearing a message,
>
> bringing news of the poem that does not exist,
> that pulses like a star, red and green, no-colour,
> blazing white against whiteness. (*CP* 129)

Perhaps uncertainty is important in the quest for justice: the invitatory other, the one who asks for justice, is always beyond what can be given. This need not mean, however, that justice has always to be subjected to cynicism and doubt. Inadequate as they might be, the moral and legal practices of justice can still be sufficient to protect principles of equality and freedom. To say justice is likely to be inadequate—even if compensation and reparation could be somehow financially exact, judgments can never quite take account of feelings, bodies, time—is not to say that it cannot still be possible and authentic. Perhaps justice, like poetry, also mediates between being and non-being and has to bear knowing how it does not exist. Perhaps justice has to admit that, like poetry, it is a word held up against death.

Dobson's poetry is profoundly elegiac (McCooey). This is not surprising, given her interest in the relation of being to non-being. She has written some remarkable pieces in which she seems prepared to look death in the face, as if to give it respect, to get it right. These poems include 'One Section' (*CP* 12), 'In a Strange House' (*CP* 160), 'Being Called For' (*CP* 161) and 'The Almond-tree in the King James Version' (*CP* 205). In these poems she does not abstract death; she represents it as something that happens from within the body. Nor does she see death as a matter of complaint or regret; she gives it due respect as something that asks of the body that it finally pay its dues to time.

Perhaps Dobson's poetry can remind justice that it too participates in elegy. Justice, as practised, seems to be predicated on loss. Whether it is making judgments on matters such as land rights, murder, injury claims or divorce settlements, justice is dealing with loss. Whatever is achieved in the battles for land rights, it will never fully restore land, spirit, dreaming. How often have we heard the family of a murder victim say a court decision is sufficient but that it cannot give them back the one they have lost? How often have we heard someone who has been compensated for injury say the money will help but will not give them back the life they had? How can divorce settlements pretend half the value of a house will heal the wound left when half a lifetime's love appears to have been wasted? There is always a sense of justice wanting as 'wanting' takes it between desire and lack. Justice, as experience and encounter, always involves some loss of innocence, which is perhaps not surprising: in Genesis justice enters as innocence and idealism are lost, companionable being gives way to those oppositions that sustain transgression and punishment, authority and obedience, as original grace gives way to redemption. We would perhaps like to think of justice as a moral ideal that the law itself obeys; we would perhaps like to think of justice as a poetics of equity. That is not, however, how justice usually manifests itself in practice.

Dobson's 'Cultural Meeting' knows that justice does not always get the exact measure of loss. The poem creates an oblique sympathy for one writer who cannot return home. That writer may represent all writers in exile, but he is primarily an individual sharing a meal with the speaker—and it may be his individuality rather than his representativeness that troubles the speaker's sense of justice. John D. Caputo remarks that the individual is a problem for ethics because the individual is ineffable, embodying that moment when proper names escape the grasp of language, when the desire to talk about someone summons the recognition that it is impossible. Metaphysics, Caputo claims, cannot speak of the individual (who is, paradoxically, too large for metaphysics because too small), and since metaphysics contains ethics, justice is (de)constructed as an impossible obligation (72–73). This poem is not, however, a philosophical argument. It is an act of sympathy, and sympathy, because it is an embodied act, responds to the individual and thus to the individual's desire for justice. To find where and how justice enters the poem, a reader has to see how, in the penultimate stanza, writer and speaker are brought together through the image of a wound:

> The cry of a word from the heart and the word is 'exile',
> It falls from the pen like a bullet-shot through the paper,
> And a charred black hole gapes like a fatal wound. (*CP* 163)

The image of the wound in the page displaces and unites speaker and hearer in an elegy of and for justice, a hunger than can be neither satisfied nor surrendered. It also recalls an image used earlier in the poem to suggest that writing itself never quite does justice to its subject. Thinking of the writers in exile, the speaker imagines their writing in these terms:

> Over the paper their black words driven, straggling,
> Summon from under restricting ice of absence
> The reedy singing of long-ago green water. (*CP* 162)

If this suggests writers in exile are like people struggling through an arctic landscape, it also prepares, by way of 'black words', for the moment when the word 'exile' will as it were pass through the paper, leaving 'a charred black hole'. In that moment the poem takes a position between aesthetic concerns with death and writing and political concerns that are real—as real as bullet holes in oppressive regimes. In that moment justice becomes a refugee, looking back to loss, unsure if asylum will be given.

The poem ends with an image of the exiled writer's hands moving over breadcrumbs (an image that picks up and comments on the earlier image of his 'Hands restless, shuffling a bundle of memoranda' as he wonders how to get his message past the red tape). Hunger seems more powerful here than any hope he might receive help: 'He ate as one whose hunger would never be filled.' The poem's sympathy, its instinct for justice, includes a realisation that writer and speaker are powerless.

Another implication in Dobson's relational and elegiac poetic of justice is that it might make us wonder about the fact that justice, as practised, so often involves one party wanting to gain power over another, demanding, not offering, what is due. Justice, that is, is often imagined, at least by complainants, as no more than a legal strategy for acquiring an individual good, for satisfying personal desire. Such complainants are unlikely to be persuaded by Aquinas, who located virtue in reason and will rather than desire, related justice to the common good, and implied that justice, like charity, disposes one to will the good of the other. Nor are they likely to be swayed by Portia's argument that 'earthly power doth then show likest God's / When mercy seasons justice' (*The Merchant of Venice* IV.i.191f, 246). Yet surely justice needs to operate in relation to other virtues if there is to be a balance between individual and common goods, if it is to guarantee that it does not become an instrument of powerful, selfish interests? Whether we call them charity, mercy or compassion, surely these open, generous virtues, inasmuch as they bring together truth, detachment and love, might be the proper virtues to mediate and moderate the claims justice makes? And surely there is a sense in which justice is most deeply received as and when we are powerless?

Such questions are likely to surface for many who read the poetry of Francis Webb. Suffering is at the centre of Webb's writing, where we find explorers humbled, sometimes scourged, by their failure before the unknown, a leper discarded by the Church, the martyr Maria Goretti, a homosexual disowned by family and dying in a psychiatric ward, along with another rejected because his Down's Syndrome affronts 'the wise world' with what appears to be idiocy. It is easy to see how Webb uses these figures to initiate what at first appears to be a reversal of power, and so readers can all too quickly attach Webb's poetry to a sentimentalised spirituality romancing marginality. Explorers become more human when they are broken. The leper confronts the walled city (one of Webb's favourite epistemological metaphors) with his tattered clothes, body and speech. Maria, dying after being raped and stabbed, is claimed by death and the Virgin Mary 'strangely at one'. The homosexual, a latter day Suffering Servant (Isaiah 52:13–53:12), judges and loves those who condemn him, as does Harry whose straggling attempt at words makes the Word present. What can easily be overlooked is that Webb's marginalised figures never acquire the kind of power that would, normally, see them justified. They remain powerless.

Webb seems to be interested in another kind of justice. More theological than political, more vulnerable than practical, his is a justice on the edge of absence, a justice that appears as the call made on 'us' by those who cannot effect what is due to them. His explorer Eyre becomes an Emmaus figure, entering a narrative that makes broken bread a symbol of vision (Luke 24:13–35). His leper never quite achieves eloquence, keeping his tattered tongue; even though he is transformed by a meeting with Francis of Assisi, that meeting is never dramatised in 'The Canticle' (*CP* 69–84), a sequence ruled over by an image of the stigmata. Maria may die a martyr, but the poem leaves her between Death, which may perform 'the embrace / Of Nothing' (*CP* 263), and the Woman, Mary, who may answer prayers figured in the poem through the rosary, the Angelus and the Miserere (Psalm 51). The homosexual may show 'in ugliness and agony a way to God' (*CP* 229), but this means he has to be kept ugly and agonised; if society stigmatises the homosexual because of his sexuality, the poem stigmatises him for the sake of sanctity. Harry's sacrament of writing may let 'us' be 'transfigured' (*CP* 225), but the poem's final line performs a Webbean fraction rite, breaking the Word back to flesh, history and writing as Harry's letter is directed 'to the House of no known address' (*CP* 225). Thus Webb's negative address brings together the ambiguities of writing and the afterlife; it keeps speech uncertain. If Webb wants justice for his characters, he is not advocating normal processes. He is figuring a mode of justice that is itself powerless, a justice that steps down. He wants justice to undergo kenosis (Philippians 2:1–11).

Webb, then, is another example of a poet who creates congruence between what he says about justice and how he says it. In his case, however, congruence is not quite achieved, because his poetry so often exercises divided speech. While it asks for compassion and justice, Webb's is also a poetry that often expects, even invites, injustice because it is so committed to the victim; and it is a poetry that constantly battles its own capacity for fascism—it is a poetry at war with itself. This means it cannot ever quite escape the oppositional, so in a sense his poetry denies even as it affirms. It wants to sacralise the homosexual but it needs to stigmatise him. It wants to make Maria Goretti as innocent as death and the Virgin Mary, but its own gaze is lewd, unable to detach itself from images of penetration. It wants the leper and Harry to challenge complacency and certitude, but confesses that it contributes to their oppression. This means that justice, in Webb's poetry, remains finally more theological desire than political opportunity. It also means that one is likely to find, in the residue left after reading, a disturbing thought: whether, precisely because it is habitually oppositional, the imaging so favoured by politicians is inclined to undermine attempts at peace and justice.

The danger in oppositional imagining is not that it generates conflict of opinion. The danger is that such imagining rests on images and metaphors that invite us to live by and within oppositions such as the Bush opposition between civilised democracy and the uncivilised (and unChristian) Other. The danger is that such images and metaphors often go unexamined, as if they had no effect on how we live. So we live in a world where the value of freedom is compromised by metaphors of force and war, where justice is something we 'get' rather than give, and where words of reconciliation are spoken from a single, empowered position. As I write, the war against terror is feeding terror; the defence of religion is making a religion of defence. The metaphors are exercising their own power, and, because they are so often metaphors of battle, that power has an enormous and unrecognised capacity for reciprocated blood.

So I have been turning more and more to poets like Wright and Dobson, because their poetry incorporates a relational and reciprocal ethic. It seems to me their poems do something more than say who deserves, who asks for, who lacks justice; they also show a way in which justice might become more approachable. I might have considered other poets. I might, for instance, have examined how James McAuley's natural law poetry sustains a hierarchical imagining with reason and will obedient to the metaphysical order, and discussed how McAuley's appeals to moral law are so often unsettled by a sense of belatedness and alienation. I might have looked at examples of postmodern poetry, which would have opened up the question of whether postmodernism undermines human rights because of its questioning of the subject, though it might also have shown that its inclination to edges, gaps and unknowns is itself an ethical activity (exposing how language itself constitutes and exercises power). I might have examined some protest poems, perhaps the obvious choice for anyone interested in how poetry addresses issues of freedom and human rights, but I doubt that many of them would, in their mode of address, incorporate a relational ethic in the manner and to the degree that Wright and Dobson do. Their poetries model those acts of power and participation that determine what we usually think of as the moral and political spheres.

I wanted to look at poems that in some way act justly, because it seems to me the need for relational and reciprocated models of political and ethical activity is urgent in a world surrendering to the poetics of terror. Here I have to confess to yet another fantasy: that the architects of terror, whether 'good' or 'evil', will give up their self-justifying oppositions and listen to Macbeth:

> If it were done when 'tis done, then 'twere well
> It were done quickly. If th' assassination
> Could trammel up the consequence, and catch,
> With his surcease, success; that but this blow
> Might be the be-all and end-all here—
> But here upon this bank and shoal of time—
> We'd jump the life to come. But in these cases
> We still have judgment here, that we but teach
> Bloody instructions, which being taught return

To plague th' inventor. This even-handed justice
Commends th' ingredience of our poison'd chalice
To our own lips. (*Macbeth* I.vii. ll.1–12)

Macbeth, of course, ignores his own counsel, becoming a student of 'bloody instructions' and a victim of their unyielding return. Macbeth, then, persuades me that the rhetoric of righteousness, which is armed with words like 'security', 'democracy', 'evil' (with or without an axis), which is ready to demonise anything that might represent 'a possible threat to our way of life', is contributing to rather than resolving the poetics of terror that creates and sustains hatred. Whatever side it makes and maintains, this rhetoric causes hatred to become pseudo-religious—in the sense that it transforms political ideas into dogmas, and then into idols. Although it might be described as wilfully relational, the rhetoric of terror is not relational in the way of the poems I have been considering. The rhetoric of terror confuses justice with power, even if it tells itself it is the power that good should exercise over evil. It does not give the sense of a waiting for, a listening to, an inclination towards the other who is addressed and is about to step into the poem, to share its space.

Works Cited

Aquinas, T. *Summa Theologiae*, 1a2ae.56. *Selected Philosophical Writings*. Timothy McDermott(ed. & trans.), Oxford: Oxford University Press, 1993. 398–409.

Buber, M. *I and Thou*. R.G. Smith (trans.), New York: Charles Scribner's Sons, 1958. (second revised edition, with a postscript by the author).

Caputo, John D. *Against Ethics*. Bloomington and Indianapolis: Indiana University Press, 1993.

Dobson, R. *Collected Poems*. Sydney: Collins/Angus & Robertson, 1991.

——. Preface to *Selected Poems* 1973, reprinted in *Selected Poems*. Sydney: Angus & Robertson, 1980.

Johnson, E. 'A Letter to My Mother.' Kevin Gilbert (ed.), *Inside Black Australia*, Ringwood: Penguin, 1988. 24.

McCooey, D. "'Looking into Landscape": The Elegiac Art of Rosemary Dobson'. *Westerly* 40, 1995. 15–25.

——. 'Rosemary Dobson: Vision and Light.' *Rosemary Dobson: A Celebration*. Canberra: National Library of Australia, 2000. 61–68.

Shakespeare, W. *The Complete Works*. P. Alexander (ed.), London and Glasgow: Collins, 1966 [1951 Tudor Edition].

Webb, F. *Collected Poems*. Sydney: Angus & Robertson, 1977.

Wright, J. *Collected Poems 1942–1985*. Sydney: Angus & Robertson/HarperCollins, 1994.

'No one but I will know'

ONCE UPON A TIME a man known as 'Uncle Hal' was babysitting for a friend when he took out his box of theatrical make-up and set to work. When the trusting mother returned home, she saw:

> He had made up her little daughter as 'a witch with wild eyebrows' and her toddling son 'as the littlest, stumbling Mephistopheles you've ever seen'. Ann was shocked that her two small children 'with their fluffy ducks and little rubber toys had been turned into two tiny unknowing monsters'. He reacted airily to her shock: 'What good are children anyway, dear? I mean, what use are they? You might as well push them through the slats of a cane-bottomed chair and turn them into lampshades as Hitler did' (Lord 55–56).

This story is found in Mary Lord's biography of her writer friend, Hal Porter (1911–1984), in a chapter called 'Enter Uncle Hal,' in a book charging that Porter engaged in sexual relations with Lord's ten-year-old son. *Hal Porter: Man of Many Parts* opens with 'A Declaration of Bias,' in which Lord reveals this and explains why she remained friends with Porter and persevered with the biography. Even though, as a practised reader of Porter, Lord must have known how he uses empirical details, confessional tones and shocking revelations to establish effects of honesty, she seems to have assumed these were merely narrative devices. She might have been more suspicious had she wondered if the

fictive strategies of his life writing were also the fictive strategies of his
writing life.

In a manoeuvre Porter would have appreciated, Lord uses her 'bias'
to secure a moral position from which she can accuse her subject of sin,
justify her work as a healing process, and finally pass judgment:

> He was a divided personality, divided in very many ways but, most
> fundamentally, divided against itself. Lacking a central core and
> having no faith except in his talent, he was amoral, a mass of
> contradictions and contrasts (302).

Even so, Lord's biography cannot contain its ethical activity within its
preferred moral position. It also becomes involved in ethical acts rehearsed
in Porter's writing, where questions of honesty, power, trust, complicity,
and evasion tangle with narratives of non-innocent children, hypocritical
adults, and writers who absolve themselves of mere morals. Lord's
biography has to become thus involved since it is a work of resistance;
it wants to provide another narrative and an alternative ethics. Hers is a
story in which children cannot be made up as monsters and Uncle Hal
can no longer get away with deception. Porter must instead feel guilt
and remorse, even though such emotions are more easily identified as
hers. She has to tell how she knew of Porter's affair with an Adelaide
schoolboy. She has to tell how, when Porter assured her he was not
molesting her son, she wanted to believe him because it allowed her to
repress her own experience of being sexually abused as a child. She has
to tell how even though Porter told her he was always the hunted, never
the hunter, she failed to interpret the warning in the fact that he 'used to
joke that Patrick was a warlock who could cast spells on people' (3). She
has to confess that, even when she knew, she 'could not confront him
directly about Patrick,' and this in the same moment that she maintains
his seductions 'would have required massive and repeated self-deception'
(10). It may seem callous and unfair to suggest that this shift from her
failure to his deception is an evasion, but it is necessary since the evasion
conceals the ambiguity of Lord's moral position: while she sometimes

indicates a belief that Porter was amoral she nevertheless demands that he have a conscience and be capable of feeling disgust, shame and guilt. It is as if she has to remind herself 'this abjection would not have been, had there not been monsters' (Bataille 19) in an attempt to make paedophilia im-possible.

At the same time, she colludes, if not with her friend's behaviour at least with her writer's ethico-textual manoeuvres. In justifying why she continued to write his biography, Lord comes dangerously close to Porter's distinction between Writer and Person, the distinction by which he raised Writer above the usual moralities (85–89). She claims Porter wanted her to write the biography because he 'hoped the truth could be told and he could be absolved' (299). Whether or not Porter is being absolved, the author is. Recognising that Porter's family will be distressed by her revelations, Lord asserts:

> Their wounds cannot be as severe as those that have been inflicted on me, Patrick and my other children for whom I am responsible. I let them down when they should have been able to depend on me and I am profoundly sorry for it. I hope what I have written will help them to understand (300).

As understandable as this might be, it is still designed to elicit an agreement that hers is a superior claim to truth and justice. This is partly (I intend no disrespect to victims of sexual abuse) an effect of Lord's story. One of Lord's fundamental narrative moves is to associate sexual abuse with shamed silence: 'I was a victim of sexual abuse. This involved actions which were not ever and could not ever be put into words' (8). She then connects her story to her son's: 'I remember becoming confused, then feeling involved in a secret that was somehow a source of incomprehensible guilt. This corresponds to Patrick's experience' (9). These moves establish the biography's ethico-narrative purpose: to arrest sexual abuse in its silence and bring it before speech. Nevertheless, while Lord's confession may, within the biography, embody a desire for honest and healing narrative, it also betrays an uncanny resemblance to Porter's fictive manoeuvres:

It was shocking to me that I was expected by my mother to behave as though nothing had ever happened. I was not allowed to express my anger, revulsion or grief; it was a non-discussable subject. Taboo. We continued to enact the happy family within our larger family of grandparents and aunts with their husbands or boyfriends and to the world at large. After a time, I more or less repressed what had happened. I see now that, in this way, I was conditioned to block out what was abominable and unspeakable, to behave as though nothing had happened (9).

As anyone familiar with his writing can see, this is Porter territory: social hypocrisy and doing 'the right thing,' civilised surfaces disguising corrupt interiors, performances designed never to reveal 'what was abominable and unspeakable.' What this suggests, in terms of literature and ethics, is that, whatever Lord may intend by exposing Porter as an object of judgment, the ethico-narrative activity of her book is not confined to or by moral judgments on paedophilia. It moves through her narratives of secrecy, shame, and justice and, since she is using these narratives tochallenge them, it enters Porter's narratives where children are predators, hypocrisy is often good manners, and God is dead. It is not, then, enough to identify and evaluate the ethical propositions operating in and between those narratives I have been calling 'Lord' and 'Porter.' It is necessary to articulate something of the reciprocity that occurs when ethics and narrative share the same space. In order to achieve this, it is useful to shift emphasis from ethical models which privilege rationalism and objectivism (which are not quite the same as rationality and objectivity) and to give some credence to a narrative model of ethics. As Hauerwas and Burrell argue, ethical ideas take on meaning within narrative and moral disagreements involve rival stories. In applying such an insight it is, however, necessary to look for that reciprocated activity by which ethics-as-narrative turns to narrative-as-ethics. In other words, it is necessary to ask how imagery, structure and perspective might be said to incorporate acts of power that have ethical as well as textual value. It is necessary to accept that to raise questions of truth, justice, and freedom in regard to representation and voice is to release powerful analogies that ask ethics and narrative to look to each other. It is necessary, then, to attempt what might be called an 'ethographic' reading, one that pays equal attention to ethical and textual qualities as a way of examining how they engage each other.

Most responses to Lord's biography overlooked the ways in which they themselves related ethics and narrative. They remained so fascinated by Porter's sexual activity that they uncritically adopted an objectivist stance that located (his) ethics somewhere on the other side of narrative. Among reviews that traded in words such as monster, betrayer and hunter, Mary Lord was quoted: she had to tell the truth because Porter 'wanted to be punished and forgiven'(Craven 3); she felt she had done him justice (Sullivan 26). Whatever Lord might have meant by 'justice,' one reviewer approved of the 'revenge,' (Elliott 12) while another relished 'the confrontation with guilt' (Indyk 96). Peter Porter tried to rescue the writing: 'In all matters but his writing, his posing was despicable and selfish. In fiction a pose is an authorial tool'(380). Leonie Kramer tried to save the writer, seeing Lord's 'Declaration of Bias' as grounds for disqualification. In a manoeuvre that left ethics standing cap in hand at the back door of Literature, Kramer invoked the notion of a purely objective, objectively pure reading and hoped for another study that would 'not be tainted by a personal grievance'(5). Peter Pierce was one of the few to relate sexuality to textuality: 'His sexual identity was elaborate and camouflaged... These deceptions of self and others helped generate the baroque splendour of his prose' (89). Pierce also questioned the 'reputation for truthfulness' that had until then been firmly attached to Porter's autobiographical volume, *The Watcher on the Cast-Iron Balcony* (89). David McCooey agreed (186), although he has now reconsidered this (*Dictionary* 298). More recently, Bruce Bennett commented that Lord's exposé might encourage readers to look again at Porter's 'fascination with secrets, gossip, rumour, masks and acting'(165). So far there is little evidence of any such interest. It may be that readers are uncertain how to proceed: such an enterprise demands discussion of the unspeakable, and might easily become a surrogate examination of the author's moral behaviour. Another factor might well be an anxiety that to use Lord's knowledge on or against Porter's writing is somehow to commit an impropriety.

If Lord had indeed been the one to make Porter's secret public, there might be some reason for hesitation, though I think the evidence within the texts is substantial enough to invite such a reading without the biography—but that is now hypothetical. The simple but significant fact is that it is the narrator of Porter's first book of autobiography, *The Watcher on the Cast-Iron Balcony*, who introduces the knowledge of paedophilia into his writing and therefore offers it to reading. This alters the ethographic starting point; it gives a permission that one might otherwise have to presume.

In a section remembering how, as a ten-year-old acting in a school fantasia, he liked the illusion of theatre and the 'shoddy disguise' of his costume, the narrator tells how one of the actors, playing King Bunyip, lost his mask. As the child-actor's mask slips, the narrator cleverly slips his own mask, so cleverly that readers seem not to have noticed:

> The next time I recall seeing that face thirty years have passed. I am now a man—at least, a man of sorts—too much a man, too little a man. I have travelled, been married, been divorced, have talked too much here and too little there, have taken my part in experiments with many lives and many bodies, have had dispassionate or stormy adventures in lying, in drunkenness, in adultery, in pederasty, in being charming and kindly, in being vile-tempered and arrogant, in being cruel, in being self-sacrificing, in being human and too human, in being inhuman and too inhuman (126).

The narrator invites, or dares, the reader to see what is hidden in full view. If there were readers who saw, they did not speak: perhaps they thought pederasty unspeakable, or his admission exaggerated, or his experiment a minor detour. Perhaps they were lulled by Porter's list into thinking pederasty no more objectionable than drunkenness, or being charming. Even though *The Watcher on the Cast-Iron Balcony* makes quite a feature of male-to-male prepubescent sexual experimentation, this was seen to guarantee the narrator's honesty. No one made the standard distinction between the adult narrator and the child self. No one applied that distinction to a book in which sex between boys, one of whom is the narrator-as-child, is being observed. No one came to the uncomfortable realisation that the adult narrator is admitting this sex in both senses: saying it happened in the past, but also bringing it back into view, into play.

The Watcher on the Cast-Iron Balcony gave such a good performance of honesty that readers suspended disbelief, even when the narrator admitted he was a liar. At the very beginning of his story he reveals that he was born with a cleft palate that was secretly mended: 'Thus secretly mended, and secretly carrying, as it were, my first lie tattooed on the roof of the mouth that is to sound out so many later lies, I grow' (9–10). At the same time as he is admitting this, he is declaring (warning?) that he alone can know if he is telling the truth:

> Of this house and of what takes place within it until I am six, I alone can tell. No one but I will know if a lie be told, therefore I must try for the truth which is the blood and breath and nerves of the elaborate and unimportant facts (10).

Perhaps the most important factor in convincing a reader to trust this narrator is the book's guiding image of the watcher, which suggests that the narrator is someone who wants to see beneath the surface and face the truth. Porter's image of the watcher obviously invites different readings, ones that focus on the book's reputation for accurate observation (and social history) and on the divided self of the autobiographical gaze. However, in a book full of references to and images of the theatre, to say nothing of disguises and secrets, the image of the watcher needs to be viewed with some suspicion. As an image it is similar to the actor's pilot, that capacity to observe and control a performance even as it is being made to seem completely genuine. Ralph Richardson, for example, speaks of acting as 'a controlled dream' in which the actor has to at once inhabit and observe the performance (Burton 71) and Noel Coward remarks that 'all acting is a question of control, the control of the actor of himself, and through himself of the audience' (Burton 165). Until now, Porter's theatrical allusions have been referred back to Porter's interest in and work in the theatre and taken as signs of the book's historical veracity. But what happens if the images of theatre are a signal for how the narrative performs?

When *The Watcher* recalls a young Hal taking up teaching, the narrator tells us that his acting skills were a great help:

> It would be as tedious to record my minor early mistakes as to record the minor successes: suffice it to say that, in no time, I am a useful teacher, even a good one—dramatic, noisy, happy, over-energetic and a disciplinarian, this last because I will put up with no childish nonsense that interferes with the display of myself or with my conception of what is due to me as an adult. One wears the disguise of manhood seriously at sixteen. The showing-off side of my being; the ability to simulate Lear-like rages I do not feel, as well as the ability to fool myself into being lovingly patient, all serve their purpose. Controlled by the canny and ruthless self-watcher, these qualities are turned into performances that trick the children into obedience (199).

Here the watcher is the pilot-self observing how the other selves perform and controlling the audience. This is how the watcher operates throughout the autobiography: the narrator is always watching a performance of the self, his gaze directed not simply at mother, father, Williamstown, Bairnsdale, Hal the cadet reporter, Alec, Miss Hart, Hal the junior teacher, and Hal the aspiring writer. At the centre of all these scenes is a non-innocent actor showing and concealing with a control that is at times chilling. When approached for sexual favours by boys, girls and older women (Hal is always approached; he does not initiate) Hal has a favourite line, 'I don't care'. This line allows him to detach and watch himself in the scene. He is 'in character' but also 'above' his performance, making sure to remember his lines and not bump into the furniture.

This notion of the actor's layered awareness helps explain the book's use of chronology. While it seems to move from early childhood, through school years and adolescence, to early career, there is a sense in which *The Watcher* stays in the narrating present. As it moves between past and present, it manages to create the impression of reaching into its own future. Often these moves are designed to cancel someone who might have been loved and to confirm the narrator in cynicism. Quite often it is their bodies that betray these people, becoming thicker, coarser, less beautiful, more corrupt—and more adult. He admits his own future in a way that suggests, not literary success, but a sexual weariness that is indistinguishable from the sexual indifference attributed to the child Hal. In this way *The Watcher* writes itself against the theme, prevalent in many autobiographies, of the loss of Eden. While it tempts a reader with an appearance of linear structure (most chapters begin and end at a point of change), its deeper structure is circular, and death is at its centre. The death at the centre is not just mortality and not just the death of the mother: it also the death of innocence. The narrator works hard to persuade the reader that his child is not innocent and that children are not innocent. They learn as they grow towards adulthood to put on masks and disguises, to perform polite, social language, to createthe illusion of innocence. There are too many instances for me to list them and they are easily identified. This is one example:

> It is suggested that adults teach children. I suggest that children teach children, and that the 'playing' they do for adults is not the real masks-off playing they do for themselves. Not until I am myself an adult do adults attempt to teach me sin. Too late. Children do not have to teach each other sin: they merely swap sins as they swap postage-stamps or dolls (73).

Whereas standard interpretations of Eden tell of the Fall in terms of before and after, opening a division between original innocence and postlapsarian knowledge, Porter writes the division within consciousness itself, erasing any notion of a before and after. Innocence always already is an ideal lost. This is why there is so little sense of change in the narrator's viewpoint. He remains throughout brutally aware, guarding the child from Paradise.

Porter's stories and novels also maintain their guard. Paedophilia appears with conspicuous frequency. More importantly, it appears in writing that, by its narrative strategies, encourages hypocrisy, condones secrecy, avoids love, and denies morality any normative power. Readers need to avoid becoming fixed on ethical propositions about paedophilia, assuming an ethographic reading involves no more than imposing these onto the text. This is not to discount the ethical propositions; it is simply to say that those propositions derive their meaning, and their force, from the ways in which they operate within and between narratives of sexuality, honesty, and responsibility. It is simply to say that such an approach, negotiating between ethics-as-narrative and narrative-as-ethics, will provide a more useful basis for an ethico-textual analysis of Porter's writing.

When Porter died Max Harris praised him for 'the loving portrait of a pederast in that first and secret and enigmatic volume he published when his heart was young and grey' (14). Harris is presumably referring to *Short Stories*, published privately in 1942, and may be using private knowledge. The book is dedicated to 'Shani ... in deepest gratitude for the authentic happiness brought by your contribution to our somewhat unusual friendship' (4). 'Shani' was Porter's name for a student with whom he had sexual relations (Lord 27). It is, however, difficult to find a 'loving portrait of a pederast' among these stories. The two that might be disguised accounts of a pederast are not loving. 'Carnival Piece' (33–34) undermines what it terms a 'scene' of happy activity by continually drawing attention to 'the old man in the ghoulish overcoat' (33) and asking 'What is he doing in this scene?' (33). As the dirty old man steals something and scuttles off, the narration follows him to a Home for Old Men where he proceeds to make surrogate love to the stolen object, a teddy bear:

> He tumbles upon his nasty bed and curls up like a baby. Horrid! He kisses the bear repeatedly; clutches it to him; squeezes it passionately; peers into its button eyes. He begins to cry noiselessly though he is smiling and smiling. He tries to say ...
> Ugh! What a wretched actor! What an impossible part! Melodrama. Bathos. Rubbish (34).

Assuming it is reasonable to claim metonymy for the teddy bear, this story is not simply an expression of that disgust Mary Lord wanted to find in Porter. If 'Rubbish' could express an ethical judgment, the emphasis on acting deliberately confuses the ethical with the aesthetic. He may only be a wretched man because he is a wretched actor. 'Scene: The Bend of a River' (39–43) inserts an old man with a strange walking stick into another 'scene,' this one of people fishing by the river. The story depends on two repetitions: the narrator keeps asking what the old man is looking at; the old man keeps replying 'Shark's backbone' when people ask him what his stick is made of. As the first question is never answered, the answer to the second begins to fill the vacuum. The old man begins to seem as predatory as a shark; the mood becomes increasingly sinister. Suddenly the old man engages a beautiful boy in conversation. Beyond saying 'Shark's backbone,' he has not shown any interest in talking until the boy appears on the scene. Their conversation, about a sporting competition the boy has won, would be insignificant except that is framed by a moment in which the narrator says of the boy 'all the while his body is glorious and young, though his voice makes him seem older, makes poignant his physical beauty' (41) and a moment in which one fisherman counsels another to use 'a black line' and 'let it drift a bit' (41) in order to better ensure a catch.

Later stories more explicitly feature schoolmasters and travellers who have affairs with boys. 'The Dream' (Porter 1962: 113–129) tells of a schoolmaster dismissed for seducing a student, though this story is a mask the narrator assumes to give controlled expression to his own attraction for the boy. Indeed, the dismissal could be read as the dream by which the narrator expels his own desire (and locates that desire beyond culpability). Desire is powerfully unspoken in 'Say to Me Ronald!' (Porter 1965: 75–91), where Perrot (Porter's favourite anagram) is uncomfortable because his wealthy Asian student, Wee Soon Wat, wants to give him golf clubs to thank him for extra lessons. The suggestion is that Perrot gave the lessons because he found the seventeen-year-old attractive and that this is what he is resisting in refusing the gift. Wee pursues him, inviting him to dinner and plying him with whiskey: whatever happens will not be Perrot's fault. 'Fiend and Friend' (Porter 1971a: 103–15) is another story in which Perrot pretends to hate the boy he likes. It stumbles, though, when Perrot finds his student, Rymill, has hurt himself during a prank and is lying wounded in the dormitory:

> And there, overzealously supported by all the Lost Boys, everyone a finger in the pie, lying in a pansyish though awkwardly sustained pose, was Rymill. One leg, on deliberate foreground display, dripped blood and stained the pyjama-leg torn like a beachcomber's at a Fancy Dress Ball (106).

Here 'pansyish' signifies something at once attractive and denied, 'deliberate foreground display' hints at the boy's seductive agency, and the stained pyjama leg might even symbolise sexual non-innocence. As a way of thanking Perrot for tending his wound, Rymill gives his teacher a python skin. Perrot meets Rymill and another student thirteen years later and, because he needs to, assumes he is the ugly one of the two. When he realises Rymill is the handsome one, Perrot covers his awkwardness by asking him did he really kill the python himself. Rymill smiles, and some readers at least are left wondering who is killing what python. 'My Pal Rembrandt' (Porter 1970: 84–108) involves one of Porter's malicious portraits of the arty homosexual: Simon Hart-Browne has come under the control of the Japanese yakuza by bedding the fifteen-year-old son of a yakuza family. What offends the narrator, who knows a lot about where and how to get sexual trade, is not that Hart-Browne has had sex with a boy, but that he has been so obvious about it. 'Rajani in Ueno—a Biography' (Porter 1970: 133–71), which tells how a famous dancer got his break when, as a handsome youth adrift in Japan, he was picked up by a wealthy Polish count, has a narrator who presents himself as someone drawn almost against his will into the world of a much older Rajani, though he knows enough to realise that Rajani's bodyguards are making money by picking up men on Hampstead Heath, remarking that they 'have not even had the decency to be hypocrites' (150). At the same time he is securing his own position by feeding on Rajani's secrets. The story flirts with a discussion of art and morality, suggesting that art might be a work of 'holiness mimed by a sinner' (142)—and 'mimed' might be the key word. 'On the Ridge' (Porter 1971a: 69–82) has a narrator who obtains a manuscript in which a writer tells how as a young teacher he lived in a house with a twelve-year-old who possessed 'the genius or insanity of evil' (77) and who stripped naked when he was to receive a flogging. The writer murders the boy and enters into an affair with the boy's mother— or rather he 'participate[s] in his own seduction by the murdered boy's mother,' (80) even though her body is 'of a sort [he] should never have chosen' (80). He assumes heterosexual disguise after killing the true object of desire, the naked boy, made responsible and evil. The writer is dead but it is clear that the narrator will expose him—as a murderer. Even 'At Aunt Sophia's'(Porter 1962: 72–84), which at first glance would seem to have nothing to do with paedophilia, has an adult narrator looking back at his/the male body becoming pubescent and barely disguising what was in the past, which is to say in the telling present, his sexual interest in another boy. These are only the more obvious examples. More could be said of stories in which children are made malevolent and sexually knowing, stories that ask readers to accept that lies are justified if they preserve good manners, stories which ridicule homosexuals so that their narrators will seem normal, healthy heterosexuals, or stories which seek narrative resolution by exposing a sordid secret that had been hidden by a respectable surface. More could be said of the many stories that use a world-weary narrative perspective, a perspective that most Porter readers mistake for ruthless honesty, to intimate that what humans do to and with each other sexually is of no consequence.

In Porter's first novel, *A Handful of Pennies*, sex justifies itself as a bodily imperative, even if the body is also responsible for corruption. The Australians working for the Occupying Forces in Japan (where Porter himself spent two years as a schoolmaster) are early versions of a figure now familiar to readers of Australian fiction set in 'Asia': Westerners for whom the East confirms uncertainties and relaxes morals. While Porter appears to be describing this process, he is also arguing that the meeting of East and West shows moral norms to be no more than hypocritical social ritual. Into this argument he introduces Maxie Glenn, boy lover to Padre Hamilton, as one of his non-innocents: 'For the youth, too mature physically, the Padre's lesson had been undisturbingly coarse because, though an umpimpled adolescence gave him an ethereal air, Maxie Glenn was coarse also.' (Lord 1980:149) The narrator goes further, making Maxie conscious of his complicity: Better than those who would forgive him and not the Padre he knew the complicity had been dual...' (152). What appears to be a novel about reciprocal cross-cultural exploitation during the Occupation is also a novel about reciprocal sexual exploitation, including that between adults and minors. The novel does not simply resist judging its reverend paedophile; it solicits sympathy for him. Expelled from Japan, Padre Hamilton stands in his farewell party, hoping desperately that the boy will look at him one last time, and is transformed into a victim: 'No man does anything consciously for the last time without a feeling of sadness; to be forced to abandon a body of which one has not tired at least quadruples this sorrow.' (152) As he is being driven to the airport Hamilton is distracted by 'a striking Oriental youth' (163). Paula Groot, sent home not so much because she had an affair with a Japanese man but because she contracted syphilis, also notices the youth, and then the two sit side by side on the plane. The effect of this is to equalise them and thereby normalise Hamilton's behaviour. What might appear to be a detached narrative perspective exposes itself as a more calculated and more cynical act.

The Tilted Cross is set in colonial Van Diemen's Land, a penal world where manners, covering brutality and venality, are more important than morals. Porter's prefatory note explaining that the novel is based on the historical convict, Thomas Griffiths Wainewright, could be read as a decoy. Porter's Wainwright, Vaneleigh, certainly has the moral cynicism of many a Porter protagonist, but he is not the one who attracts narrative interest. This is directed to the beautifully male Queely Sheill. Indeed *The Tilted Cross* might be worth investigating as an exercise in homoerotic displacement since the sexual interest taken in Queely by Lady Rose Knight and Lady Asnetha Sleep might well reflect the narrator's interest. The narrator is always looking at him, handsome as a god (23), and they are always trying to bed him. Lady Asnetha succeeds. Queely, whose innocence is so natural as to make him 'incapable of acting' (126) and therefore inculpable, whose sexuality is so instinctive as to be unregulated, thinks it a kindness to fornicate with her since she is a cripple and wants it so much. At the same time, Porter's description of sexual passion is, characteristically, shadowed by a distrust of the body: sexual intercourse is imaged in terms of rage and, perversely, crucifixion. Intercourse is 'the interlocked affront and striving and battle of flesh' (100). For Queely it is 'a crucifixion hedged with tears ... mortality preserving itself in the forgetfulness that is too instantly mortal' (100) and consequently 'his violence and frenzy were not those of the one who hungers but of the one who is sacrificed' (100). In thus providing Asnetha with his pity, Queely offends Vaneleigh's doctrine of mistrust: 'Sympathy buys shame' (31), and 'You'll suffer, as I did, not because you erred, but because you trusted' (111). Vaneleigh's moral cynicism extends into his art. As he prepares to paint Lady Knight's portrait, he voices a thought that will later occur to the narrator of *The Watcher on the Cast-Iron Balcony*: 'If what was sought turned out to be a lie, that was what he and his pencil would find and manufacture into a truth' (53). This sits uncomfortably with the fact that Queely is falsely condemned when Teapot, the thirteen-year-old black servant of Lady Asnetha, who can lie like truth, accuses him of theft. Teapot is written in a manner that emphasises his knowing sexuality: he denounces Queely so as to preserve his own role as Lady Asnetha's toy and entertains the idea of sex with Polidorio Smith, the homosexual actor, so as to acquire a toy of his own. He is yet another of Porter's child monsters.

While in prison Queely conducts himself with Christ-like forgiveness and forbearance, though Porter's gestures towards the Christifiction of Queely are, I think, cynical. They are used to align religion with hyprocrisy. Adrian Mitchell has argued that: 'The point is not in the parody, the inverted Christian myth and morality, but in inversion itself.' (4) I would suggest that, in this case, pointlessness is the point: the allusions disempower Christian morality. While this might appear to be in keeping with the novel's vision of a penal and venal hell, it also has the effect of neutralising any position that might want to make distinctions of kind and degree in regard to sexual behaviour (Porter's writing very often hides its sexual agenda behind its social criticism). This is, after all, a book that has made church bells complicit with ankle-chains: 'Sunday in Hobart

Town bore its starveling resemblance to Sunday in the London which had exported to it the chimes of church bells along with the chimes of ankle-chains, the one to accompany and uplift duplicity, the other to accompany and weigh down obscenity' (137). When the dying Queely says 'Queely thirsts' (256), this is taken over by the shadows in his mind, the shadows of 'the blasphemous and filthy' (256) feasting off his death. Among those shadows is 'the undying god who grants all—Death' (257). As Queely prays for those who condemned him, Porter reintroduces his titular image of 'The Cross tilted to fall' (257). Part of the inversion Mitchell describes lies in the fact that Queely dies at Christmas, but Porter does not confine himself to this. Immediately after Queely's death, he inverts the story of the Annunciation. Recounting how Asnetha's maid has fallen pregnant, he remarks: 'Ferris the groom was suspected of being the Welsh hussy's Holy Ghost, but unjustly, for he was too experienced a man, and had fornicated with too many women, to be so carelessly immoral' (261). Porter also has his own take on the Incarnation, making Queely's innocent carnality so edible that it assumes the status of a eucharist: 'So, to him, carnality was carnality. It had not extra value for him since his beauty had never let it fall into irritating disuse... He felt he knew when the wine and bread of his body could not be denied' (94–95). But denied it is, and by the writing: the beautiful Queely is disfigured and dies. If *The Tilted Cross* were simply a story about how a moral innocent is sacrificed so that society can feed its hyprocrisy, it does not need to have Queely break his leg in an escape attempt, have the leg turn gangrenous, have the leg amputated, and have the beautiful man become 'the one legged ugly man' (255). The beauty of innocence is, through Queely's death, destroyed and secrecy is saved. It is a process that eerily fulfils the description of Queely entering Asnetha, that 'monstrous caricature of Eurydice' (Mitchell 6): 'With eyes closed, mouths agape and askew, brows plaited in tameless agony of expression, the deathmask-in-life of consummation, they were to destroy what had infuriated them' (100). This is a book that so associates sexuality with Eurydice's underworld that it wants to kill love. It might be social criticism, a portrait of a society that has tilted the cross so that it is ready to fall. It might also be that it is the novel itself that tilts the cross.

According to Gavin Ogilvie, the least unbelievable character in *The Right Thing*, '[t]he innocent are always guilty' (100). In this novel Porter mixes a third-person narration of the Ogilvies, who think themselves a pastoral aristocracy, with the first-person diary entries of the prodigal Gavin (who has worked in London as an actor and been a homosexual). The effect is unconvincing. In the third-person narration the women speak as if they are performing in a competition for Bette Davis impersonators, while the young lovers, Angus Olgivie and Maureen O'Connell, are simply the instruments of an unintended and unmarried pregnancy, a sexual shame that has to be expelled in the interests of property and propriety (something that is achieved, to the profound satisfaction of the Olgivies, when Maureen tips herself over a cliff). Gavin's diaries are more persuasive, particularly when he is recording how his younger nephew, Alastair, confesses to having had sex with men—though 'confess' is not the right word since Gavin implies that Alastair's confession is an exercise in seduction. Gavin (so he says) halts the boy's 'game' (162). This is not because Gavin disapproves of boys having sex with men. It is because he is another watcher: having been literally an actor, he maintains that a good society depends on 'playing,' on 'doing the right thing' (107). When he saw the slums of Colombo just before he was himself sexually initiated by a dark and polished older man, he recognised that '[e]vents do not change man; they merely unmask him' (103). It is worth noting that his account once again links sexual satisfaction to putrefaction. At Colombo too, while he is watching little girls going into his ship 'where Hindoo and Pakistani and Goanese men waited randily to appease themselves' (112), he decides that moral codes are only cultural habits. He is not, then, a moral voice: that role is reserved for and satirised in Maureen's friend, Elvira. After the suicide, Elvira sets out to shoot Angus, but kills Alastair by mistake. The novel, as published, ends: 'She had, nevertheless, done the right thing' (264). This is the narrator's comment; the character does not know Alastair's secret. The extraordinary thing about *The Right Thing* is that Alastair barely appears in it yet the whole story is designed to murder him. In ethical and narrative terms his death functions, not as a wrong, but as a propitiatory sacrifice: it justifies those who believe 'the right thing' is good perfounance.

If my reading gives proper respect to Porter's texts, then clearly the discussion within and about *Hal Porter: Man of Many Parts* is a distraction. It creates the false impression that Lord gave us the knowledge of Porter's evil, when in fact it is Porter himself who offers, however furtively, this knowledge to his reader. Moreover, by imagining paedophilia as an isolable and objective action, the discussion tends to remove it from narrative. Porter's texts—and here I am deliberately merging autobiography and fiction on the grounds that they employ the same fictive strategies—permit a reader to return paedophilia to narrative and examine how it functions within stories that make a virtue of secrecy even as they evacuate those notions of goodness and responsibility that make virtue credible. Porter's is, after all, a writing of corruption. Its originary moment is the death of the mother, the moment that contains *The Watcher on the Cast-Iron Balcony*, a book that is, as it were, written over her corpse, a book that explicitly identifies her death with the death of God and the death of love (254), a book in which the narrator finally calls himself 'the dead one' (255). It is possible that Porter's is a narrative that has looked so long at corruption that it feels no remorse as it turns children into lampshades.

Works Cited

Bataille, Georges. 'Reflections on the Executioner and the Victim.' Claire Nouvet (ed.). *Literature and the Ethical Question*. Yale French Studies no. 79, 1991. 15–19.

Bennett, Bruce. *Australian Short Fiction: A History*. St Lucia: University of Queensland Press, 2002.

Burton, Hal (ed.). *Great Acting*. New York: Bonanza Books, 1967.

Craven, Peter. 'Porter: friend and betrayer'. *Australian*, 15–16 January 1994, Review 3.

Elliott, Helen. 'Loyal to a sinful friend'. *Australian Book Review* 157, 1993/94, 1112.

Harris, Max. 'Divided spirit that was Hal Porter'. *Australian*, 13–14 October 1984, 14.

Hauerwas, Stanley and David Burrell. 'From System to Story: An Alternative Pattern for Rationality in Ethics.' Stanley Hauerwas and L. Gregory Jones (eds.). *Why Narrative? Readings in Narrative Theology*. Grand Rapids: William B. Eerdmans Publishing Company, 1989, 158–190.

Indyk, Ivor. 'Looking Beyond the Subject: Some Recent Biographies'. *Australian Literary Studies*, 17.1, 1995. 96.

Kramer, Leonie. 'Too many facts, not enough truth'. *Australian*, 4–5 December 1993, Review 5.

Lord, Mary (ed.). *Hal Porter*. St Lucia: University of Queensland Press, 1980.

——. *Hal Porter: Man of Many Parts*. Sydney: Random House, 1993.

McCooey, David. *Artful Histories*. Cambridge: Cambridge University Press, 1996.

——. 'Hal Porter'. *Dictionary of Literary Biography*, vol. 260: Australian Writers 1915–1950. Selina Samuels (ed.). Detroit: Gale, 2002. 295–306.

Mitchell, Adrian. 'Introduction,' Hal Porter, *The Tilted Cross*. Adelaide: Rigby, 1971, 1–7.

Pierce, Peter. 'Haunted and hunted'. *Bulletin*, 7 December 1993. 89.

Porter, Hal. *Short Stories*. Adelaide: privately published, 1942.

——. *The Tilted Cross*. London: Faber and Faber, 1961.

——. *A Bachelor's Children*. Sydney: Angus & Robertson, 1962.

——. *The Watcher on the Cast-Iron Balcony*. London: Faber and Faber, 1986 [1963].

——. *The Cats of Venice*. Sydney: Angus & Robertson, 1965.

——. *Mr Butterfly and other Tales of New Japan*. Sydney: Angus & Robertson, 1970.

——. 1971a *Selected Stories*. Leonie Kramer (ed.). Sydney: Angus & Robertson, 1971.

——. 1971b *The Right Thing*. Adelaide: Rigby, 1971.

——. 'Gavin's Diary: An Unused Last Chapter of The Right Thing'. *Southerly* 33:4, 1973. 355–63.

——. *Fredo Fuss Love Life*. Sydney: Angus & Robertson, 1974.

Porter, Peter. 'Porter on Porter'. *Meanjin*, 53.2, 1994. 376–80.

Sullivan, Jane. 'Doing justice to Uncle Hal'. *Sydney Morning Herald*. Wednesday 27 October 1993. 26.

Sacrificing Grace

CHRISTOS TSIOLKAS'S *DEAD EUROPE*

Abraham Unblessed

> Isaac, my father would bellow at me when I had made him angry,
> interrupted his reading, when I was full of boisterous energy. Isaac,
> I will sacrifice you to bloody God! —*Dead Europe*

CHEEKY, POSSIBLY OUTRAGEOUS, THIS allusion to Abraham's intended
sacrifice of his son Isaac (Genesis 22:1–18) becomes a minor tease by the
time Christos Tsiolkas's *Dead Europe* reveals the full extent of its investment
in blood, retaliation, sacrifice and scapegoating. Even so, the allusion does
signal the way in which the novel deploys religious references to contest
religion. Abraham believes he is doing the will of his God, who intervenes
and promises: 'all the nations of the earth shall bless themselves by your
descendants' (Genesis 22:18). Isaac's father does not believe in God and
will insist on being buried without religious ritual. Abraham's God accepts
faith in favour of sacrifice; *Dead Europe* surrenders faith to sacrifice.

At first sight, it might seem that this novel is reworking, albeit more
powerfully, preoccupations rehearsed in *The Jesus Man* (1999). It too
is fascinated with evil: its central horror, Tommy's murder-suicide, is

positioned beyond understanding, even as it enters the family consciousness like a virus. In addition, *The Jesus Man* investigates cursed bloodlines (338), ghosts (402), the interdependence of god and satan (180), and the destructive consequences of (always oppositional) religious allegiances (206). Finally, it already insists that, despite the alleviating influence of personal love, the history of hatred is so long and deep that nothing can undo it. Asked what might be done about racism, Luigi thinks:

> It is a good question and the only answer I have is that there is nothing to be done, that it is not only the night, but the weeks and the months, the years and the century, that need to be undone. I know the embarrassment of being racist, the consciousness of another's skin, the oddity of manners to which I am unaccustomed. But I don't get the hatred; the hatred, its intensity, that's a sickness. It's psychotic (361).

What makes *Dead Europe* so much more powerful than *The Jesus Man* is the way it moves between texts to activate those analogies that allow it to turn history into hatred and Europe into Hell. What makes *Dead Europe* so much more shattering is that it sacrifices Isaac's mother in order to seal its bargain with hopelessness. This terrible ending is a step *The Jesus Man* does not take. Tommy's mother, Maria, does make a sacrifice in the hope of recovering his lost soul: travelling to her ancestral birthplace she crawls on her knees to the church of the Prophet Elijah in order 'to plead with her God that her son's suicide, his sins, would not deny him God's grace' (250). While her husband and son reject this action, the novel itself does not cancel it. It keeps it as one among a number of different attitudes to religion, neither more nor less privileged than Artie's atheism, Neil's lethal fundamentalism, or Tommy's apocalyptic psychosis. It even finds a faint counterpart when, at book's end, Luigi lights candles with his niece, Betty, and asks a God in whom he does not believe 'to look after, to protect, to make safe this little girl' (402). *Dead Europe*, however, goes further: the mother makes her sacrifice, and she is herself the sacrifice by which the book finally cancels grace.

Promise Cancelled

> With cities it is as with dreams: everything imaginable can be
> dreamed, but even the most unexpected dream is a rebus that
> conceals a desire or, its reverse, a fear. Cities, like dreams, are made
> of desires and fears (Calvino 44).

Dead Europe is a book of cities, spaces in which sexual, economic, political,
and religious architectures relate to each other, architectures that
accommodate or refuse those human values that arrive with names like
freedom, love and justice. As Isaac moves from city to city, he descends into
ever darkening circles of his Inferno. In one of many demonic epiphanies
that give the book structural and thematic power, what at first appears to
be a familiar story of an Australian in search of his European roots turns
out to be a story of an Australian possessed by a Europe that is not so
much dead as undead. When Isaac arrives in Athens, it seems that he is
to be hero of a journey based on 'the theme of homesickness, of exile and
return' (35), a hero in mourning since 'the Greece [he] knew in Australia
was indeed largely irrelevant to these modern Europeans' (35). This is
confirmed as the book demonstrates its interest in Europeanisation (or is
it Americanisation?), consumerism and poverty, the fall of Communism
and the disintegration of national states. Yet something else happens. In
Athens Isaac meets Serge, a displaced Russian youth who sells sex, but
any expectation that the novel might offer a gay guide to sexy Europe is
averted. Instead the reader is introduced to the notion of 'illicit memory', a
notion that prefigures what Europe will become even as it describes what
Isaac feels:

> I had arrived in Greece aware that I was going to fuck people, eager
> to engage in a bout of promiscuity, but the memory of the last
> few hours in the hotel room now shamed me. The experience of
> paying the youth for sex, while tantalising as fantasy—in fact, a
> fantasy in which I happily and often indulged in [sic]—in reality
> had proven clichéd. It had been sordid and had made me feel old

and disappointed. Not even the illicit memory of the boy's tough
beauty could lessen my regret (29).

As the reader reaches for Cavafy, whose 'Ithaka' Isaac quotes when
speaking at the exhibition of his photographs (37), something strange
occurs. Helping a boy who has been beaten in a back street, Isaac ends
up in Serge's flat, where he discovers the boy is Yuri, Serge's brother, and
where he meets their grandmother, Elena. After spending time with them,
he decides to return with his camera. When he does, he is told they no
longer live there: the grandmother died some years beforehand and the
brothers moved away. The first of many reverberations has been sounded;
Europe has its own illicit memories.

Isaac's experience of other cities follows a similar pattern. Instead of
seeing the Venice that 'had always been a romance' (131), he is drawn
into the Jewish ghetto where an old Jew insists he photograph 'the crude
symbols of continuing racism' (151). Seeing a crucifix Isaac is wearing, the
Jew suddenly becomes aggressive, snatching his camera. In the ensuing
struggle, he bites Isaac on the wrist and Isaac, in what is an unrecognised
sign of his future, becomes 'transfixed by the raw pink wounds' and by
the fact that '[t]here was no blood' (153). As the struggle continues, Isaac
curses the old man as a 'fucking Jew' (154). Characteristically, Tsiolkas
takes the incident beyond an individual's racism: 'I had never uttered this
curse before. A rush of power surged through every particle of me. It was as
if I had been yearning to utter that curse since the beginning of time' (154).
Even in this story of the cursed Jew there is, however, an unexpected turn.
When Isaac learns the old man has had his tongue cut out and his wife has
been blinded, he assumes they are victims of the Holocaust, but Tsiolkas
turns aside, indicating that he does not want his treatment of racism to
become contained in a single horror, however great. The old couple's story,
it turns out, is closer to that of Romeo and Juliet: it was their families who
violated them; she was an Arab and he a Jew. As well as signalling how
the novel engages with contemporary conflicts, this demonstrates one of
the novel's major strategies: to oppose the large history of hatred with the
frailer possibilities of personal love.

It is also in Venice that Isaac remembers Signor Bruno Parlovecchio, the sixty-year-old Italian who first told him the beauties of Venice and whose name (Mister Old Talk) now returns changed into ancient curse. Bruno initiated Isaac sexually, though in Isaac's account their architecture of desire is an effect of reciprocated forces: Bruno gets consolation; Isaac gets culture. As Isaac discloses more, he recalls his first love, a fully sexual relationship involving anal penetration of a minor by an adult male, Paul Ricco, a relationship abruptly terminated when Isaac turns sixteen and no longer satisfies Ricco's heterosexual fiction of the boy as 'pretty girl' (146). In a parodic version of Abraham's sacrifice, Isaac's father sanctions his son's sexual activity, advising him not to have sex for money and declaring: 'I wish God had granted me a love for cock instead of damning me with the desire for cunt' (142). Neither the narrator nor the novel seem concerned about the morality of this relationship, though it is possible that these benign representations of paedophilia are being positioned as morally other than the exploitative paedophilia Isaac encounters as he makes his way deeper into Europe.

Venice also delivers an unrecognised sign: in the photographs he took of his mother's birthplace Isaac sees ghostly figures, but then convinces himself that the haunted images are the result of a technical printing error, an effect of superimposition (which might itself serve as a metaphor for civilisation). At this point I was not as reader sure if I believed him. I was still troubled by his description of his arrival at the Grand Canal: 'I climbed onto the first ferry I saw and began my journey through the guts of the city' (132). In that image I could hear Charos breathing. It was clear by now that narratives of hell and underworld were shadowing the novel, just as it was becoming clear that the ghosted photograph was a metaphor for the novel's structure, the way in which the haunted narrative of Reveka's past was starting to press into the present, into presence, in Isaac's narrative.

In Prague Isaac remembers his first visit, in which he found 'the idyllic inner city,' 'a European city that had just emerged from a fairytale.'(179). Ten years later, he finds something different: McDonald's and whores (180). As with Athens, the city engenders disillusionment. The sex acquires a new intensity and Isaac hears a voice saying, 'You are in Hell' (223). He watches the stage show in which Pano fucks a boy, a boy whose face exposes the demon Isaac first saw in his mother's village:

> The boy's thin body shuddered and as I looked down at him it seemed that his skin had fallen away and his very bones were visible; and when I searched his face it had darkened, his hair was now black, not fair, and the gaunt face that leered up at me was looking straight into my eyes and his eyes were shining, they were laughing, and I knew those eyes, had always known those eyes (226).

It is in Prague too that Isaac is sexually attracted to the under-aged and promiscuous Milos. Resisting the attraction, Isaac indulges in a masturbation fantasy that anticipates the stage show, connecting violence, sex and blood (192–3). This thirst for blood is a sign that Isaac is being taken over (at least to readers familiar with vampire stories). It is also a sign of the book's interest in sacrifice, which is to say its interest in the primitive violence of sacrifice. It is this interest that persuades the book to deny sacrifice any redemptive efficacy. This denial will, at story's end, have a devastating effect; here it is simply signalled in the way the images of sadomasochistic sex are also images of Christ's suffering and in the way the language of vampiric appetite appropriates Christ's 'eat my body' and 'drink my blood'. While the language of Eucharist extends the book's analogical activity, it also, because of its parodic force, cancels grace.

Something of the novel's resistance to grace and redemption is revealed just after the fuck show as Maria, Pano's mother and mistress of ceremonies, tells Isaac she is not named after the Christian Mary. She hopes she is named after Miriam, who at the fall of Jerusalem, killed her children and 'ate from their flesh' (232). Then, speaking in ancient Greek (perhaps she is as much Medea as Miriam?), she charges Isaac: 'Eat, for I have already eaten. Can it be you are afraid? Are you weaker than a woman, weaker than even a mother?' (232). Again vampiric and eucharistic discourses are confused. By novel's end, the final question has gained added power and significance. For the moment, though, the denial of hope seems mild. Isaac tells Maria and her daughter-in-law to leave Prague. Maria asks would they be safe in Australia if Isaac took them there. 'And for one moment, a grace of a moment, I thought I saw hope in her eyes. Then there was only a mocking tenderness' (233). Maria is without hope. As Isaac watches the two women walk away, he becomes like them, a wanderer in Hell:

> I walked the dark city, past whores and beggars, drunkards and dopers, revellers and madmen shouting out the varied names of Paradise and of Hell. I crossed streets and alleys and boulevards and bridges and I kept walking, exhausted, all the while repeating to myself, I once had a teacher, I once had a teacher, and he taught me there was a city called Prague and that once hope existed in this city, and I kept walking and walking but dawn came and I had found no hope (233).

Even Paris, favourite of so many photographers, appears damned. Isaac sees not 'the gloriously pretty city of classical architecture and narrow sloping streets' (277) but 'a harsh place, a tough, crumbling, decaying, stinking, dirty city' (277). By now the novel's analogical affinities have started to exert considerable pressure; Europe is opening avenues to the underworld—and the underworld is not confined to Europe. It is in Paris that Isaac has to explain to a refugee (Sula) that Australia is no longer a welcoming country (in doing so he abandons the hope contained in his father's nickname, 'Lucky'). Isaac's guide to the darker side of Paris is an old friend of his father's, Gerry. Photographing him, Isaac remarks: 'There is no expression on his face, it can't be read. He is Charos' (303). The significance of this is clouded until Reveka goes to London to save her dying son. Recognising Gerry in Isaac's photos, she tells Colin that he killed himself (his funeral is mentioned at the beginning of the book) and that, although called Gerry, his real name means Isaac. Her son has been assumed into the name of one who is damned:

> She clutched at the photograph of the old man all night. She could not sleep. What odyssey have you been on, Isaac? she murmured to

herself. How will I bring you back from the underworld? What am I to sacrifice? (406)

I will return to the mother's sacrifice, but for the moment I want to linger with photographs. The photographs Isaac takes in Paris are determined by the novel's intention to make a space where the three competing religions of the book have cancelled their claims to represent God and offer a final happiness:

> I take a photograph of two Arab men smoking cigarettes in a Halal pizza shop. There is no God but Allah and his Prophet is Mohammed. I shoot the luminous spires of Notre Dame. Jesus Christ was the Son of God crucified and Resurrected on the third day in order to redeem us from sin. I capture the Hebrew lettering on the windows of a bakery in an alley off the Bastille. There is one God and the Jews are his Chosen People. The savage mythologies of ignorant, obsolete tribes. I am not tired, I am still elated. I am of this world, only in and of this world. Revelation. Every photograph I take is an act of defiance against God (302).

This makes sense within Isaac's story. It also reveals how the book depends on its own oppositions, in this case an opposition between romance and realism. Perhaps there are also hidden here oppositions between the ordinary and the transcendent, the beautiful and the ugly that might have surprised other photographers of Paris. Some years before Isaac, the 'real' photographers, Henri Cartier-Bresson and Brassai explored a city that is more than and other than Isaac's image of a 'gloriously pretty city of classical architecture and narrow sloping streets' (277). Cartier Bresson, for instance, took a photograph of the Marais district in which a gate featuring Medusa's head opens onto a shadowed archway leading into a dark interior; it is at once alluring and disturbing and might almost provide a visual counterpart to the novel's journey (112). Introducing his *The Secret Paris of the '30s* (2001), Brassai might almost be describing Isaac's experience:

And yet, drawn by the beauty of evil, the magic of the lower depths, having taken pictures for my 'voyage to the end of night' from the outside, I wanted to know what went on inside, behind the walls, behind the façades, in the wings: bars, dives, night clubs, one-night hotels, bordellos, opium dens. I was eager to penetrate this other world, this fringe world, the secret, sinister world of mobsters, outcasts, toughs, pimps, whores, addicts, inverts. Rightly or wrongly, I felt at the time that this underground world represented Paris at its least cosmopolitan, at its most alive, its most authentic, that in these colourful faces of its underworld there had been preserved, from age to age, almost without alteration, the folklore of its most remote past.

Among the photographs Brassai took are images of cesspool cleaners, urinals used as beats, a prostitute washing herself at a bidet while her customer returns to his trousers, a homosexual couple one of whom wears only trousers and the other only a coat (and hat), a bare breasted dancer from the Folies-Bergère being fondled by a fireman, lesbian, gay and drag clubs, opium dens, and mobsters who might easily have killed their photographer. It is a Paris more 'harsh' than 'pretty', even if it does resist Isaac's opposition of pretty and dirty.

Isaac's photographs of Paris are not, then, as unusual as the narrator pretends, but the reader needs to think they are. They serve a fictive need: they are another means of cancelling hope. This is especially evident when, viewing the photographs he took in Amsterdam, Isaac finds himself mocked by a deity whose malignancy mirrors that of the emerging demon. These photographs too do not come out as Isaac expected; they are full of twisted bodies, described in terms that suggest images of concentration camps:

Every photograph is an apology, every photograph I take is an act of contrition before a mocking malignant God. With every shot His laughter rings out. I am nothing in this world (304).

Isaac momentarily bows before the (heretical) notion of a God who is, through religion, the cause of evil.

Haunted Story

Isaac's dark odyssey is ghosted by a family story that is moving towards him even as he goes in search of it. These narratives are reinforced in the stories of the displaced and disillusioned characters Isaac meets. They are further extended and intensified through Tsiolkas's use of intertextuality: other, older stories rise to the surface and slip through the frames of the main text (as they do through the frames of Isaac's photographs), particularly those stories of blood and sacrifice that, just as they seem about to invoke Hebrew and Christian belief, unlock the language of demons and vampires. The book derives its considerable power from these analogical affinities. While it is always tempting to isolate and identify influences, this would be reductive (and might give a false impression Tsiolkas's text is obeying some simple law of linear transmission in its relation to 'first' texts). Tsiolkas's use of such stories is never specified to a degree that might fix and familiarise them, and his writing absorbs rather than obeys their authority. Allusions generate a shadow network of association, which makes their effect in the book all the more powerful.

A reader familiar with Greek folklore will not be as surprised as I was when Tsiolkas introduced Reveka's family story. It emerges like a horror story, drawing on superstitions of long ago and creating a blackly religious text. Yet studies have shown that the beliefs embedded in this layer of the novel are not as remote as they might at first appear. Writers such as John Cuthbert Lawson and John L. Tomkinson give an account of Greek folklore that clarifies why even Isaac protects himself with the sign of the Cross:

> But he had disappeared. I swung around and looked at the path. I walked to the gate and peered below. The ground sloped down to a precarious drop. The cemetery was perched on the cliff's edge. I drew back and looked behind me but the gypsy child had disappeared completely. And then for the first time in years, as I walked out of the church grounds I found my hand had flown to my forehead and to my heart. I had made the sign of the Cross. And again I heard laughter (107).

Among the beliefs and practices which continued to be active in modern Greek culture are some which establish themselves in Tsiolkas's tale: evil spirits and vampires (whose bodies had to be burned), sacrifices and scape-goats used to lift curses (curses that could be passed along the generations), blood-guilt and revenge (especially that exacted by those who have been murdered), wise old women working with priests to exorcise demons, evil spirits often appearing in the form of snakes, spirits who had a particular appetite for young children, sometimes drinking their blood, sometimes suffocating them by sitting on their chests. Lawson observes that since ancient Greek religion did not identify godhead with goodness, popular belief has inherited a reluctance to separate angels from demons. In this argument, Greek Christianity becomes something like a surface culture while the older traditions remain active, pushing up from underneath.

Tsiolkas's interest in spirits and superstition represents, then, not so much a gothic departure from realism as an ethnographic account of family lore. Yet for all his political and cultural realism, Tsiolkas manages to keep the novel unlocked. He does not use Greek folklore as a privileged source of narrative (which is perhaps why, structurally, the novel resists being arranged as if it were a simple linear account of a curse moving from generation to generation). So the folklore does not constrain or confine the novel, but rather releases it into and releases in it a remarkably active and allusive memory. A reader familiar with Abraham's story, the legends of Lilith and the Wandering Jew, Christian theology of redemptive sacrifice, as indeed with the *Odyssey*, *The Divine Comedy*, Marlowe's *Faustus*, and C.P. Cavafy's 'Ithaka', is likely to approach this work as a story where many other stories meet. Similarly, a reader familiar with the many books, films and television shows devoted to vampires may well decide to examine how the novel exploits the sexually transgressive possibilities of the vampire, and might even identify a surprising political counterpart in Paul Morrissey's *Blood for Dracula* (1974), which has Dracula trying to feed off a corrupt class system.

Even so, while vampire shows are an obvious influence, one of the novel's major cinematic influences may well be Roman Polanski, who, (coincidentally?) was a Jewish boy hidden by a Catholic family in wartime Poland (Feeny/Duncan 9). *The Tenant* (1976), for example, employs a poetics of terror that corresponds closely with Tsiolkas's aesthetic: darkened interiors, descending stairs, strange apparitions that may or may not be caused by fevered imagining (apparitions that are framed by windows as if they are photographs), escalating malevolence, epistemological destabilisation, and the use of sexuality to figure a world defamiliarised to the point of horror. *Repulsion* (1965) depicts hallucinations caused by the irruptive energy of repressed sexuality and, again, shows people passing through darkened spaces. It also ends with an image of a photograph as the camera moves in to show darkness in the eye. Even the more conventional thriller, *Frantic* (1987), shows Paris as an underworld, using images of night-time traffic to define the contemporary traveller. In an essay on *The Pianist* (2002), Tsiolkas writes of the 'sense of unnameable horror' that pervades so much of Polanski's work, admiring a capacity to investigate evil 'as psychological and as existing in the everday'. At the same time he suggests that a major reason for Polanski's success with evil is that he removes it from morality: anti-Semitism is not a story of good versus evil but 'the consequence of specific European histories and struggles, rooted in defined religious differences and hatreds, and emerging from individual and cultural identities'. *The Pianist* is then interpreted as an atheist's vision of a 'completely man-made' Hell, with Tsiolkas interpreting the survival of the protagonist, Szpilman, as an accident: 'In refusing to make survival a matter of morality and ethics, but instead a matter of accident, Polanski refutes the rhetoric of Good and Evil' (*senses of cinema*). Other readers are, of course, likely to refer to other movies: my point is simply that reading this book is like stepping into a room where analogies are engaged in a progressive dance. The appropriate response is not to grab hold of one of them, but to enjoy the dance.

It might be tempting for a reader to decide there is a divide between the novel's first and second chapters, a divide between its 'contemporary' and 'mythological' narratives, as also between its 'realist' and 'gothic' modes. The opening of the novel, however, suggests otherwise; it suggests that stories of blood and sacrifice cross the divides we draw when we imagine discourses such as history and geography. *Dead Europe* opens with a story about how Jews on Christmas would take a Christian baby and pierce its body to 'drain the child of its blood': 'While Christians celebrated the birth of Jesus, Jews had a mock ceremony at midnight in their synagogues, before images of their horned God, where they drank the blood of the sacrificed child' (3). This could be read simply as indicative of Reveka's prejudice, setting the reader on a path that will eventually lead to the question of whether the book itself is anti-Semitic. I suspect this is a misreading because it separates one story from the novel's analogical network. While *Dead Europe* does have race-hatred as one of its major concerns, the blood story equally represents popular Greek belief in scape-goating, sacrifice, and the thirst for blood that drives demons and those possessed by them. Similarly, if it is read simply as an example of Jewish/ Christian antagonism, it might incline a reader to accept the cliché that religion has offered human history little more than an excuse for hatred and violence. This may well be what the narrator believes, but the text is doing something more: it is initiating a connection between the alleged Jewish ritual and Christmas, which celebrates the birth of the scape-goat Christ, the one who will offer his blood in sacrifice. The effect of this is that the old Greek belief in blood-sacrifice begins to absorb Jewish and Christian blood rites, effectively disempowering them. This opening, then, inaugurates an analogical activity that will include different stories of blood and sacrifice as a way of demonstrating the power and permanence of hatred.

In another example of the novel's analogical intensity, Tsiolkas's depiction of the demon derives from popular Greek superstition but is not confined by it. When he first appears, the demon can only be seen by Maritha, who is the wise old woman. He is seen wrapping himself around the feet of the child Christo. He is also responsible for the death of village children, whose blood he licks. When Maritha learns the Hebrew has been murdered and buried in Christian ground, she persuades the priest to exhume and burn his body; she believes he has become a vampire, a belief confirmed when his body is found to be incorrupt. When she realises that Christo is his son, she kills the child because she thinks he has already drunk blood. Yet, this material is reaching back to the opening story of

Jews drinking the blood of Christian babies and forward to the chapter that follows, Isaac's account of Prague, which includes Sal Mineo telling him of parents who sell their children, Isaac's sadistic fantasies about Milos and Pano, the story of Miriam eating her children, and discussion of anti-Semitism and the Holocaust. It is reaching back to the moment when Lucia, Isaac's grandmother, convinces her husband Michaelis that he should kill the Hebrew boy placed in their care during the war:

> Our child is a child of God. The Hebrew belongs to the Devil. Don't you see, Husband? God has given us an opportunity to redeem ourselves for our sin. You must murder that fiend we have been protecting. Her hand had crept to his groin. It is God's will (118).

When Michaelis succumbs, he reminds Lucia that God will judge her, to which she replies: 'Yes, let his blood be on me' (120). This immediately reverberates beyond the confines of the text, as few readers will not remember this is what the Jews say to Pontius Pilate (Matthew 27:25). If they do forget, Colin will remind them when he cites this incident as the basis of blood libel (387). Other readers will remember what Rebecca says to Jacob when he questions whether it is right to deceive Isaac and get his blessing: 'On me be the curse, my son!' (Genesis 27:13). In addition, after the murder there is an encounter between Michaelis and Lucia that is, especially in its references to washing hands and troubled sleep, reminiscent of the encounter between Macbeth and his wife after the murder of Duncan (127–9). At the same time, the story of blood is reaching further forward, making its way to Australia: on the boat to Australia Angelo drinks the menstrual blood of Stella whom Reveka has 'cursed' (322); in Australia Reveka is finally exorcised by another crone. It reaches its climax when Isaac, just before killing James and Nikolai in a London hotel in order to drink their blood, declares his satanic credo, which is also his vision of undead Europe:

> What I believe is that we will kill each other, that we will hurt each other. We will destroy our neighbours and we will exile them.

We will sell our children as whores. We will murder and rape and punish one another. We will keep warring and we will keep hating and we will believe that we are just and righteous and faithful. We will keep killing and selling one another and we will believe that we are just and fair and good. We will pursue pleasures and destroy one another in these pursuits. We will abandon our children. We will do all this in the name of God and in the name of our nature. We will create poverty and illness and we will create obscene wealth and the depravities that arise from it. We will think ourselves just and righteous, faithful and sane. We will hate and kill and piss and shit on one another. We will continue to do so. We will create Armageddon. In the name of God or in the name of justice or, simply, because we can. This is what I believe (379).

'Damned Perpetually'

The laughter Isaac hears when he blesses himself is the laughter he hears when he looks upon his photographs of Amsterdam. It is a laughter made possible by the fact that in this story God is not ethical. He is, throughout, confused with Satan. When the Hebrew youth says that God protects him, Lucia replies that it is the Devil who protects him. When he chants over his food, Lucia asks, 'Is that how Satan speaks?' to which he replies, 'And God as well' (62). When Lucia finally has him impregnate her, she wonders: 'Was that spirit evil, or from God? She did not care' (63). Before this, when Michaelis Panagis goes to America, he receives from God what he asks: enough money to go back to his village and silence those who mock his parents, and marriage to Lucia. But is it God who is answering his prayers? His work in America is described in terms of Hell, indeed a Hell that is hungry: 'The dark pits with their charred walls and roaring furnaces had seemed like Hell and he was to spend thirteen years stoking those furnaces, shovelling coal into their ravenous mouths' (109). The troubling thing about the image of hellish furnaces is that, in this book of analogical affinities, Tsiolkas might also be here describing the extermination furnaces; the image implicates Michaelis and America in that evil, just as it implicates America in terror, refusing the civilised/barbaric opposition invoked in 'axis of evil' rhetoric. On her way to Australia, Reveka remembers her mother telling her the demon accompanying her is called 'Angel' and has been sent by God to protect them (315), even though Angelo's behaviour towards the other passengers is malevolent. By making god and satan, angel and demon, interchangeable Tsiolkas undoes standard Western ethical oppositions. While one effect of this is to expose how such oppositions are used to create a poetics of terror, another is to call ethics itself into question.

Even as they are used to enlarge the novel's narrative scope, Jewish and Christian scriptures are disempowered. It is not uncommon to refer to the entire Hebrew bible as Torah, the name also given to the books of the Law. Nevertheless, Isaac's tendency to do this does, in the context of this novel, reinforce an impression that religion is mainly concerned with sexuality and sacrifice (these are the books that contain instructions for sacrifice and prohibitions about sexuality and, significantly for Isaac and Colin, homosexuality). Obviously, the emphasis on Law accords with the novel's interest in the theo-political effects of dogmatic religions. Nevertheless, what is excluded does constitute a substantial part of and different image of Jewish scripture, such as the erotic passages from the Song of Solomon, the redemptive vision of Isaiah and his Suffering Servant, Hosea's vision of a divine love that forgave infidelity, the psalmist's image of the Lord as shepherd, and these few lines describing Jonah's journey:

> I went down into the countries underneath the earth,
> to the peoples of the past.
> But you lifted my life from the pit,
> Yahweh, my God. (Jonah: 2–7)

Dead Europe needs to deny the second half of this quote, but the first two lines are a reminder that Jewish scripture is not unaware of the descent into darkness that characterises Tsiolkas's Europe. Selective memory is also at work in the novel's account of Christianity, and again because the novel is more concerned with the theo-political effects of Christian moral agendas than with gospel stories. The result is that the poetics of Christianity is ignored in favour of its politics, and that politics is itself represented as if it is a single expression of a simply unified message. What is also, therefore, ignored is that the gospels are not a simply unified text but a product of complex redaction employing a process of intertextuality as sophisticated as that used in *Dead Europe*. They also display a capacity for difference. It is a commonplace of gospel scholarship to recognise the differences of the three synoptic gospels: Matthew wants to show, through quotation, how Christ fulfils the prophecies; Mark is intent on the 'messianic secret' and the slow recognition of Christ as the mysterious Son of Man; Luke is the story of God's 'loving kindness' (Luke is the only evangelist to tell the parables of the Good Samaritan and the Prodigal Son.) I am not suggesting that Tsiolkas should have attended to all the ambiguities, paradoxes and contradictions of these scriptures. I am noting his exclusions because they clarify the narrative's commitment to its infernal gaze; without them, Isaac's story is able to take evil beyond the chance of redemption.

What interests me, then, is the question of narrative intention. So I find it intriguing that what is done to Jewish and Christian scripture is also done to Cavafy's 'Ithaka' (47). Isaac quotes Cavafy's 'Ithaka' at his Athens exhibition (37). It is a significant, albeit brief, allusion, if for no other reason than the poem offers advice to Odysseus, who ghosts much of Tsiolkas's fiction. 'Ithaka' favours the journey over the destination ('Ithaka has given you your lovely journey'). In that sense the poem might be seen as having an arrested teleology that corresponds to the novel's refusal of hope; but 'Ithaka' also advises its hero:

The Laistrygonians, and the Kyklopes,
Angry Poseidon, —don't be afraid of them;
You will never find such things on your way,
If only your thoughts be high, and a select
Emotion touch your spirit and your body.

Dead Europe could almost be read as a denial of this advice. Whereas *The Jesus Man* seems to be listening to 'Ithaka' as it ends—'I'm requiring no destination. I simply wish for motion, the struggle against wind and sea, to keep moving and to never stop' (403)—*Dead Europe* gives its journey over to the fears, the furies, just as Isaac carries them in his soul. For Cavafy tells Odysseus:

> The Laistrygonians, and the Kyklopes,
> Poseidon raging —you will never meet them,
> Unless you carry them with you in your soul,
> If your soul does not raise them up before you.

'Ithaka', then, is used as selectively as the scriptures. So too, of course, is Dante: Isaac never reaches heaven, just as his Lucia does not, as she does in Dante's *Paradiso*, represent mercy.

'fucking aesthetics and ethics'

If Hell lies all about us and hatred is so irresistible, is it possible for the novel to exercise ethical judgment? *Dead Europe* derives great power from its sympathy for people accustomed to unspeakable horror and from its unflinching and infernal gaze; it also derives great power from its insistence that hatred and bloodlust lie at the very foundations of European culture. Yet the sources of its narrative power are also the sources of its ethical dilemma. The novel presents hatred and scape-goating as if they are irresistible determinants of history, yet depicts people like Michaelis, Lucia, and Colin making choices and suffering their consequences. It goes beyond good and evil, yet it is always looking back to notions of sin, retribution and redemption. In particular, it wants to lift anti-Semitism and paedophilia into the other dimension of metaphor, yet it particularises them in Isaac's life choices: he has no qualms about his pre-adolescent affair with Paul; he disapproves of anti-Semitism. Even if it could be argued that a determinist worldview dominates the novel's representation of personal choice and so permits racism by default, this does not support a conclusion that the book actively justifies anti-Semitism. *Dead Europe* challenges moral conventions, and quite radically, yet is preoccupied with what might almost be called the instinct for ethics, the unformalised desire for a better world.

Dead Europe has too much control of character and narrative to be simply anti-Semitic. The opinions expressed by individual characters are clearly theirs and are clearly understood as such, while the narration itself adopts an impartial stance. Since the characters represent very different experiences and opinions (even though they are also unified by their displacement), Tsiolkas is able to show how complex anti-Semitism is, as he does when Isaac is refused permission to take photographs at the Jewish Museum of Thessalonika. In the space of a brief telephone conversation to his partner, Colin, Isaac goes from declaring he was hurt because the museum guard 'was making no distinction between [him] and an anti-Semite' (89) to admitting he wanted to tell the guard, 'Fuck off, you paranoid Jew, I have nothing to do with this history' (90). This is symptomatic of the way Tsiolkas approaches other characters. He appreciates that real people are capable of contradiction, that they can quickly feel a retaliatory hatred even though another part of them says this is wrong. He wants, in a sense, to show how easy hatred is, and in that sense the book is making the ethical point that to imagine anti-Semitism as if it is an almost transcendent hatred is ironically to undervalue it. Similarly, for all its insistence on scape-goating, the novel refuses to typify the Jew as history's victim. One of the dangers in ethical readings of literature is that characters are forced to become representative (such readings are, like political readings, often covertly allegorical), so the idea that individuals of whatever race, colour, gender can be inadequate and downright evil is unacceptable. In this novel, however, Syd, the Jewish businessman in Prague, does not correctly represent the race; he represents a post-religious, post-Holocaust character who takes refuge in material possessions. His parents perished in the gas chambers and if he had any faith it disappeared with them. He is now a purveyor of pornography with a particular inclination to paedophilia. It is Syd who says:

> I am the real Jew, mate ... You don't know Jews, do you? You think we should be the nice old fella in the back of the store, wouldn't

hurt a fucking fly. Salt of the earth and God's chosen people. I'm not that kind of Jew, cunt. That kind of mumza Jew is finished. I hope that mumza has gone forever (219–20).

He will not accept the role of scapegoat (even if he seems willing enough to pass it on to his boys).

Finally, the novel is not anti-Semitic because it keeps its eye on the larger analogical game in which anti-Semitism becomes another instance of blood sacrifice. Whether the horror is that visited on the Hebrew by Michaelis and Lucia, or on the Israeli-Arab lovers by their families, or on refugees by small-hearted governments, or on the Jewish people by the Third Reich, it is placed in a long memory of hatred. While some might think this de-theologises the Holocaust, it seems to me appropriate and respectful. One of the major achievements of this book is how it shows that histories cannot be contained by ethnic and nationalist borders. Instead, histories reach into each other. And if many of the histories included in this book do rest on fundamental acts of scape-goating, this ought to be a warning against simplistic, oppositional judgments, and a reminder of how easily holocausts can happen.

The depiction of sexual decadence is also controlled, though more ambivalent. While exploitative sex operates as a realist referent to displacement, poverty and power in post-Communist Europe, the novel's attitude to paedophiliac sexual relationships is divided. When he remembers Mister Parlovecchio and Paul Ricco, Isaac seems not to harbour any regrets or anger. The narrative appears not to judge. After watching the fuck-show between Pano and the boy, Isaac does judge. He is disgusted:

I did not know where my shame was coming from. I had seen sex acts before, and hadn't I even paid for sex with an Athenian whore only a few weeks ago, who, if I was honest with myself, would not have been much older than the boy Pano was fucking on the podium? But whatever its source, the contempt I felt for myself was rich, righteous and mortifying. If I could not be sure if I was ashamed of being a man, or of being a man who was a fag, or of both, or of being a white man in an Eastern city, or of all of it, I knew enough to know that I was ashamed of being human. You are in Hell (226).

Clearly Isaac sees the demonic paedophilia of Prague as different from the tutelary paedophilia of Melbourne. Traditional moral thinking might find this unconvincing since it is a distinction in degree parading as a distinction in kind. This is not, however, the basis of the novel's judgment. That seems to emerge when Sal Mineo undercuts Isaac's scruples with a reiteration of a Marxist critique of ethics:

> Look around you, Isaac. Look where you are. Do you know what contempt these blokes have for you, with your headstart in capitalism and you're still fucking mouthing off about silly ideas you learnt at college. Beauty and art and fucking politics. They'd sell their fucking children for a buck. And you want to talk about fucking aesthetics and ethics (203).

It seems to me the book substantially agrees with Sal. If, as I have argued, its inter-textuality undermines hope and if its narrative perspective and analogical character support a determinist view of history, this would seem to suggest that ethics is a luxury the poor cannot afford.

It may, of course, be that the hopelessness associated with racism and sexual exploitation is designed to make readers want some belief, some story, capable of facing evil. In what might almost be a comment on the novel's representation of sexuality, Tsiolkas remarks: 'There is a danger in excess and the danger is a spiritual and moral emptiness' (www.paperbackbooks.com). If the book does evoke a reaction against excess and emptiness, then at that level it can be considered a profoundly ethical work. It is not clear to me that it does. Moreover, representing evil does not amount to redeeming it and, given the historical, economic, and indeed religious, forces ranged against it, ethics is hardly a powerful force for good. It might turn out to be little more than a wish that people were not so cruel.

Is, then, the love between Isaac and Colin capable of resisting the destructive and corrosive effects of history and its hatred? I cannot see that their love is as strong as it needs to be. This is largely because of the way the novel confuses good and evil. Colin bears a swastika tattoo. Although he did not choose it and although he wears it with shame, he cannot erase the 'history' and 'power' that Isaac hates (10). The significance of this tattoo is developed when it is clear that Isaac is in Hell and when the book has firmly established racism and sexual decadence as signs of a decaying Europe. What is then significant about Colin's tattoo is how it confirms the book's sacrifice of hope. Colin is explaining what he means when he says he has 'exiled' himself from the Jews:

> —You know how you can see a black man on the street or an Aboriginal woman or an old Vietnamese geezer and the first thing that you are aware of is their difference from you? You understand that?
>
> His tone had become cold and distant, but there was an urgency to it. I reluctantly nodded.
>
> —And then you know how you can talk to the stranger, get pissed with them, ask about the weather, the football, talk about a film, and the difference just disappears? It's no longer about skin colour or language, it's just you and the other person, does that make sense?
>
> —Yes.
>
> —Well, that can never happen between me and a Jew. He tapped his arm. This tattoo, it's not ever going to go away (254).

Isaac is angry with this explanation, thinking Colin is using the Jews as a 'scapegoat for the idealisation of [his] own poverty and pain' (254). '[D]etermined to leave him' (254), Isaac instead gives way to Colin's look of 'acute sadness' (255) and the desire 'to give him peace again' (255). Isaac himself has to take on shame in order to love:

> If with me Colin had found someone prepared to accept his shame, I now shared his exile. As I was holding him, loving him, my own

dark arm brushed against his pale flesh, and against his tattoo. The ink was on my skin too (255).

If this represents the hope of redemptive love, it is immediately undermined: this memory occurs immediately before Isaac, on the train from Prague, drinks menstrual blood, which is probably the book's most perverted version of blood sacrifice. The strategies here are the strategies by which the book itself sacrifices hope. There is also the difficulty that the book clearly indicates the love Isaac has for Colin is shadowed by distrust (99). Colin's declares his love for Isaac in the final section, 'The Book of Lilith'. Lilith, in the Jewish apocrypha, is the first wife of Adam who refused to be subservient, left paradise before eating the forbidden fruit (before the curse of mortality), gave birth to demons and still roams the earth where 'God allows her to eat the blood of uncircumcised children' (389). In the first chapter of this section, Colin choses Isaac over God, aligning this choice with an option for Lilith and Lucifer. He who is supposed to signify the hope of love is saying that he prefers to be in Hell with his love: 'I promise you, Isaac, if God is the righteous prick from the Bible, I choose Hell over Him. Fuck him. I choose to be with you. I choose Hell' (390). Admittedly, the chapter is called 'Purgatory' and it is not clear whether it is a nightmare sequence, coming immediately before the chapter in which Colin receives the phone call saying Isaac is dying in London. It is also an unsettling sequence since the one declaring his love for Isaac sounds a little like the demon, prefiguring how the demon will talk, finally, to Isaac's mother. For these reasons I cannot see the love between Isaac and Colin as a hope big enough to withstand the bloodthirsty powers pushing up from beneath the civilised surface of Europe.

'On me be the curse, my son!'

> See, see where Christ's blood streams in the firmament!
> One drop would save my soul, half a drop. (Marlowe xix, II.146–47)

Much of this book depends on interrupted intertextuality, but the one text that *Dead Europe* carries through to its damned end is Marlowe's *Doctor Faustus*. Both Faustus and Reveka are denied the blood of the eucharist. After making her deal with God ('If you save my son, Lord, the Devil can have my soul.' 409) and after Isaac has recovered, Reveka enters the church. She does not find the forgiveness and compassion she hopes for, but the realisation that her pact is sealed:

> Once inside she stood in front of an icon of Christ, her God, and looked into his face. It was not the Christ Child but the stern mature face of the Christ Pantocrator. The unforgiving eyes of the creator and judge stared down at her and she bowed her head. At the end of the service the congregation began to queue for Holy Communion. The severe Father, still gazing down at her, admonished her as she unthinkingly went to take her place in the queue.
>
> Rebecca pulled away from her daughter, and turned and fled the church. The trees had begun to shed their leaves. She understood now the extent of her punishment. She was never again to see the light of the Saviour's face, she would never again taste of His blood, partake of His flesh (410–11).

This scene has its precursor in the one describing the damnation of Reveka's grandmother, Maritha (176). After killing Christo in the hope of lifting the curse placed on her family Maritha too goes to the Church for forgiveness and finds herself 'beyond grace' by the uncompromising will of that 'stern, unforgiving God' who sustains Tsiolkas's image of bloodthirsty monotheism. The difference is that Rebecca has the demon keep her company. He has the last word, uttering his malignant promise of eternal companionship.

Of all the sacrifices mentioned in this novel, the eucharist is the one blood sacrifice that might, at least in Rebecca's belief, save her. There is no absolute theological reason why it should not (a conventional theology of mercy could see to that). The fact that it is denied her is more a narrative than a theological necessity. In order to seal the book's analogies, so preoccupied with destructive sacrifice, so privileging hate over hope, the book needs to sacrifice the mother. In a narrative full of sacrifices, she is the last scape-goat, the sacrifice through which the book ensures its dark purpose.

Note: my thanks to Bernadette Brennan and Stephen Fahey for ongoing conversations about this book.

Noel Rowe completed this essay one year prior to his death. It has not been published previously.

Works Cited

Brassai, *The Secret Paris of the '30s*. New York: Thames & Hudson 2001. Originally published: Paris: Editions Gallimard, 1976. No pagination.

Calvino, I. *Invisible Cities*. William Weaver (trans.). London: Vintage, 1997.

Cartier-Bresson, H. 'The Marais 1952'. *A Propos de Paris*. New York and Boston: Bullfinch Press, Fifth Printing, 2004.

Cavafy, C.P. *Poems by C.P. Cavafy*. John Mavrogordato (trans.). London: Chatto & Windus, 1974.

Feeney, F.X./Paul Duncan (eds.). *Roman Polanski*. Köln: Tachen, 2006.

Lawson, John C. *Modern Greek Folklore and Ancient Greek Religion*. New York: University Books, 1964. [CUP 1910].

Marlowe, C. *The Tragical History of the Life and Death of Doctor Faustus*, sc.xix, ll.146–7. *The Revels Plays* edition, John D. Jump (ed.). Manchester: Manchester University Press, 1978.

Morrissey, P. (dir.) *Blood for Dracula*. Force Entertainment, 1974.

Polanski, R. (dir.) *The Tenant*. Paramount, 1976.

——. *Repulsion*. MRA Entertainment, 1965.

——. *Frantic*. Warner Bros, 1987.

——. *The Pianist*. Universal, 2002.

Tomkinson, John L. *Haunted Greece: Nymphs, Vampires, and other Exotica*. Athens: Anagnosis Books, 2004.

Tsiolkas, C. *The Jesus Man*. Milson's Point: Random House, 1999.

——. *Dead Europe*. Milson's Point: Vintage, 2005.

——. 'The Atheist's Shoah—Roman Polanski's *The Pianist*'. senses of cinema, May 2003.

——. http://www.sensesofcinema.com/contents/03/26/pianist.html Accessed 25/5/06.

——. http://www.paperbackbooks.com.au/christos.htm. Accessed 25/5/06.

Critical Works by Noel Rowe

A SELECT BIBLIOGRAPHY

Modern Australian Poets. Melbourne: Oxford University Press, 1994.

Windchimes: Asia in Australian Poetry. Edited with Vivian Smith. Sydney: Halstead Press, 2006.

'The Misty Ways of Asia'. *East by South: China in the Antipodean Imagination*. Charles Ferrall, Paul Millar and Keren Smith (eds.). Wellington NZ: Victoria University Press, 2005. 70–86.

'Just Poetry'. *Just Words?: Australian Authors Writing for Justice*. Bernadette Brennan (ed.). St Lucia: University of Queensland Press, 2008. 46–61.

'Justice, Sacrifice and the Mother's Poem'. *The Poetry of Les Murray: Critical Essays*. Laurie Hergenhan and Bruce Clunies Ross (eds.). *Australian Literary Studies* 20:2, 2001. 142–56.

'Les Murray and the Unseen Opponent'. *Southerly* 51:2, 1991. 319–330.

'Intending Wholeness'. Review of Lawrence Bourke's *A Vivid Steady State: Les Murray and Australian Poetry*. *Southerly* 52:2, 1992. 165–74.

'Deviation and Devotion: Francis Webb's "Homosexual"'. *Departures: How Australia Reinvents Itself*. Xavier Pons (ed.). Melbourne: Melbourne University Press, 2002. 184–91.

'Francis Webb and the Will of the Poem'. *Southerly* 47:2, 1987. 180–196.

'Vincent Buckley: The City and the Sacred'. *Australian Writing and the City*. Fran de Groen and Ken Stewart (eds.). Sydney: ASAL 1999. 96–100.

'Believing More and Less: The Later Poetry of Vincent Buckley'. *Meridian* 10:1, May 1991. 4–18.

'James McAuley and the Possibility of Despair'. *Southerly* 60:2, 2000. 26–38.

'James McAuley and the Grammar of Existence'. *Australian Journal of Law and Society*, 9 (1993). 107–117.

'The Catholic Element in James McAuley's Poetry'. *Quadrant* 28:5, May 1984. 45–48.

'Theology and Myth in James McAuley's Captain Quiros'. *Pacifica* 4, 1991. 307–326

'Landing the Sacred'. *A Grain of Eternity: 1997 Australian International Religion, Literature and the Arts Conference Proceedings*. Michael Griffith and James Tulip (eds.) Sydney: Centre for Studies in Religion, Literature and the Arts, 1998.179–88.

'Giving a Word to the Sand'. *Westerly* 45, 2000. 151–60.

'The Choice of Nothing'. Michael Griffith (ed.). 'Special Issue: Religion, Literature and the Arts in Australia', *Literature and Theology* 10:3 September, 1996. 224–229.

'Poetry, Theology and Emptiness'. *Australian EJournal of Theology*. No. 5, August 2005.

'How to Gossip with Angels: Australian Poetry After the Gods'. *Antipodes* 19:2, 2005. 177–183.

'Are There Really Angels in Carlton? Australian Literature and Theology.' *Pacifica* 6, 1993. 141–164.

'The Place of Poetry: The Work of Vivian Smith'. *Southerly* 56:2, 1996. 46–66.

'Patience and Surprise: The Poetry of Vivian Smith'. *Southerly* 47:2, 1986. 178–194.

'"Sounds in print, worlds below": Seamus Heaney's deepening words'. *Sydney Studies in English* 26, 2000. 70–91.

'Much More You Could Say: Bruce Dawe's Poetry'. *Sydney Studies in English* 24, 1998–9. 102–117.

'Reticent Desire: The Poetry of Bruce Dawe'. *Outrider: A Journal of Multicultural Literature in Australia* 9:1–2, June 1992. 82–97.

'Emotions of a Destiny: The Poetry of Philip Martin'. *Southerly* 46:1, 1986. 93–113.

'Friendly Diversity: Six Friendly Street Poets'. *Southerly* 48:3, 1988. 306–325.

'"Will this be your poem, or mine?" The Give and Take of Story'. *Australian Literary Studies* 23:2, 2007. 1–14.

'Abominable Scripts: Hal Porter's Plays'. *Journal of the Association for the Study of Australian Literature (JASAL)* 4, 2005. 23–34.

'"No One but I will Know": Hal Porter's Honesty'. *Australian Humanities Review* 41, February 2007.

'Hardly Centred: Peter Kenna's *A Hard God*. *Seeking the Centre RLA Conference Proceedings 2001*. Colette Rayment and Mark Byrne (eds.). Sydney: RLA Press, 2002. 204–17.